M U

Ruth Hamilton

MUNTU

African Culture and the Western World

JANHEINZ JAHN

Translated from the German by Marjorie Grene
With an Introduction by Calvin C. Hernton

Grove Weidenfeld
NEW YORK

Published by Grove Weidenfeld
A division of Grove Press, Inc.
841 Broadway
New York, NY 10003-4793

Originally published in 1958 in West Germany by
Eugen Diederichs Verlag under the title *Muntu*.

Library of Congress Cataloging-in-Publication Data

Jahn, Janheinz.
[Muntu. English]
Muntu : African culture and the Western world / by Janheinz Jahn ;
translated from the German by Marjorie Grene ; [introduction by
Calvin C. Hernton]. — Rev. Grove Weidenfeld Evergreen ed.
p.   cm.
Translation of: Muntu.
Reprint, with new introd. Originally published: New York : Grove
Press, 1961.
Includes bibliographical references and indexes.
ISBN 0-8021-3208-1 : $12.95
1. Africa, Sub-Saharan—Civilization.   2. Negritude (Literary
movement) I. Title.
DT352.4.J3613   1990
967—dc20   90-47010   CIP

Manufactured in the United States of America

Printed on acid-free paper

First American Edition 1961
Revised Grove Weidenfeld Evergreen Edition 1990

10 9 8 7 6 5 4 3 2 1

The publishers acknowledge with thanks the assistance of Mr. William Fagg of the Department of Ethnography, The British Museum, in the transliteration of African names, particularly in Chapter 3.

CONTENTS

Introduction to the Second Edition
by Calvin C. Hernton   xi

1. SKOKIAN?—Problem and Method
    I *Quo Vadis Africa?*   11
    II *Traditional and Modern (Jaspers' Theory of History)*   12
    III *'Skokian' (Malinowski's Theory of Cultural Change)*   14
    IV *Neo-African Culture (All history is myth)*   16
    V *'Muntu' (The problem of Man)*   18
    VI *The 'Real' African*   19
    VII *Black Souls in a White World*   21
    VIII *The Arrangement of the Book*   25

2. VOODOO—The Embodiment of the Gods
    I *Old Accounts of the Cult*   29
    II *The Voodoo Ceremony in the Arada Rite*   33
    III *The Gods (Loas)*   39
    IV *The Embodiment of the Gods*   47
    V *Religion and Politics*   51

3. RUMBA—The Meaning of the Dances
    I *The Santería*   62
    II *Ñañigismo (The Secret Society)*   69
    III *The Origins of Rumba*   78
    IV *Rumba Rhythm in Lyric Poetry*   90

4. NTU—African Philosophy
    I *The Basic Principles*   96
    II *The Four Categories*   99

Contents

III *God*   104
IV *Life and Death*   105
V *Death and Re-birth*   109
VI *Religion and Ethics*   114

5. NOMMO—The Magic Power of the Word
    I *Man is Master of 'Things'*   121
    II *African Medicine*   127
    III *The Words and Exorcism*   132
    IV *Négritude and Surrealism*   140
    V *Négritude and Expressionism*   146

6. KUNTU—Immutability of Style
    I *Image and Form*   156
    II *Rhythm*   164
    III *Masks*   169
    IV *The New Art*   176

7. HANTU—History of Literature
    I *Writing*   185
    II *Culture in Time and Space*   190
    III *Residual-African Literature*   195
    IV *Neo-African Literature*   204
    V *Modern Literature in Africa*   209

8. BLUES—The Conflict of Cultures
    I *Residual African Elements in North America*   217
    II *States of Conflict*   225
    III *Europe, the Partner*   234
    IV *Conclusion*   237

NOTES   240

BIBLIOGRAPHY   252

INDEX OF NAMES   261

SUBJECT INDEX   265

MAP   268

ILLUSTRATIONS

Plate

1. Carved head in a Shango shrine in Ilobu, West Nigeria. (Photo: U. Beier)   *facing page* 32

2. Dance mask of Kra. Liberia. (Collection of the Frobenius Institute, Frankfurt-am-Main. Photo: R. Bouvier)   33

3. Horse and rider. Yoruba, Nigeria. (Photo: Helmut Lander)   48

4a. Ancestral figure. Bakota, Gabon. (N. Städtisches Museum für Völkerkunde, Frankfurt-am-Main)   49

4b. Bronze figure. Ife, Nigeria. (Antiquities Service, Jos, Nigeria. Photo: U. Beier)   49

5. Head of a Queen Mother, from Benin, West Nigeria. (British Museum, London)   80

6. Woodcarving of antelopes for a head-dress. Bambara, West Sudan. (N. Städtisches Museum für Völkerkunde, Frankfurt-am-Main)   81

7. Sara dancers, Republic of Chad. (From *Les Hommes de la Danse*, Editions Clairefontaine. Photo: Michel Huet)   96

8. Christ carrying the cross. Panel of door of Catholic chapel, University College, Ibadan, Nigeria. (Photo: U. Beier)   97

9. Cement grave sculpture. Ibibio, East Nigeria. (Photo: U. Beier)   128

Illustrations

10. Woodcarving by Felix Ídubor of Benin. Door of Co-operative Bank of Ibadan, West Nigeria. (Photo: U. Beier) *facing page* 129

11. Painting by Ben Enwonwu, Nigeria. (Federal Information Service, Lagos, Nigeria) 144

12. *The Magic Table* by Enguerrand Gourgue, Haiti. (Stedelijke Museum, Amsterdam) 145

13. Sculpture: *Bull* by Pablo Picasso. (Photo: Chevojon) 176

14. *Diviner for Obatala*. Silk screen by Susanne Wenger (cover of *Yoruba Poetry* by B. Gibadamosi and U. Beier) 177

15. *Umbral*. Oil-painting by Wifredo Lam, Cuba, 1950. (Photo: Marc Vaux) 192

16. *The Jungle*. Gouache by Wifredo Lam. (Museum of Modern Art, New York) 193

Introduction to the Second Edition

Perhaps it was fate? Perhaps it was centuries of anesthetized impulses, unconsciously revived as a result of an unplanned visit to Nigeria. I had gone simply because a friend said let's go. When I returned to teaching at Oberlin College, in Ohio, I was asked to increase my course offerings, and I replied that I would add a course on African literature. I had not thought of it before. The idea had jumped out of my mouth spontaneously. Over the years I think I had read two or three books by African authors, most recently *Blame Me on History* by Bloke Modisane, because I had met Bloke when I lived in England. Also, in addition to having already read *Facing Mount Kenya*, I had read a book on Nigerian history and politics while there. Of course, during the 1960s I had read Frantz Fanon's *The Wretched of the Earth* and *Black Skin, White Masks*. But that was the extent of it. Yet I had said I would teach African literature, fiction, drama, and poetry.

Upon returning from Nigeria, I had to go to Washington, D.C., a few weeks before school began. It was summer, early 1970s. There, in Washington, I sought out C. L. R. James, whom I had come to know and regard as a great twentieth-century scholar and intellectual. James was seventy years old. He gave me a list of books: *Things Fall Apart, The Beautiful Ones Are Not Yet Born, A Question of Power, The Voice, Weep Not, Child, The Palm-Wine Drinkard, God's Bits of Wood, The Radiance of the King, Jagua Nana*, and others. When I was in the hall leaving, James peered out the door and bade me back. He said there was a book that was imperative for me to read. The book was *Muntu*, by Janheinz Jahn.

My first awareness of Africa came through the Tarzan movies. Every Saturday, in my hometown, Chattanooga, Tennessee, along with some two hundred other black boys and girls, I ate popcorn and watched the depiction of Africa as nothing but a jungle. Monkeys scampered among the trees, while animals and snakes menacingly roamed. Africans were portrayed as half-naked, voodoo-crazed, cannibalistic savages. Then came King Kong. Africa was still a jungle, the people were still savages, and mighty Kong was captured by a group of crafty white men who brought the big beast to America, where his lust after a white women, the beauty, led to Kong's demise.

The next boyhood memory I have of Africa also came from the movies. In between showings of the major film I saw a short feature in which a jungle was depicted in "Technicolor." Torrential rains poured steadily down as a regal lion purposefully stalked the jungle, as though it were searching for something. Throughout the short feature a baritone voice-over rose and fell in rhythmic intonation:

> What is Africa to me:
> . . . .
> Jungle star or jungle track,
> Strong bronzed men, or regal black
> . . . .
> *One three centuries removed*
> . . . .
> *Spicy grove, cinnamon tree,*
> *What is Africa to me?*
> . . . .
> So I lie, who always hear
> . . . .
> Great drums throbbing through the air.
> . . . .
> I can never rest at all
> When the rain begins to fall;
> . . . .
> In an old remembered way
> Rain works on me night and day.
> . . . . ·.
> Lord, I fashion dark gods, too,
> . . . .

Dark despairing features where,
Crowned with dark rebellious hair,
. . . .

Lord, forgive me if my need
Sometimes shapes a human creed. . . .

The theater was quiet, so quiet that you could have heard the
sound of a pin had one fallen to the floor. I sat as if riveted to my
seat. The jungle was there, and the lion and the rain. But the
words and the strong, rhythmic voice, coupled with the rain
falling and the lion searching the jungle, which was more like a
beautiful forest, made powerful emotions rise and fall and
surge in me. A lot of the words escaped me, and I did not know
what they all meant; but some of the words and the images
stuck in my mind, and I never forgot them. But I recognized
the voice of Rex Ingram, the black man who played the genie in
The Thief of Baghdad and *A Thousand and One Nights*. Twenty
years would pass, though, before I read the poem that he was
reciting, "Heritage," authored by the famed Harlem Renaissance poet Countee Cullen. At the time, however, I possessed
no knowledge to give the images and words any meaning beyond the nameless yet powerful feelings they evoked in me.

The first year I was in college in Talladega, Alabama, Langston Hughes came and read his poetry. Before he read, though,
the choir rose and sang a song:

I've known rivers:
. . . .

I've known rivers ancient as the world and older
    than the flow of human blood in human veins.
. . . .

I bathed in the Euphrates when dawns were young.
I built my hut near the Congo and it lulled me to sleep.
I looked upon the Nile and raised the pyramids
    above it.
. . . .

I've known rivers:
. . . .

My soul has grown deep like the rivers.

The rendition was Langston Hughes' prizewinning poem "The Negro Speaks of Rivers," set to music. By now I was aware of Africa as the place from which my ancestors were brought as slaves to America. I had read of the Euphrates and the Nile in high school history as the place where the "Cradle of Civilization" had been. But the book and the teacher forgot to mention that the rivers were in Africa and that the Phoenicians and Egyptians were Africans. The singing of Langston Hughes' poem made me feel the same as when in the movie I had experienced Countee Cullen's "Heritage." Still not fully aware of the meaning, I knew now, however, that those rivers were in Africa and that they had something profound to do with me and all Negroes in America. Then one day quite accidentally I pulled from the library stacks *The World and Africa*, by W. E. B. Du Bois. Africa, indeed, was as old as human blood in human veins. Though its people and land had been conquered and exploited by Europeans for the better part of four centuries, its resources were the richest on the earth and the fate of its people augured the destiny of the world. As I read this book, *The World and Africa*, a retroactive understanding came to me. I left Talladega College and went to Fisk University as a sociology graduate student and took part in a Monday night extracurricular study group of students who met at a professor's house. A student from Liberia told us about neocolonialism in his country. He said that the Tubman government was a puppet regime in the service of American rubber corporations that held the Liberian population in bondage in their own country and worked the natives on rubber plantations at per capita incomes of about two hundred dollars a year.

It was now the mid-1950s. African names—Jomo Kenyatta, Tom Mboya, Kwame Nkrumah, Julius Nyerere, Patrice Lumumba, and many others—flared in the media. While the struggles for freedom throughout Africa occupied the agenda of our study group at Fisk, we noted how the popular media insinuated the same old "jungle" concept of Africa—infested with uncivilized heathens. Particularly the Mau Mau liberation struggle in Kenya and the war in the Congo were sensationalized as being the most "savage," "bloodthirsty," and "Communistic" on the part of the Africans. I was once again reminded of the way white people viewed Africa, such as in Vachel Lindsay's poem "The Congo (A Study of the Negro Race)":

> Fat black bucks in a wine-barrel room,
> . . . .
> Beat an empty barrel with the handle of a broom,
> . . . .
> Boom, boom, BOOM,
> . . . .
> THEN I SAW THE CONGO, CREEPING
>   THROUGH THE BLACK,
> . . . .
> Then along that river-bank
> A thousand miles
> Tattooed cannibals danced in files;
> . . . .
> "BLOOD!" screamed the skull-faced, lean
>   witch-doctors,
> . . . .
> BOOM, steal the pygmies,
> BOOM, kill the Arabs,
> BOOM, kill the white men,
> HOO, HOO, HOO.
> . . . .
> "Be careful what you do,
> Or Mumbo-Jumbo . . . will hoo-doo you. . . ."

Of course, our study group at Fisk absolutely rejected the "jungle" conception of Africa. Influenced by Marxism, we debunked the stereotypes and myths and favored a revolutionary vision of African reality. Earlier one of my Talladega College professors had told us that Jomo Kenyatta—depicted in the press as the savage leader of the bloodthirsty Mau Mau—was an intellectual scholar with a Ph.D. in anthropology and the author of *Facing Mount Kenya*. Reading the book, I was enthralled by the *sacred* relationship between Kenyan society and the land that the British arrogantly disregarded. They had privatized and plundered the land and reeked devastation on not only the land but on Kenyan culture and the Kenyan psyche as well. By the time I reached New York with my graduate degree from Fisk, the summer of 1957, my awareness of Africa was far removed from the image I had received during my adolescence. That summer, 1957, the "Gold Coast" won independence and Africanized its name to Ghana. I wrote the following lines in a poem: .

> I see a black continent rising across
> The ocean.
> I see a sun going down in the west,
> Dripping blood like a predatory bird
> With a hole in its breast.

Looking back, I realize there was a shortcoming that at the time I was not able to see. Through reading and discussion groups I had educated myself, and my feelings toward Africa were intellectually informed, politically inspired, and racially motivated. That was a significant step forward. But it was not enough. I had acquired no backgrounding in what being African meant. I lacked understanding of the time-honored ways by which the people conceptualized and structured their world and lived in it. I knew next to nothing of what made African people *African*. My racial identification with and my political vision of Africa were sincere. But I was nonetheless a Westerner, and I viewed and felt toward Africa with the views and feelings of a Western creature politely called a "Negro." My consciousness of Africa was missing a vital link.

I had always sensed this missing link. When I read *Facing Mount Kenya*, for example, I was enthralled by the binding spirituality between the land and the people. I was struck by the mystical, the magical, the strange, and the beautiful. Yet there was an alien undertow in the way *Facing Mount Kenya* made me feel. My inarticulate but gut feeling of alienation was confirmed when I read Richard Wright's *Black Power*. Wright was there, in Ghana, during the heyday of the independence struggle. He was a friend of Nkrumah and went with him in the towns, villages, and countrysides. Wright shared the African zeal for freedom. Africans were black, and Wright was black.

He knew oppression; he knew colonialism. Before he went, he had read a score of important books. He wanted so much to share a common spirit and outlook with his African brothers. Instead, he experienced a formidable estrangement in human temperament and political sensibility between himself and the Africans that irked and angered him. In West Africa, as in Ghana alone, Wright encountered many different tribes, languages, and finely distinguished heritages that disillusioned his particular intellectualism and political sensibilities, which were the intellectualism and sensibilities of a Mississippi-born Negro profoundly influenced by Western culture and racism. I think to his chagrin Wright discovered that in their integrity Africans do not conform to any preconceived paradigms from outside, no matter how educated such preconceptions may be or how deeply one is in love with the Africa of his or her particular sentiments.

For five years in Europe I met and fraternized with men and women from various parts of Africa. I came to know them mainly as Westernized human beings and only slightly as Africans. We communicated and related in Western terms, for these were the only terms in which I could communicate. When they began to relate out of their own heritage, I felt left out. Though I was with them, I was not of them, and I found myself on the fringes of their togetherness because, for one thing, I did not know any of their languages. All I knew were Western languages, European languages, mainly English with a little French and Spanish thrown in.

When slavery outlawed the speaking of African languages, the slaves were cut off from the most vital medium of cultural heritage and transmission. When I went to Africa and lived for several months in Nigeria and a week in Senegal, I experienced the historical "missing link" between me and the world from which my ancestors came. In Lagos, Nigeria, I lived for a while in Suru Lere, which was a vast, sprawling dwelling area. I imposed on this area the interpretation of my own experiences in the Southland of America. The stucco low-level dwellings and shacks reminded me of my own neighborhood in Chattanooga, Tennessee, or any "ghetto" in the North, like, for example, Newark, New Jersey. When, however, I encountered the *inside* of Nigerian culture, my feeling of familiarity was abruptly shattered. The first night I heard the drums in Suru Lere I thought a great party was going on. But all night long the drums continued their rhythmic pounding. Though I was informed that the drums were the nightly ritual of the Muslims, I kept getting flashes of the deeply ingrained impression of Africa as "savage jungle" that I had received during my childhood. In Dakar, Senegal, hardly anyone would speak English, only French. There, in Dakar, where the desert is creeping down from the north, I saw people wearing clothes ranging from the most Western to the most traditional. At noon they suddenly stopped everything and bowed down in the streets, buildings, anywhere they were, and paid homage to Mecca. In Lagos, Nigeria, I roamed about the teeming city, sweltering in the heat of a constant sun. In the aftermath of the bloody internecine war known as the Biafran conflict, the city of Lagos also sweltered in the heat of transition between the old ways of Africa and the new ways of the West. Many nights into morning I sat with a former Ibo commander in the Biafran Army, huddled over bottles of scotch whiskey, and I listened to the details of that debauching war. Everywhere I witnessed the psychic pain of Africans undergoing the exigency of uprootedness and transition. At the time, the early 1970s, throughout Lagos and the rest of Nigeria, as well as in other parts of Africa, the hot contrapuntal, polyrhythmic, Afro-beat musical sound of Fela Ransome-Kuti boomed in the hotels, bars, nightclubs, and joints. Fela's music boomed along every street and alley in the markets and sprawling dwelling areas of the poor. In his music I heard James Brown, I heard Sonny Rollins, I recognized the fiery Baptist Church, and I heard Jelly Roll Morton, Mama Yancey, and Scott Joplin—the spirituals, the gospels, the blues, the rhythm and blues, the rag, and the jazz. The music had journeyed across the ocean and returned with the trappings of the alien experience. Yet it retained the essence of its own self. Now it spoke of not just one experience but of the African/European/American experience as well, the diasporic experience.

Though my sense of familiarity among the people was growing, only Africa's music was thoroughly recognizable to me.

The larger identification I felt was still basically racial, basically political and ideological. I was in Africa, but only one residual of Africa was in me. One day, as I sauntered along the sun-drenched road, some Nigerian children pointed at me and yelled, "Oyinbo!" I had been apprised of the expression. It meant an African of black complexion whose constitution was unable to countenance the eating of pepper and the pepper had changed the African's complexion to a lighter shade of brown, my complexion. "Oyinbo" indeed.

> One three centuries removed
> From the scenes his fathers loved.

Although I was back on the scene, I was not really of the scene. I was missing the African-rooted experiences and understand-ings of what it meant to *be* African.

I got my first effective understanding of what it means to be African when I read Janheinz Jahn's remarkable book. *Muntu* provided my first grounding in the primary assumptions, prin-ciples, and concepts upon which African culture and worldview are structured and which constitute the philosophy of existence in which African feelings are born and nurtured. Human be-ings create culture to bring sense to existence and meaningful ways of viewing the world and living in it. Sense and meaning are salient qualities and vital functions of African culture. But you have got to feel, comprehend, understand, and respect the fundamentals of African culture before you can see the sense and appreciate the meaning. Relying on the work of six major sources, three Africans and one African-American, along with a French ethnologist and a Belgian monk, Janheinz Jahn identi-fies and elucidates four categories and two principles of basic African ontology and world order. The four categories are:

1. Muntu (human being; plural: Bantu)
2. Kintu (thing, object, animate and inanimate, including animal; plural: Bintu)
3. Hantu (place and time)
4. Kuntu (modality, quality, style, rhythm, beauty, etc.)

These categories are universal categories of existence. "All being, all essence, in whatever form it is conceived," writes Jahn, "can be subsumed under one of these categories. Nothing can be conceived outside them." Jahn is relying specifically on the work of the Bantu scholar of Bantu philosophy and language Alexis Kagame. Not only do everything in existence and everything conceivable belong to one of the four categories, but the categories are categories of not mere substance; more important, they are categories of *forces*. ". . . all things are forces. . . . Man and woman (category Muntu), dog and stone (category Kintu), east and yesterday (category Hantu), beauty and laughter (category Kuntu) are forces and as such are all related to one another. The relationship of these forces is expressed in their names, for if we remove the determinative the stem NTU is the same for all the categories [pp. 100–101]."

The first principle then is NTU, which may be considered the principle of essential coherence or compatibility among all things or among all the disciplines. Here Jahn relies on the Yoruba writer Adebayo Adesanya and quotes him: "Philosophy, theology, politics, social theory, land law, medicine, psychology, birth and burial, all find themselves logically concatenated in a system so tight that to subtract one item from the whole is to paralyse the structure of the whole [p. 97]." But NTU must not be confused with a supreme force at the top of an hierarchical pyramid, for it does not and cannot exist independent of its manifestation in the forces of the four categories of Muntu, Kintu, Hantu, and Kuntu. In other words, NTU is simply existence, universal and particular. It is at once "God" and man and thing and time-and-space and modality. NTU is everywhere and everything. Nothing exists outside NTU, and NTU never exists outside anything because, Jahn asserts, "NTU is what Muntu, Kintu, Hantu and Kuntu all equally *are*. Force and matter are not being united in this conception; on the contrary, they have never been apart."

At its roots African philosophy is the philosophy of unity of all things, of ontological harmony and coherence in the world. NTU affects the being of the forces, and the forces affect the being of NTU. In and through the manifestations of NTU, being is possible, and in and through being, NTU is possible.

Therefore, in traditional African culture, life and death, secular and sacred, night and day, black and white, ugliness and beauty are not antagonistic polarities, but they all are constant and continuing forces.

None of the forces, however, including Muntu (human being) are self-activating forces. Rather, they are "sleeping," "dormant," "anesthetized" forces. That brings us to the second principle, the principle of Nommo. Jahn writes: "The driving power . . . that gives life and efficacy to all things is Nommo, the 'word,' of which we can only say that it is word and water and seed and blood for the moment [all] in one [p. 101]." Nommo—the spoken word, the sound of the drums, the laughter of the throat, the poem, and the song—constitutes the "magical" force that activates and enlivens all other forces. This force, this awesome power, Nommo, the word, is the exclusive property of Muntu. Muntu, human being, is the only force that is capable of possessing the magic and power of Nommo. This is because Muntu is the only force endowed with intelligence, or ubwenge.

Bintu (animals) have a kind of "intelligence," but it is not the quality of the intelligence of which human beings (Bantu) are capable. Muntu is not automatically a muntu by virtue of being biologically born. The ontology of the human being is a double process. The biological body must unite with a "shadow," the process of which is indicated by the principle of buzima. At the same time a spiritual force, Nommo-force, unites with the body, and the human being is originated in terms of a body with a *spirit*. This is the principle of magara: life, designating the union of Nommo-force with a human creature, resulting in a Muntu. Illustrating the African significance of the Nommo-force, Jahn quotes from a three-hour conversation that an old but vigorous Dogon sage had with a French ethnologist, Marcel Griaule. The sage expounded in great poetic language on the nature and role of Nommo:

> "The Nommo," says Ogotommêli, "is water and heat. The vital force that carries the word issues from the mouth in a water vapour which is both water and word. . . . The vital force of the earth . . . is water. . . . Even in stone there is that force, for dampness is everywhere. . . . The word is for all

in this world; it must be exchanged, so that it goes and comes, for it is good to give and to receive the forces of life. . . . The good word . . . brings and maintains the moisture necessary to procreation and by this means Nommo . . . transforms into a germ the water of the word and gives it the appearance of a human person . . . [pp. 124–25]"

The Nommo-force process is indispensable to produce a *complete* human being with intelligence and a soul. Jahn explains that the newborn child becomes a Muntu only when the father or the "sorcerer" gives the child a *name* and *pronounces* it. Only the giving of a name adds the magara principle (spirituality) to the buzima principle (living human being). If, for example, a biological child dies before its name is pronounced, the child is not even mourned. The full-fledged human being is produced, writes Jahn, "not by the act of birth, but by the word-seed: it is designated."

Thus, just as images, objects, works of art, animals, and so forth get their particular meanings by *speaking* the meanings into them, the humanity (Muntuness) of the human animal is designated by virtue of pronouncing or speaking the word-name. Even the specific nature of the gods, or loas, are determined in and through the word or words that designate their significance. Ergo, we may speak of the *designation* of the human being, the *designation* of the object, the image, the animal, the tree, the stool, the mask, and so on. Because fluidity is a property of the word, all fluid things—rivers, streams, lakes, blood, breath, moisture, semen, and the like—and all things that conduct fluid, such as trees (Kuntu force), are likely to be imbued with divine significance or may even be designated as "honorary" Muntu. Depending, moreover, on the Nommo-force of one's ancestors and the extent to which one acquires the Nommo-power (*spirit*-force) of ancestors, individuals may possess varying degrees of Nommo-power, and since the word is all-powerful, a powerful Muntu, such as a griot or shaman, may be capable through Nommo-power of effecting anything. This is what we in the West disparagingly refer to as "black magic" or as "primitive mumbo jumbo." It is no more primitive or mumbo jumbo than the sacrament ceremony in our own churches. To wit, the monotheistic religions of the West, as well as the so-called science of logic and reason, are nothing more than our own brand of "mumbo jumbo," a culturally sanctioned "white magic."

The four basic categories and two basic principles—Muntu, Kintu, Hantu, Kuntu, NTU, Nommo—plus all the subcategories and other concepts and principles, are explored and illustrated in great detail by Janheinz Jahn. *Muntu* gives good insight into the foundation and workings of a culture out of which both traditional and modern Africans are coming. Although the cultural system that Jahn breaks down and describes is based largely on the Dogon, Yoruba, and Bantu cultures, his analysis and treatment are convincingly applicable to the whole of Africa below the Sahara, often referred to as Black Africa. What we call Africa comprises hundreds of tribes, clans, ethnics, and languages. Jahn does not assert a monolith of African culture. What arises from his treatment, among differences and diversity, is a common denominator, a unity of philosophy and epistemology at the core of the African world. *Muntu* weaves the thread of meaning through African diversity, it makes sense out of "mumbo jumbo," and it provides a window through which we may comprehend the integrity of what we see but do not otherwise understand.

At Oberlin College, we were halfway through my newly added course, Modern African Literature, and had enjoyed lively discussions of the books we had read when over fall break I assigned *Muntu*. The students returned, and we spent several class meetings rediscussing the books we had read in the light of *Muntu*. Our reading of *Muntu* brought to our reanalyses of the books we had covered a deeper comprehension of them and revealed a rich, "hidden" landscape we had not recognized before. *The Palm-Wine Drinkard*, by Amos Tutuola, no longer appeared "foreign," "strange," or "weird"; it was no longer thought to be some kind of African "fairy tale." We grasped the profound agency in black culture of song, dance, and drum. We witnessed the systemic complexity, the sense and meaning of Clarence's journey through the African "bush" in Camara Laye's *Radiance of the King*, and despite Clarence's white skin, we entered into the process of Clarence's becoming a full-fledged African. At the end, when he is embraced by the divine boy-king, we, too, were spirited away. For the rest of the course *Muntu* brought to our discussions a deeper, broader, more meaningful comprehension of the novels, plays, and poetry we read. We realized and understood that we were experiencing a literature that was coming out of what Jahn called "neo-African culture."

The subtitle of *Muntu* is *African Culture and the Western World.* As discussed so far, the book is given to transliteration of the fundamentals of traditional African culture into European terms. Since first reading *Muntu* and first teaching the Modern African Literature course, I have read many books, papers, articles, monograms, and other literature pertaining to Africa. Some relevant ones are *African Religions and Philosophy*, by John S. Mbiti; *African Philosophy*, by Richard A. Wright; *The Mind of Africa*, by Willie E. Abraham; *An African Treasury*, edited by Langston Hughes; *Whispers from a Continent*, by Wilfred Cartey; *Toward the Decolonization of African Literature*, coauthored by Chinweizu, Onwuchekwa Jemie, and Ihechukwu Madubuike; and *Ngambika*, edited by Carole Boyce Davis and Anne Adams Graves. All the books I have read, especially the ones mentioned above, are valuable. But the book that means most to me is singularly *Muntu*. Its great value lies in its utility in grasping the traditional African ethos and idiom. *Muntu* illuminates and clarifies the deep structures underpinning traditional African culture. It explicates the integrity of African ways. But this, traditional Africa, is not Jahn's thesis. His thesis is the *new* African culture, not the old. On page 16, Jahn writes:

> . . . it is said that they are trying to revive the African tradition . . . the past as it was. . . . On the contrary, African intelligence wants to integrate into modern life only what seems valuable from the past. The goal is neither the traditional African nor the black European but the modern African. This means that a tradition . . . whose values are made explicit and renewed, must assimilate those European elements which modern times demand; and in this process the European elements are so transformed and

adapted that a modern, viable *African* culture arises out of the whole . . . a genuine Renaissance, which does not remain a merely formal renewal and imitation of the past, but permits something new to emerge [Jahn's emphasis]. This something new is already at hand; we call it neo-African culture.

This is Jahn's thesis. It is also his problem. But Muntu evinces little evidence that Jahn perceives his thesis as being difficult and hazardous. Proceeding rather optimistically, Jahn dismisses or overrides the problematics of his thesis. On pages 17 and 18 he writes, quoting Egon Friedell:

"All history is saga and myth, and as such the product of the state of our intellectual powers at a particular time. . . ." The Africa presented by the ethnologist is a legend in which we *used* to believe [my emphasis]. The African tradition as it appears in the light of neo-African culture may also be a legend—but it is the legend in which African intelligence believes. . . . Moreover . . . the tradition . . . is nevertheless the only true one, since it is the one which will from now on determine the future of Africa. For several centuries Africa has had to suffer under the conception . . . formed by Europe. . . . But the present and the future . . . will be determined by the conception that *African* intelligence forms of the African past [Jahn's emphasis].

Unless I misread him, Jahn seems to fall prey to his own category of Skokian, a glorification of the nature of the past and its role in the making of the future, without regard for the powers in the world that seek to discredit, undermine, dominate, exploit, and destroy everything that is truly African.

Three chapters—"Voodoo," "Rumba," and "Blues"—are devoted to piecing together the synthesis between traditional African culture and European culture, resulting in what Jahn calls the neo-African culture. There are specific subsections in six chapters of the book in which the dialectics of race and culture contact in Africa and in the European/American settings are conceptualized, explained, illustrated, and set forth. Jahn's thesis of the New African Culture is sufficiently illustrated by the use of African canonical literature, authored by the folk as well as by francophone and anglophone Africans and by African-Americans. Negritude, for example, is illustrated, and its European critics are criticized for their cultural imperialism. The so-called voodoo of Haiti is illuminated in its dialectical aspects of African and European (Catholic) syncretism, and is treated as a *religion* the essence of which is like any other religion, and its role in the liberation of Haiti at the turn of the eighteenth century is attested to. In some chapters subsections are entitled: "Négritude and Surrealism," "Négritude and Expressionism," "The New Art," "Neo-African Literature," "Residual-African Elements in North America," and "Europe, the Partner."

Jahn's facts are substantial. But his assertions about the facts seem overly optimistic to me. Granted, Jahn published *Muntu* in 1958, and his good faith is remarkably demonstrated. The present reissuing of *Muntu* alone speaks to its classical quality. And it is ample and well that *Muntu* celebrates the rediscovery and repossession of the African consciousness on the part of all peoples of African descent. But the force of white supremacy and the might of its violence are still at large in the world. Not alone is this force cultural. It is political, economic, and most of all, it is militarized to the hilt. There is little evidence that Europe will become a faithful partner with Africa. The religious, ideological, economic, and military forces of white supremacy are vultures eating up not merely the culture but the very lives of African peoples.

There is also the problem, the dilemma, of the African "intelligence" itself, as to which traditional and what Western stuff to bring with it into the modern world. What pangs must molest the "African personality" in making the transition from traditional to modern, as there are those who proclaim already that we are in the "postmodern" age. There is the other dilemma of Africans writing in the language of their oppressors or former oppressors. Even though they might use the European languages in an African way, many Africans are asking, "Just whom are we writing for?" To make a long story short, in the words of the South African writer Bessie Head, the bottom line is a question of power.

Culture is or can be a form of struggle. But cultural struggles are doomed to frizzle, accommodation and co-option if they are not attended by or are not part and parcel of a political struggle and, if need be, a military struggle. Cultures may be transformed from within by virtue of the dialectics of their own elements. But the indigenous history of African cultures was interrupted and arrested from without by cultural, political, and military means of European white supremacists. African writers, such as Ngugi wa Thiong'o (*Petals of Blood*) and Ousmane Sembene (*God's Bits of Wood*), and African-American writers, such as John A. Williams, Ishmael Reed, and Audre Lorde, are aware of the inextricable relation between the cultural struggle and the political struggle. I do not believe that neo-African or African-American culture will save themselves, let alone save the West, unless the culture struggles are part of political struggles.

Although *Muntu* does not incorporate these problems into its treatment, it is a hallmark work, a cartography of traditional African and neo-African culture. The book is a demystification of the so-called black African mystique. Equally significant, *Muntu* can serve, by comparative application of Jahn's methodology, as an eye-opener to the machinery of white Western culture that is in and all around us.

—*Calvin C. Hernton, 1990*

Chapter 1

SKOKIAN?

Problem and Method

Whatever human beings think and do and
produce concerns all other human beings.

KARL JASPERS

I. QUO VADIS AFRICA?

Africa is entering world history. There is a flow of books and articles dealing with this process in its political, economic, sociological and psychological aspects. But all these expositions have in common a single conviction; they are all persuaded that one single pattern of cultural change is forming. Through the influence of Europe, it is believed, Africa is adapting herself, giving up her traditions and adopting foreign ideas, methods of work, forms of government and principles of economic organization. The time of transition, whether short or long, is thought to be a time of crisis which will confront all Africans with the decision either to accept modern civilization and survive, or to perish with their own traditions. Some observers believe in a gradual, as others in a sudden, transition, but all are agreed that a fully Europeanized Africa will be the end product of the process. Europe is alleged to provide the model, Africa to copy it; Europe to be spiritually the giving, Africa the receiving partner.

Since Europe is held to be the teacher and Africa the pupil, Europe is to decide when Africa is ripe: ripe for a faith, ripe for action, ripe for freedom. Europe is thought to know what is good for Africa, better than Africa herself. Admittedly, Europe offers different and rival doctrines—democracy or communism, Christianity or atheism—and in choosing between these the pupil may gain status for herself—a process which is usually regretted; yet this alters nothing in the general pattern. Whether Africa accepts the doctrines one recommends or those one warns her against, she must give up her own traditions: there are no other possibilities to be considered.

The justification for this is that the age of technology has produced on the earth conditions from which it is no longer possible for any nation to escape. The combine harvester, it is argued, is superior to the hoe and machete, the gun to the bow and arrow. The combine and the gun originated in the sphere of Western, or Christian civilization. Therefore those who wish to give up hoe, machete, bow and arrow and to have combines and guns, must also give up healing by witchcraft, polygamy and 'superstition'; in short, they must give up their whole culture and demand in its place newspapers, monogamy and Christianity (or communism). If this argument is valid, then the pattern of African assimilation to Europe is valid also. But if it is not valid, and a third possibility is conceivable—if Africa can master modern technology yet retain a modified African culture—what then are all the prognoses, discussions and projects worth which fail to take this culture into consideration?

Thus the question of the future of Africa becomes the question of the existence of an African culture.

II. TRADITIONAL AND MODERN (JASPERS' THEORY OF HISTORY)

The example of Japan teaches us that a people can appropriate modern technology and modern forms of organization without abandoning their traditional culture; that modernity can be assimilated to a non-European culture without destroying it. Could something of the same kind happen in Africa?

It will be objected that Japan and Africa are not comparable, since their cultures lie on different levels. According to Jaspers, history has shown two great advances. First, after the age of myth, which includes pre-history and the history of the great early cultures, reflective thought began[1] between 900 and 800 B.C. in Greece and Asia Minor, simultaneously but independently.* It was this advance that really set history in motion, transformed it and determined its direction. The second advance is the age of science and technology, which now in its turn is everywhere taking the lead and transforming all mankind. Japan, like Europe, is said to have been affected by the first advance and thus to be a land of higher culture, while Africa is only just being brought into the main stream of history. Here all signs of a higher culture are wanting. This part of the globe is inhabited by primitive peoples who may choose between extinction or—what? Jaspers' thesis does not even allow these primitive peoples a chance of adaptation. If even Mexico and Peru, higher cultures untouched by the first advance, failed to survive the contact with Europe—'they vanished in the mere presence of Western culture'[2]—how can primitive peoples survive contact with the scientific-technical age?

Jaspers foresees for them no adjustment, but only their extinction or the fate of becoming mere raw material to be processed by technological civilization.[3]

For the Australian aborigines, the South Sea Islanders, and the American Indians, the thesis of Jaspers seems largely valid. For the Africans it clearly fails to hold. For they managed to survive despite the most intense pressure of slave trading and slavery; nor does it look as if they were prepared to furnish the raw material for a technical world civilization. The present flood of literature on Africa arises precisely from the disquieting fact that the Africans are not behaving as those planners and prophets who arrogantly dispose of them predicted they would behave. So the reader rushes from one analysis to another, for he cannot shake off the feeling that the Africans themselves have a part to play; he wants to know what the Africans are really feeling and thinking, yet the shrewder authors leave him with a question mark.

Is Jaspers' thesis mistaken then? Or are the Africans perhaps not a primitive people? And are they perhaps even able to achieve the rationalization of their pre-historical existence (the axial period) and from this rationalization the assimilation of western civilization at the same time?

* Jaspers calls this the 'axial period'.

13

The question, therefore, whether in confronting Western culture Africa reacts differently today from the way she did in the past, and differently from Mexico or Polynesia, involves once more the question of the existence and nature of an African culture.

III. 'SKOKIAN' (MALINOWSKI'S THEORY OF CULTURAL CHANGE)

Malinowski sees culture not as something static but as something that is constantly changing. The simple conception of the transformation of Africa is too simple for him. It is, he believes, only on the surface that the transition produces 'hybrids'; in reality these are new forms, taken neither from the European nor the African tradition. Take for example *Skokian*, a 'cocktail' of methyl alcohol, calcium carbide, treacle, tobacco and so on, which is drunk in the slums of Johannesburg: such a thing has never before been adopted in either Europe or Africa. Thus Skokian is something new, the legitimate offspring of African slums and European moral principles. The Boers' Puritan aversion to the harmless African beer and the police regulation which forbade its use forced the African inhabitants to invent a drink that could be made and stored in small quantities, easy to hide, which could be matured in a few hours, and could have its alcoholic effect quickly.[4] Similarly, in Malinowski's view, all new objects, facts and forms of life in Africa are the results of European pressure and African resistance. Even African nationalism, which invokes and revives an African culture, is, according to Malinowski, nothing but 'Skokian': the African, he believes, is seduced by the enticements of Western Civilization, and accepts new forms of life. His ultimate aim is to be 'if not European, then at least a master or part master of some of the devices, possessions and influences which in his eyes constitute European superiority'.[5]

But if he has been permitted to attend a European or American university, he must finally make the discovery that in legal, economic, social and political matters, equal rights and status are in fact denied him. And when once a share in the ideals, interests and blessings of a co-operative effort are denied them, the Africans naturally fall back on their own systems of belief, value and feeling. The more independent, far-sighted and sensitive the African, the stronger will be his reaction. Elements of an old culture, such as for example the ritualistic attitude to livestock, to African music, to dances and amusements, are revived with a new, almost ethnographic interest in racial history, traditional law, and the artistic and intellectual achievements of their own races. This sophisticated nationalism, in Malinowski's view, draws all its strength from the 'enormous residue' of old tradition.[6]

Malinowski's functional theory of cultural change—which like most theories of Africa is intended in the last analysis to ensure 'a stable and effective rule by a minority',[7] that is, by a European minority—sees in the revival of African traditions an unhealthy and 'sophisticated' nationalism, a product of psychological retreat before European pressure, 'modern myth-making', a drug, that is, 'Skokian'. But is there another possibility? Is it here a question of that very development of increasing awareness to which Jaspers ascribes such power? Could this renewal, this rationalization of tradition, in fact be the crucial period in African development, which is making it possible for the Africans to assert themselves, and to escape the fate, assigned to them by Jaspers and Malinowski, of 'becoming tools'? In other words, is that nationalism, though so unhealthy for European rule, perhaps not so 'unhealthy' at all for the Africans—considering that it has already begun to bring about the emergence of independent African states? We ask what the Africans are thinking, what they are planning, what they believe, how they can survive the crisis, why the historical process fails to conform to the predicted pattern—but we pay no attention to the rational revival of the African tradition by African intelligence, or else we dismiss it as the drug of psychological self-intoxication, as 'Skokian'.

The psychological situation of the Africans does indeed play a part in stimulating the cultural revival, but it cannot be its only cause—especially since the most creative and productive leaders of the revival are not those whose equal rights and status are denied, but precisely those to whom nothing has been denied, who are officials or ministers in Europe, and who have not the slightest personal reason to be dissatisfied with their lot.

But if the revival of the African tradition is no 'Skokian', no self-betrayal, no intoxication, no deception—if it is a reality which can no longer be ignored, a reality which plays a role in politics, economics, art, and literature, ought we not to give it its correct name: African Renaissance?

If we abandon the scheme by which the African wants to become a 'black European' but is permitted only to become a tool for technology, and if we adopt the only point of view worthy of European culture, that every human being has and must have the right to become what he wants, then our eyes are opened. Then the African is no longer an object to which one gives instructions, but a partner, whom one can interrogate about his aims, his ideas, his view of the world, and from whom one gets answers. Instead of relying on the usual method of questioning the 'man in the bush' or the 'boy' as the representative of Africa, it is certainly more advisable to turn to those Africans who have their own opinion and who will determine the future of Africa: those, in other words, of whom it is said that they are trying to revive the African tradition. For it is soon evident that none of them is thinking of reviving the past as it was; that would be 'Skokian'. On the contrary, African intelligence wants to integrate into modern life only what seems valuable from the past. The goal is neither the traditional African nor the black European but the modern African. This means that a tradition seen rationally, whose values are made explicit and renewed, must assimilate those European elements which modern times demand; and in this process the European elements are so transformed and adapted that a modern, viable *African* culture arises out of the whole. It is a question, therefore, of a genuine Renaissance, which does not remain a merely formal renewal and imitation of the past, but permits something new to emerge. This something new is already at hand; we call it neo-African culture.

IV. Neo-African Culture (All its History is Myth)

This book attempts to present a systematic exposition of neo-African culture. It is a culture built on two components. The

European component is generally known, so that it will be recognizable to the reader without difficulty. The traditional African component is treated in greater detail, and is in fact presented as it appears in the light of neo-African culture.

This needs justification, for it will be objected that there has never been a traditional African culture as a whole, but only a plurality of different 'primitive' cultures, and this objection will be supported by pointing to more or less accurate investigations by ethnologists. But the question of whether or not a plurality is understood as a unity is to a great extent one of interpretation. European research has always had the plurality in view and has scarcely noticed the common denominator. In the light of neo-African culture, on the other hand, it is the unity that is slightly stressed. Moreover, the valuable components of the tradition, which find their continuation in neo-African culture, are emphasized, and the others left aside. It will be objected that this produces a false picture of the past, a myth instead of an objective picture of history. But this is the case with every history. 'Every age has a definite picture of all past events accessible to it, a picture peculiar to itself,' writes Friedell. 'Legend is not one of the forms, but rather the only form, in which we can imaginatively consider and relive history. All history is saga and myth, and as such the product of the state of our intellectual powers at a particular time: of our capacity for comprehension, the vigour of our imagination, our feeling for reality.'[8] The Africa presented by the ethnologist is a legend in which we used to believe. The African tradition as it appears in the light of neo-African culture may also be a legend—but it is the legend in which African intelligence believes. And it is their perfect right to declare authentic, correct and true those components of their past which they believe to be so. In the same way a Christian, asked about the nature of Christianity, will point to the Gospel teaching 'Love my neighbour' and not to the Inquisition.

Moreover, if it is not objective, the conception of the tradition as it appears in the light of neo-African culture is nevertheless the only true one, since it is the one which will from now on determine the future of Africa. For several centuries Africa has had to suffer under the conception of the African past formed by

Europe. As long as this was so, that European conception was 'true', that is to say, effective. But the present and the future on the other hand will be determined by the conception that *African* intelligence forms of the African past. Neo-African culture appears as an unbroken extension, as the legitimate heir of tradition. Only where man feels himself to be heir and successor to the past has he the strength for a new beginning.

V. 'MUNTU' (THE PROBLEM OF MAN)

Muntu, the title of this book, is a Bantu word and is usually translated as 'man'. But the concept of 'Muntu' embraces living and dead, ancestors and deified ancestors: gods. The unity expressed by the inclusive concept of Muntu is one of the characteristics of African culture, and further peculiarities are derived from it. That concept therefore seemed an appropriate title for the book. Yet at the same time the concept 'Muntu' points to the fact that all differences in the nature of man have their common denominator. True, in the course of argument differences are stressed, contrasts revealed—which are necessary in order to clarify the peculiarities of a culture. But when the reader finds that these peculiarities are not so extraordinary, that much that characterizes African culture also occurs in other cultures, then the title 'Muntu' may remind him that nothing superhuman can be expected of human cultures. If in places the reader is inclined to object that what we are expounding as an aspect of African culture plays a part also in other cultures, that the meaning of life is also stressed in European culture, that the spoken word has the greatest significance also in other cultures, above all in illiterate ones, that rhythm has its functions among all peoples, that even in the Christian Middle Ages the picture has also functioned as symbol, ideogram, and sensory image, and that therefore all these so emphatically African matters are not after all so original —then let him recollect that all human cultures resemble one another up to a point, that different cultures only value their common elements differently, in so far as one puts the accent here, another there, and that it is the ordering, the relation of the

18

elements to one another that determines the difference between the cultures. The one looks for basic images, because image and idea precede the word; the other makes the word produce the image. In one rhythm is monometric, in the other polymetric. But only the sum total of all the particular ways of doing things, any one of which may also occur in other cultures, produces the big 'How', the aggregate ordered by a particular philosophical conception, which constitutes the unique character of a culture.

That is precisely what this book is intended to convey: namely, that cultural differences rest on the different ordering and emphasis of something basically similar and not on biological differences between men. Neo-African culture clearly demonstrates that culture is not biologically inherited, that one can voluntarily abandon or acquire a culture, that customs and capabilities, thoughts and judgements are not innate. The static culture of a society of bees is inherited, but human culture, in contrast, is preserved by being handed on from one generation to another.[9] Neo-African culture reveals itself to us as a spiritual phenomenon. If therefore the reader discovers in the course of the exposition that the mystery of African culture, the magical practices of medicine men, the demoniac possession of the Haitian Voodoo cult are not so mysterious after all, and can be interpreted according to a conception of the world intelligible to all men—if, in other words, the reader is led to human understanding instead of to enjoyable but meaningless thrills and shudders, he should not be disappointed: rather let him rejoice in recognizing rational behaviour in the action of his fellow men.

VI. The 'Real' African

'Africa' in this book means Africa south of the Sahara, 'Black Africa', and the inhabitants of this region are referred to as Africans—the people 'in the bush' as well as the intellectuals. In the course of European history Africans have sometimes been called 'heathens', 'savages' or 'primitives', sometimes extolled as 'pure, natural human beings'. This vocabulary arose out of certain prejudices, which were in turn confirmed by the vocabulary, so that every assertion was justified. For those who expect to see in their fellow men fools, blockheads or devils, will find evidence to confirm their prejudices. If we are convinced the other fellow cannot sing, we have only to call his song 'a hellish row' in order to justify our claim. Simply by applying a certain vocabulary one can easily turn Gods into idols, faces into grimaces, votive images into fetishes, discussions into palavers and distort real objects and matters of fact through bigotry and prejudice. We speak in this book, therefore, not about 'savages', 'primitives', 'heathens' or 'Negroes' but about Africans and Afro-Americans, who are neither angels nor devils but people, among whom—as everywhere—there are good and bad, stupid and clever, geniuses and boneheads, honest men and scoundrels. But since this book deals with culture, it is above all people of a certain intellectual level who are quoted.

This seems obvious. But prejudice has created types in the mind of the public. Only the most highly cultivated person, humane, cosmopolitan, enlightened, progressive, counts as a 'real European'. A 'real African', on the other hand, lives in the bush, carves 'primitive' sculptures, can neither read nor write, goes naked, lives carefree and happy from day to day and tells fairy stories about the crocodile and the elephant. The more 'primitive', the more 'really African'. But an African who is enlightened and cosmopolitan, who presides in the most cultivated fashion over congresses, who makes political speeches or writes novels, no longer counts as a 'real' African.

Yet we should not measure with two different kinds of yardstick. We should admit that in Europe also a great many people let themselves be led by 'group concepts' and are incapable of thinking logically. It is no different in Africa. But if people want to learn about European culture, they study the works of European authors and artists. And since in this case we are trying to learn about African culture, we shall turn to the corresponding group of people.

When I published the collection *Schwarzer Orpheus* a critic remarked that these fascinating poems were 'unfortunately' influenced by European thought and no longer 'really African'.

Now this book has set itself in fact the task of attempting to determine what *is* 'really African', and then of examining neo-African poetry, literature and art, to see to what extent they are 'really African' and to what extent they are not.

VII. BLACK SOULS IN A WHITE WORLD

Millions of Afro-Americans in South America, the Antilles and the United States grow up in a European-American environment and without any knowledge of African culture. Except for the colour of their skins they are Americans like any others. Yet the others think this colour a blemish and let those in question feel it. Thus the Afro-American is constantly reminded of his origin, which has otherwise often lost all meaning for him.

Such an Afro-American, the physician and psychologist Frantz Fanon of Martinique, has presented in a stimulating book the reactions of the Afro-Americans.[10] He explains that psychologically the majority of Afro-Americans are ill, and he shows how they react to the terrible spiritual pressure placed upon them. One group want to become white, to liberate themselves from the burdensome memory that a more highly pigmented skin represents: in the Negro press of the United States there are countless advertisements for salves and mixtures which are allegedly able to bleach the skin. The others seek their salvation in the acquisition of the African heritage of which they have been deprived. Through an emotional stimulus a conscious step is taken—the first step into neo-African culture. The emotional need admittedly, is for an intoxicant—'Skokian'—yet when it is voluntarily sought it produces an attitude that is of interest to us here as the approach to neo-African culture. Frantz Fanon presents the psychological process in the first person:

'The knowledge of the body is uniquely negative knowledge. One is acquainted with oneself in the third person. I know that if I want to smoke, I must extend my right arm and pick up the packet of cigarettes at the other end of the table. The matches are in the left-hand drawer, so I must lean back a bit in order to reach them. I do not carry out all these movements simply out of habit, but through an implicit knowledge. The slow construction of myself as a body in the midst of a spatial and temporal world: this seems to me to be the pattern.'[11]

Fanon then shows that the basic pattern does not apply to a black-skinned person in the 'white' world. The natural physical pattern is overlaid with historical-racial conceptions, with conceptions imposed by a hostile and biased world: ' "Look, a Negro!" It was an external stimulus that impinged on me as I was passing. I suppressed a smile. "Look, a Negro!" It was true. I was amused. "Look a Negro!" The circle narrowed more and more. I was openly amused. "Mummy. Look, a Negro! I'm afraid." Afraid. Afraid. So they were beginning to fear me. I wanted to split my sides laughing, but it was no longer possible. I couldn't laugh any more. For I knew that there are legends, stories, that there is history and especially historicity, as Jaspers had taught me. So the schema of normal body-experience was dissolved, attacked at several points, gave way and was replaced by a schema that is racial and epidemic. In the train I was acquainted with my body, no longer so to speak in the third person but in three persons. In the train, instead of one seat, I was left two or three. I was responsible at one and the same time for my body, for my race, for my ancestors. I looked at myself objectively, discovered my blackness, my ethnic characteristics. And I understood all that was thus being held against me: cultural backwardness, fetishism, slavery, cannibalism. I wanted to be a human being, nothing more than a human being. Nothing binds me to my forebears, enslaved and lynched as they were. Yet I decided to take them upon myself. It was on the universal level of the intellect that I understood this inner ancestry. I am the descendant of slaves just as President Lebrun is the descendant of serfs. But does anyone say, for example, to President Lebrun, "Do you know, my friend, I have no race prejudice", or "But do please come in, Doctor, we have no prejudice here . . ." Or: "So you're a doctor? I always knew there were some intelligent Negroes." What should I do with myself? What corner could I creep into? My body seemed to be on display, dissected, inspected, put together again. The Negro trembles because he is cold. The white world, the only respectable world, denied me

22

any share in itself. It is demanded of a man that he bear himself like a man. But of me it was demanded that I bear myself like a black man, like a Negro. How is that? Although I had every reason to hate and despise them, *they* rejected *me*. If they loved me, they said they loved me in spite of my colour. If they hate me, they tell me it is not because I am black that they hate me. So I am the prisoner of this infernal circle.'[12]

Fanon investigates the psychological consequences of this situation, the self-hatred, the disgust. He proceeds to an ever sharper analysis. 'Neither my polished manner nor my literary knowledge nor my understanding of quantum theory met with favour. I complained; I demanded explanations. I was facing something irrational. The psychoanalysts say that nothing is more traumatic for a child than the contact with reality. But I say that for a human being who has no weapon but his reason, there is nothing more neurotic than an encounter with the irrational.[13] The scientists have admitted that the Negro is a human creature; physically and mentally he has developed analogously to the white man: the same morphology, the same histology. On all fronts reason has assured our victory. But this very victory was making a fool of me. In theory it was agreed: the Negro is a human being. But what good was that to me? Too late! All the discoveries were made, the till was empty. Too late! Between them and me stood a world—a white world. For they were not capable of wiping out the past.'[14]

Fanon then describes what, in this mood, the encounter with African culture, with neo-African poetry, means: 'I had rationalized my environment, but it had rejected me in the name of colour prejudice. Since there was no understanding on the basis of reason, I threw myself into the arms of the irrational. I became irrational up to my neck. The tom-tom drummed out my cosmic mission. The arteries of the world, torn open, have made me fertile. I found, not my origin, but the origin. I wedded the world! The white man has never understood this magical substitution. He desires the world and wants it for himself alone. He considers himself predestined to rule the world. He has made it useful to himself. But here are values which do not submit to his rule. Like a sorcerer I steal from the white man a certain world which he cannot identify. Above the plantations and the banana trees I gently set the true world. The essence of the world was my property. The white man suddenly had the impression that I was eluding him and taking something with me. They turned out my pockets but found there only familiar things. But now I had a secret. And if they questioned me, I murmured to myself:

"Thou Tokowaly, thou hearest the unhearable, thou explainest to me what my forebears say in the quiet of the constellations. Infinite is the milky way of the spirits in the celestial shallows, but there is the wisdom of the moon goddess and the darkness throws off her veil, thou African night, my black night, mystical and black, clear and full of splendour."[16] I made myself the poet of the world. As an American friend said to me, I had become, "in the mechanized world of the white men, the guardian of humanity". At last I was recognized, I was no longer nothing.[17] The whites clapped me on the shoulder, they were enchanted, in me they had recovered the fundamental, the natural, naiveté. Full of zeal I threw myself into the black past. But what did I find? Schoelcher, Frobenius, Westermann, Delafosse, white, and only white scholars had stirred up, investigated, excavated everything already. And what had they discovered? That there had been a mistake, that there never had been a primitive man. I had never been a primitive, still less a half-man. I belonged to a race which had been working gold and silver for two thousand years.[18] Thus I could direct the white man to his proper boundaries, could demonstrate to him that I was no late comer, that my history was just as rich as his. I shouted, I jumped for joy. But he growled and muttered, he was uncomfortable. What is the point of all these historical analyses? Stop thrashing around in the past and try instead to adjust yourself to *our* rhythm. In our over-industrialized society there is no longer any place for your sensibility. One must be hard in order to survive. It is no longer a question of playing "the game of the world", but of subjecting oneself to the arrangement of integrals and atoms. Everything else is child's play. To my irrationality they opposed reason, and to my reason the "higher reason"!'[19]

The 'living experience of the black' which Frantz Fanon here so vividly portrays, exhibits the two facts which he emphasizes: 'It is a fact that the whites think they are better than the black. And it is also a fact that the black want at any price to prove to the whites that their thought is just as rich, their intellect as powerful.'[20] So long as one tries to produce this proof by seeking in African culture values which correspond exactly to the standards valid for European culture, one is bound to fail. But if one measures by the standards proper to African culture—and that is what this book attempts—then this question of valuation is shown to be falsely put, since there is no universal standard for the evaluation of cultures. According to its own standard—who does not know this?—every culture is superior to every other.

Race prejudice is a problem of Western culture and is not therefore the subject of this book. It cannot be resolved from the side of the African. He is its victim, and in fact as Frantz Fanon has shown, it drives many an Afro-American, who is culturally a European-American, to neo-African culture. Fanon explains also to those who describe the poetry of this culture as a 'situation',[21] or as an intoxicant for the intellectual Afro-American, as Skokian: 'In this poetry I have found not only my situation, but *myself*. I feel in myself a soul as large as the world, a soul as deep as the deepest of rivers, my breast swells to infinity. And then they recommend to me the modesty of a sick man. Irresponsible, mounted between nothing and the infinite, I begin to weep.'[22]

It is fitting therefore to keep the discussion clear of the area of value judgements, free of hate as much as of adulation. Let us proceed according to those sentences of Frantz Fanon which represent the heart of his analysis and which could equally well stand as motto at the head of this book: 'For us the man who worships the Negroes is just as "sick" as the man who despises them. And conversely the black man who would like to bleach his skin is just as unhappy as the one who preaches hatred of the white man.'[23]

VIII. THE ARRANGEMENT OF THE BOOK

Since in every sphere African culture—traditional or modern —becomes intelligible only when its basic conceptions are familiar, we ought really to begin, after this introductory chapter *Skokian*, with African philosophy. However, the reader is expecting a living portrait, not a textbook. He expects doctrines only when, thanks to his own experience, he can visualize something in connection with them. The second chapter *Voodoo*, therefore, constitutes an introduction to African religion—by means of an especially stimulating example, partly because Voodoo is considered to be an especially impious cult, and partly also because we can show here how Christian elements are Africanized and assimilated. Instead of in Haiti, the same problem could have been presented in Brazil, Guiana or La Plata. Thus the book follows throughout the African method of using a picture as a sign—just as above the concept 'Skokian', an intoxicating drink mixed of European and African products, is taken to stand for heterogeneous ideas which contribute to auto-intoxication. Where such pictures appear, they are not exclusive but inclusive: in the sign we find the sense.

The third chapter *Rumba* is centred in the dance and the locale is Cuba. It extends from the cult, through the secret society to modern Afro-Cuban lyric poetry and presents incidentally a history of the African dances that have reached Europe.

Thus in two extensive chapters, which like all the chapters move from the traditional to the modern, enough material is presented so that we can risk the leap to Africa.

We must make this leap, for philosophy, which is presented in the fourth chapter, *Ntu*, is the foundation of African culture. It will be objected that philosophy presupposes critical awareness, an awareness which was lacking in the African past; in the past there were only myths. We have already answered this objection. As soon as awareness is present, the world view that people have accepted, dimly perceived, and actually lived becomes philosophy. 'All things have their philosophy,' writes Friedell, 'more than that: all things *are* philosophy. Man must seek out the idea that lies hidden in every fact, the thought whose mere form it is.'[24] Kagame, Ogotommêli, Tempels have expounded and systematized the philosophy of the Bantu, the Ruandese, and the Dogon. Their basic principles agree, although the peoples from whom these ideas stem live in different parts of Africa. Thus we are presenting here that common denominator which allows us to interpret the whole of African culture, both old and new. The justification of such a generalization of philosophical principles is demonstrated by its outcome. Since it is a question of an African and not a European philosophy, it is difficult to put it in terms of European concepts. The essential concepts can only be indirectly described in European language. They have to be approached first from one side, then from another, until at last the concept in question has been circumscribed. The reader should not linger therefore over the first interpretation, which is usually only a hint. All the concepts are clarified in the course of the exposition.

The concepts are taken from the language in which they are first mentioned. Thus *Magara* is a concept of the Kinyaruanda, *Nommo* a concept of the language of the Dogon. If a term has once been used it is retained even though the thing it designates has an entirely different name in some other area. Since African culture appears as a unity, it makes no difference from which African language a term is derived. Nor do the terms need to come from a single language; thus we are able in each case to choose terms that are easy to remember. The reader should not be alarmed if, for example, Bantu and Dogon concepts are used in speaking of a Yoruba mask.

Philosophy provides the basis of African culture. As soon as its principles are clear, they are applied in order to investigate and interpret with their help the other spheres of culture. In the fifth chapter, *Nommo*, the magic force of the spoken word is expounded. This chapter explains the nature of African medicine and African poetry. Here too, as in all the chapters, we have proceeded from tradition to the modern period. The difference between the two is a matter of awareness, not of time. Tradition that still survives unconsciously today is referred to as 'residual-African'; tradition that consciously persists or is consciously revived is called 'neo-African'.

The sixth chapter, *Kuntu*, investigates African art—sculpture, painting, mask—and so evolves an African aesthetic. The seventh chapter, *Hantu*, provides a history of African literature. The eighth chapter, *Blues*, is concerned with the conflict of cultures, the border zone between the Western and African cultures. It points out the political consequences and shows what meaning African culture may have for a future world culture.

From this sketch it is clear that the reader cannot expect a complete exposition of the subject, for the subject of each chapter would be worth a comprehensive study of its own. Thus it is a question here only of the outlines of African culture, not of an exhaustive presentation. We could, admittedly, have made room for a more extended exposition by cutting the quotations, but it seemed necessary for the general reader, who starts with prejudices but no previous acquaintance with the subject, to provide just such a first acquaintance.

For the most part, moreover, the quotations are in fact abbreviated, though for the sake of better readability this is not indicated by the use of dots. On the other hand, the meaning has not been distorted by this procedure, as the reader may ascertain by consulting the sources referred to.

The book is a beginning, the first attempt to sketch neo-African culture as an independent culture of equal value with other cultures. It is a culture which is shaping the future of a continent and which should be overlooked by no one who wants to live with all his fellow men on this shrinking globe in peace and with respect for the freedom of his neighbour.

Chapter 2

VOODOO

The Embodiment of the Gods

This is the long road to Guinea . . .
JACQUES ROMAIN

I. OLD ACCOUNTS OF THE CULT

Voodoo! Word of dark vowels and heavily rolling consonants! Voodoo! Mysterious nocturnal sound of drums in
the Haitian mountains, that makes the tourists shudder and
reminds them of abominations they have read about! Voodoo,
idolatry, sorcery; Voodoo, epitome of all impiety, all depravity
and terror, witches' Sabbath of the infernal powers and ineradi-
cable heresy! What is it all about?

Some people have tried to derive the word from the dance of
the Golden Calf (*veau d'or*), and it has also been related to the
heretical side of the Waldensians (*Vaudois*) who were reputed to
practise witchcraft. In fact, the whole practice of witchcraft in
the Middle Ages was called 'vaudoisie'.

The word is written in many different ways: Vaudou, Vaudoux,
Vodoo, etc., but it comes from Dahomey in West Africa, where it
means 'genius, protective spirit'; in the Fon language it is called
'Voduh' and in Ewe 'Vudu'. The name of the cult, like the cult
itself, is of West African origin, for the Haitians for the most part
come from there.[1] The reason why it was the religious conceptions
of Dahomey in particular that came to prevail in Haiti is apparent
from a London report of 1789[2] which tells us that ten to twelve
thousand slaves were exported yearly from the kingdom of
Dahomey. The English exported only seven to eight hundred of

29

these, the Portuguese about three thousand and the French the remainder,[2] in other words more than six to eight thousand a year, who were shipped to the French Antilles, above all to Saint-Dominique, as the principal French colony of Haiti was then called.

The earliest indication of the survival of African cults in Haiti we owe to an anonymous French report, which says: 'The slaves are strictly forbidden to practise the dance which in Surinam is called "Water-Mama" and in our colonies "Mae d'Agua" (Water mother). They therefore make a great secret of it, and all we know is that it highly inflames their imaginations. They make immense efforts to do evil things. The leader of the plot falls into such transports that he loses consciousness.'[3]

Moreau de Saint-Méry, an enlightened scholar, lawyer and politician who was born in Martinique and practised law for nine years in Haiti before playing an important part in the French Revolution, employed the leisure hours of the North-American exile forced on him through his quarrel with Robespierre in describing in detail the geographical, social and political conditions in Haiti.[4]

In his works of several volumes this relative of the Empress Josephine describes, among other things, a Voodoo ceremony. 'According to the Arada Negroes Voodoo means a great supernatural being, a snake that knows the past and the present and, through the medium of the high priestess and of a Negress, foretells the future. These two are called King and Queen, Master and Mistress, or Papa and Mama.'

The meeting takes place, he says, only secretly and at night, far from profane eyes. The initiated put on sandals and wrap themselves in red cloths. The King and Queen wear girdles. A chest, through the boards of which one can see the snake, serves as an altar. The faithful present their wishes, then the Queen leaps upon the chest, falls at once into a trance, begins to prophesy and gives her commands. Sacrificial gifts are brought, the King and Queen receive them. The receipts are used to meet the expenses of the community and to assist needy members. Then follows an oath similar to that at the opening of the meeting and 'as fearful as the first', an oath of secrecy and obedience.

Then the dance begins. The king draws a circle, in which the disciple who is to be initiated is presented, herbs, horse hairs 'and other abominable things' in his hands. At a sign from the king the congregation begins to sing, while the youth begins to tremble and to dance. If in so doing he should happen to leave the circle, the singing stops and king and queen turn their backs on him, in order to banish this inauspicious portent. The dancer recovers himself, is brought back into the circle, dances again and at last falls into 'convulsive palpitations, to which the Voodoo king puts an end by tapping him lightly on the head with his rod'. The disciple is led to the altar, takes the oath and is received. Then begins the communal dance which, with the help of intoxicating beverages, becomes a 'bacchanal'. 'They tear the clothes from their bodies, bite their own flesh'; some are brought 'unconscious' into a side room where 'the most abominable prostitutions' take place. Exhaustion concludes these 'demoralising' scenes.

If we make allowance for the want of understanding and the prejudice which Moreau shares with his European contemporaries, he has well observed the external aspect of the ceremonies. Moreau emphasizes that Voodoo and Don Pedro—'an even worse dance with quicker movements, which was introduced in 1768'—were danced without instruments. Hand-clapping and drums were introduced only to 'deceive the police' and give the ceremonies the colouring of entertainments. From this an American author, Williams, concludes, as late as 1932, that Voodoo was originally a snake cult, a secret cult without drums, in which the dance, which had served only as a disguise, gradually moved into the foreground and spoiled the cult proper.[5] This view follows from the assumption that, as is the case in modern Europe, dance and music have nothing to do with sacred matters and serve only for amusement and pleasure.

We shall see, however, that in the Arada rite as in the Petrus rite the drums are, and always have been, an essential part of the ritual. For the drums are by no means a late addition. That they were missing in the ceremony described by Moreau does in fact have reasons closely connected with the wish 'to deceive the police'. The slave-owners had no suspicion that certain specified, dedicated drums belonged to every ceremony: but the faithful

31

had no way of knowing that their masters had no idea that each ritual action was connected with special sacred drums. So in order not to give themselves away, they omitted the ritual drums, from which the black police in the service of the masters could have recognized every detail of the ritual; and after the ritualistic part they performed half profane dances like the *calenda*, for which only less sacred drums are used. In this way they thought they could count on a lighter punishment in case of discovery.

However, the oaths which bound the faithful to secrecy must also be separated from the cult proper. They were necessary only in order to meet the harsh laws of the infamous *Code Noir* of 1685, which declared that slaves must after a short time be instructed and baptized in the Catholic faith, whereupon they were forbidden to take part any longer in any other religious ceremony. According to the *Code Noir*, masters who allowed slaves to take part in other than Catholic religious ceremonies were just as guilty as if they had themselves taken part in such gatherings, that is to say, they were punished as heretics. Any meeting whatsoever of slaves of different masters was forbidden, 'by day or by night, under the pretext of a wedding or under other pretexts, on the estate of the master or elsewhere, in the street or in hiding'. A police order of Port-au-Prince in 1772 prohibits even 'free Negroes and those of mixed breeding' to dance the calenda, which was considered profane.

The social function of the sacrificial offerings did not escape even Moreau, although he let it appear that the gifts were intended above all to enrich the priest and priestess, who according to him had nothing else in mind but to subject the 'foolish crowd' to their 'whims' and their 'private interests' and to force the 'most abominable nonsense' on them as 'unalterable law'.

To the Haitian scholar Jean Price-Mars belongs the credit of recognizing in the Voodoo-cult a genuine religion, after his compatriot, the physician Dr. J. C. Dornsainvil, had declared Voodoo to be 'a deep psycho-nervous disturbance of a religious kind, bordering on paranoia'.[6] 'Voodoo is a religion,' writes Price-Mars, 'because the initiated believe in the existence of spiritual beings who live partly in the universe, partly in close contact with men, whose activities they control. These invisible beings form

1. Carved head in a Shango shrine in Ilobu, West Nigeria. (Photo: U. Beier)

2. Dance mask of Kra. Liberia. (Collection of the
Frobenius Institute, Frankfurt-am-Main. Photo:
R. Bouvier)

an Olympus of Gods, the highest of whom bears the title "Papa" or "Great Master" and claims special veneration. Voodoo is a religion, because the cult developed for its gods demands a hierarchical body of priests, a community of believers, temples, altars, ceremonies and finally an oral tradition, which has certainly not come down to us unchanged but has fortunately preserved the essential part of the cult. Voodoo is a religion because out of the chaos of legends and distorted fables we can extract a theology, a system of concepts with the help of which our African forebears explained in primitive fashion the natural phenomena —a system which laid the foundations for the anarchistic faith on which the corrupt Catholicism of the mass of our people rests.[7] Voodoo is a very primitive religion, founded partly on the belief in all-powerful spirits—gods, demons, disembodied souls— partly on the belief in sorcery and magic. With respect to this double character we must consider that these beliefs were more or less pure in their country of origin and that in our country they have been modified by a century of contact with the Catholic religion.'[8]

Price-Mars' recognition that Voodoo is a religion brings us a decisive step forward, yet we must still try to discover whether the mixture of different African cults has in fact diluted the original conceptions or whether, on the contrary, the mixture emphasizes the original basic concepts. We may ignore the fact that Price-Mars paid tribute to the animistic theory of Tylor, already refuted by Lévy-Bruhl, according to which 'the primitive' peopled nature with souls in order to 'explain' natural phenomena.

II. The Voodoo Ceremony in the Arada Rite

In the course of the nearly two hundred years that have passed since Moreau's report, the Voodoo rites have undergone some changes. Price-Mars, who attended more than a hundred Voodoo ceremonies, emphasizes that a living snake is not used any more,[9] while Williams believes Price-Mars must have been mistaken, since the snake to him is the 'Fetish' of the snake cult in ancient Whydah in Dahomey and therefore the core of the whole ritual.

But if Price-Mars is right, then Voodoo has changed. Williams comes to the conclusion that 'the religious elements of the cult were yielding to social influences'. As time passed, the 'accompanying dance', he says, has moved more and more into the foreground, with the consequence that Voodoo in the strict sense of the word begins to wane and is Voodoo in name alone. 'We have before us,' he writes, 'a general conglomération of all the old cults, combined with dances of every description, all imbued with every form of witchcraft and sorcery, posing under the generic term of "Voodoo". The religion of the Whydahs has become the witchcraft of the Haitians.'[10]

Before we discuss this view, let us watch the performances of a ceremony of the Arada ritual as it appears today. We shall follow in principle the presentation of Michel Leiris,[11] which he himself has supplemented by reference to the observations of Alfred Metraux of the sociological division of U.N.E.S.C.O. and to recent literature in this special field.[12] We have also added further details from other sources.[13]*

The Voodoo ceremony can take place by day and by night in the open or in certain rooms. At the present time Saturday is preferred, and the ceremony is usually celebrated in a special building, the Voodoo-temple, called *Hounfort*. The hounfort is distinguished externally from an ordinary farm building only through a barn-like addition, the peristyle, the roof of which is supported by pillars, mainly by the middle pillar, the brightly decorated *poteau-mitan*, the centre post about which the rites are carried out and from above which the *loas* descend from heaven. The peristyle is decorated with the coat of arms of the Republic of Haiti and with the picture of the President. Particular peristyles are often dedicated to different rites: for instance, one to the Arada and another to the Petro rite. At the entrance stand tables with bread, biscuits, fish and so on, a kind of buffet at which the faithful can buy refreshments during the ceremonies.

Small altar spaces called *bagi* are arranged around the peristyles. Bagi is the holy of holies, the *Caille Mystère*, the house of the 'secret ones', the loas. In the simplest form it is drawn as a

* In what follows we give the usual spelling of the Creole terms, but there are many other spellings too.

rectangle on the ground, but generally the hounforts have several such spaces, each dedicated to a particular *loa* (loi) and often containing several altars. The walls are plastered with bright little chromolithographs representing the saint with whom the particular loa is identified. The altar in the bagi is called *pè* or—in the simplest form, when bagi and pè are simply traced on the ground—also *soba*. The pè is surrounded by a ditch into which the food, the *manger* brought to the loa is placed. On the pè stand jugs with the souls of the initiated and plates holding votive offerings of all kinds as well as the decorated gourd rattles of the priests. The libation—that is, the pouring of the sacrificial drink offered to the appropriate loa at the beginning of the ceremony—takes place before the pè. Some water is poured to the left, some to the right, and some in the centre, and this is done twice, first on the left and then on the right side of the altar. In doing this one cries 'Abobo!', an exclamation which corresponds more or less to the German 'prosit'. Before every libation the jug is 'oriented', that is, it is lifted towards each of the four points of the compass in turn.

Meanwhile a *houngan* has drawn on the ground with black ashes or white flour a large *vèvè*, which stretches from the door to the poteau-mitan—a heraldic work of art. Every loa has its vèvè, or coat of arms, but different symbols such as circles, triangles, zig-zag designs and other signs, resembling those of our freemasons, can also be combined. The outlines or symbols of the animals one intends to sacrifice are also painted in, and so one gets a large vèvè, a figured, symmetrical composition, which one might call the programme, the artistic plan of the coming ceremony. Therefore also, in the course of the ceremony, a libation is repeatedly made at various points of the vèvè, in order to ascertain at what place in the ceremony one is at the moment and what is to come.

The priest is called *houngan*, the priestess *mambo*. There are usually several houngans and mambos present. A *papaloa* on the other hand is a high priest, a dignitary of the Voodoo religion, approximately of the rank of a bishop. In every ceremony one houngan acts as *La-place*, that is, as master of ceremonies; he is also referred to as the 'emperor'. He is always flanked by two women who hold flags with the symbol of the loa in whose honour the meal, the *manger*, is being held. The *badgigan* or acolyte is the assistant of the High Priest. Only a papaloa has a badgigan.

We recognize the priests by their solemn, usually black robes, but above all by their *asson*, their gourd rattle. This consists of a small, hollowed-out, sun-dried gourd of a longish shape, the stem of which serves as a handle. Inside are seeds or small pebbles or even small bones from the backbone of a snake. Only La-place and the priests are allowed to use the asson, which the High Priest, on the occasion of their solemn investiture, has given them as sceptre and emblem of dignity, and with which they direct the course of the rite, as we shall see.[14]

The orchestra, consisting of four men, has now taken its place. The highest houngan rattles with his asson and the instruments begin in turn, first the *ogan*, a triangle-like instrument which the oganist holds in his left hand and strikes with a small stick in his right hand. Then follow the drums, *tambours rada*: first *boula*, the small drum, which the *boulailler* holds horizontally and plays, seated, with two drumsticks. Shortly thereafter *second* begins, the middle drum, which the *secondier* holds inclined, almost vertically, between his legs. He beats this drum with his fists or his fingers, or with an ordinary or a special drumstick, the *aguida*. Finally the big drum joins in, *manman* or *assotôr*, a drum about $2\frac{1}{2}$ to 3 feet high and 9 to 12 inches in diameter—twice as big as the Boula. The seated drummer holds manman—which he may also play standing—at such an angle that it is supported at 45 degrees on his left knee, while he beats its wooden surface or drumhide with a special bobbin-like stick, the *badyat kon*. These three drums, which in some districts are called *ajaounto, honto* and *hountogri*, are made of hollow trunks of valuable wood, oak, cedar, mahogany; they are specially dedicated and may be used only for purposes of ritual. Before the trees were cut prayers had been said to the loas, and before they were used the drums had been wrapped in white cloths and purified of all evil powers.

Behind the orchestra the *hounsi*, the initiated, have taken their places in a semi-circle: girls, maidens, women, men too, in snow-white robes. There are about fifty. They form the ballet and the choir. Most of them are *kanzo*, that is, they have completed all the rites of initiation. Before the chapel stands the choir leader, the *hounguénikon* who is also called *Impératrice*, Empress. She too is provided with an asson. Sometimes also a man can be hounguénikon; it depends on the voice. She (or he) has to sing the solo parts in alternating chant, unless a special soloist, the *chanterelle*, comes forward out of the choir of the hounsi. The first song begins, calling together the company of the faithful, the *societé*:

> *La famille, semblez! Agoé!*
> *Eya! Guinin va aider nous!*

> *Family, assemble! Agwe! [a loa]*
> *Eya! Guinea [= Africa] will help us!*

Only now does La-place, the master of ceremonies, enter the room, and the *virer*, the circling begins, a graceful ceremony of greeting, in which the hounsi, that is, the initiated, greet the priests, houngans, mambos, La-place and Hounguénikon. They advance towards one another, every priest takes the right hand of a hounsi in his raised left hand and lets her turn slowly first to one side and then to the other to the rhythm of the orchestra, each turn ending in a light curtsey on each side. At the same time the priest has clasped with his right hand the left hand of another hounsi, who performs the same movements in the opposite direction. Then both hounsis move on to another priest or priestess until all hounsi and priests have introduced themselves to one another.[15]

The La-place makes the sacrificial animals known to the faithful. He takes a cock in each hand and walks dancing along the line of the faithful, swinging the birds up and down before him. This is called *ventaillage*. Then follows *foula*, the spraying. A houngan takes some *clairin*, a white sugar-cane brandy, spiced with pepper, into his mouth, blows out his cheeks and sprays it on all sides. This is the African method of making a sacrifice with an alcoholic drink. A strong smell of alcohol and pepper spreads through the room, the tension rises, the drumming and the songs, which have never ceased, become louder. Soon several hounsi fall into a trance, leap, dance, and begin to scream. One initiate after another is taken possession of by a loa, or better is 'ridden', as

37

the special term *chevauché* implies. The hounsi becomes the horse of the loa which is embodied in him (or her). Hounsi who are not 'ridden' are called *chrétiens vivants*, 'living Christians'. They look after those who are 'ridden' to see that they do not injure themselves.

To the unitiated observer this ecstatic dancing presents itself as a disordered jumble of movement, an unorganized chaos of shouting, for the different hounsi are 'ridden' by different loas. This unleashing of 'drives' in spontaneous seizures, which seem to occur collectively and yet have individually different effects, the whole procedure appearing quite uncontrolled, has time and again filled onlookers with terror and has given Voodoo its evil reputation. 'Mass madness', 'paranoia' are among the milder judgements on these events. In view of the obvious exclusion of reason and control, must we not ascribe any and every excess to the individuals so let loose?

We must therefore give an exact account of these events. We said above: 'The music becomes louder.' We should have said: the rhythm changes, or more exactly: the rhythms change, in fact the rhythms change within a rhythmic system which is constructed on a polymetric musical foundation. Alfons M. Dauer, to whom we owe this knowledge, writes: 'The difference between our rhythmic conception and that of the Africans consists in the fact that we perceive rhythm by hearing, while they perceive it by movement. In this off-beat technique of the African we have before us an ecstasy in the truest sense of the word; for its essence is to disturb the state of static self-contained repose which distinguishes both metre and rhythm in addition to their character as time-spans. This it does by overlaying their static accents with ecstatic emphases, producing tensions between the two. The same thing happens in all forms of African combinations of rhythm; it should probably be considered their true aim and meaning. From this point of view the innermost object of African music consists in producing, through rhythmic configurations of a specific kind, an uninterrupted ecstasy.'[16]

If we add to this that every loa has its particular rhythm, that is, its specific beat, the ordering principle of this apparently disordered ecstasy becomes visible. 'The drummers change the rhythm and beat a *yanvalou* in order to honour Legba,' observes Odette Rigaud.[17] The initiate who knows the specific beat of one or more loas—and the communication of this knowledge constitutes the initiation—needs only to concentrate on the rhythmic beat of his loa and surrender himself to it, in order to carry out the movements appropriate to the loa. Thus he carries out, not any arbitrary movements, but exactly those which correspond to the peculiarity of the loa and to its specific beat. It is also possible, therefore, that several dancers may be ridden by the same loa if they react to the same specific beat.

Thus the loas can only 'mount' the dancers when one after the other is 'called' by the specific beat of the orchestra of drums. If an uncalled loa, a *bossal* or 'wandering loa' should mistakenly manifest itself—an occurrence that is considered unlucky—the orchestra plays a *mazon*, a 'leave-taking rhythm', which at once makes the bossal leave his choual again. Also if a loa stays too long and disturbs the meeting, by letting the dancer he is riding create a disturbance—an extremely rare occurrence—a mazon is played.

Thus the music of the drums, the polymetric basis of which serves to allow a number of different beats to sound at one time, guides all the ecstatic events of this apparent chaos down to the smallest detail. But it is not the drummers who supervise the ceremony, but the houngans or priests, among them La-Place and Hounguénikon ('Emperor' and 'Empress'), who, with the help of their sacred rattles, the assons, give the drummers the right beat. Hence the significance of the assons; hence the rule that no one but a priest may possess an asson. The priests with their precise and hierarchical functions are as it were the directors of a sacred operatic dance. Their assons are the batons, the drummers the orchestra, the hounsis the chorus, the dancers the soloists. There can be no question of disorder.

III. The Gods (Loas)

The importance of the genuine African polymetric foundation of this music is evident from a comparison with the forms of ecstasy that occur in North American Negro churches. Since in these, as Dauer demonstrates, the polymetric basis has been lost,[18] the participants are no longer ridden by several loas but only by one—Christ. Moreover, one priest or director is sufficient, while for Voodoo several houngans are necessary. In the Negro churches a collective state of possession occurs, while in Africa several *Voduns* or *orishas* (loas) never manifest themselves at one time and the possession never leads to 'wild dances', but usually to a quiet 'sinking into oneself'. Thus in its type of possession, Voodoo stands midway between Africa and the Negro churches.

Thus Voodoo is no 'mass madness'; moreover, in view of all this organization, this system of priestly functions, orchestral functions, song and cult, one cannot speak of paranoia even in the case of the solo dancer. His possession and lapse of consciousness are of quite another kind. For the initiate is following laws of behaviour deeply grounded in his culture and almost completely inaccessible to European understanding. According to Dauer, these laws force him to express his immense excitement in a catharsis, in rhythmic action embracing sound and movement. Yet the possessed person maintains contact with his environment throughout. His physical and mental powers remain entirely un-touched: they even seem to be intensified. It may be, indeed, that in this ecstatic condition mental conflicts of the possessed person are unintentionally and involuntarily removed or smoothed out, and thus an inner harmony is achieved. This would explain to some extent why the dancer seems to be most refreshed after the most violent seizure. Thus the effect is healthful and not harmful. 'Accordingly,' writes Dauer, 'one must not speak of this phenomenon as hysteria, neurosis or epilepsy, as has often been done.'[19] And Métraux writes: 'We may even say that this represents the normal behaviour of the believer, in fact that it is expected of active participants in the cult. It is rather the believer who is never seized by the god who deserves to be called ab-normal.'[20] In Africa, too, a person who has never been seized, never possessed by a divinity is not accepted into any cult.

The heightening of the physical and mental powers of man, which Dauer here suggests, seems to us the true aim of all Voodoo ceremonies; here lies the meaning, the social function and the value of Voodoo. The symbolic actions, the libations, invocations, animal sacrifices, fire-baths and so on, in which the possessed take part in a completely conscious state, as well as the states of possession themselves, all serve only to increase the physical and mental powers of man. In what way and by what means this intensification begins, we shall recognize if we investigate what it is that 'mounts' those possessed: if we determine, in other words, who and what these loas really are.

The highest ruler of all loas is *Bon Dieu*, the good lord. He is the creator of the world, but so high above man that he is not concerned with him. He is so far away that he only laughs at the sufferings of men.[21] One says 'If God wills' (Si dié vlé) and resigns oneself therewith to one's fate, but one does not pray to Bon Dieu. Even in the Catholic church many worshippers prefer to pray only to the Virgin or the saints.

So much the more, however, does one honour the loas, those supernatural beings who are also in some districts called *saints* (saints) or *anges* (angels). Yet even when they are equated with the saints of the Catholic church, one knows that they come from Guinin, that is from Africa (Guinea). For they are neither only good like angels or saints, nor only bad like devils. They are, like the heart of man, neither good nor bad.[22] They like good meals, which is why one offers them sacrifices; they can be suspicious, insolent, jealous and irritable, above all if the food they are offered does not appeal to them. They can boast, swear, drink too much, and quarrel. Yet they are good to their servants, they protect and help them, advise them when ill and appear to the hungry man in a dream saying, 'Do not lose courage, you will find work and earn money', and then he does earn money. Every loa has his preferred seat, his *reposoir*, a tree, a plant, a spring. Hence the branches in the hounfort, on which the loas sit and from which they descend, when summoned, on to the people who become their 'horses'.

According to the particular rites, there are different groups of loas which, however, often intersect. Originally each ritual belonged to a particular people; but as the African peoples mixed in Haiti the gods too mixed, at least to a lesser extent. Smaller groups were assimilated to larger; the largest group belongs to the *Arada* or *Rada* rite, which comes from Dahomey. The *Nago* (Yoruba) and *Ibo* rites, which also come from Guinea, have been almost altogether absorbed in the Arada rite, while the Petro rite from the Congo remained, and various other rites from the Congo or from Angola were fused with it. But the Petro rite and the Arada rite have also come closely to resemble one another. Since most Haitians come from Dahomey, the Arada rite has the greatest number of adherents.

In the Voodoo ceremony the first loa to be invoked is *Legba*. He is the lord of roads and streets, the Hermes of the Voodoo Olympus, the protector of crossroads and doors, the protector of the herd. His wife is *Ayizan*, the Goddess of the markets and the highest goddess of the Arada Olympus. Legba's symbol, his vèvè, is the cross—a cross which has, however, only its form, not its meaning, in common with the Christian cross. The vertical board means the street, which joins together the deep and the heights, the street of the loas, the invisible ones. The foot of this vertical world-axis is rooted in the waters of the deep. Here on the 'island under the sea' is Guinea, Africa, the legendary home; here the loas have their permanent places, from which they hasten straight upwards to the living. Every vertical, above all every tree, and especially the poteau-mitan in the hounfort, symbolizes the 'tree of the Gods' which unites the damp earth, from which all things spring, with heaven. The horizontal bar of the cross signifies the earthly and human world. Only at the crossroad, where the human and divine axes meet, does contact with the divinities take place. And this crossroad is guarded by Legba.[23] In Dahomey and Nigeria he is the interpreter of the gods, who translates the requests and prayers of men into their language.[24] In Haiti he has the function of opening the *barrière* that separates men from the loas. He is invoked in the *yanvalou*—rhythm and dance:

Aitibo Legba, Luvri bayè pu mwẽ
Papa Legba, luvri bayè pu mwẽ
Luvri bayè pu m'kapab rãtré
    A tu bon Legba, ouvre la barrière pour moi
    Papa Legba, ouvre la barrière pour moi
    Ouvre la barrière pour me faire capable de rentrer.

Lò m'a tunẽ, m'a salié loa-yo
Vodu Legba, luvri bayè pu mwẽ
Lò m'a tune, m'a remésyé loa-yo
*Abobo!**

> *Lorsque je retournerai, je saluerai les Loas*
> *Vodou Legba, ouvre la barrière pour moi*
> *Lorsque je retournerai, je remercierai les Loas*
> *Abobo!*

>> *Atibon Legba, open the barrier for me,*
>> *Papa Legba, open the barrier for me.*
>> *Open the barrier, that I may enter.*
>> *Voodoo Legba, open the barrier for me.*
>> *When I return I shall salute the Loas.*
>> *Voodoo Legba, open the barrier for me.*
>> *When I return, I shall thank the Loas.*
>> *Abobo!*

Meantime La-place hurries again and again to the door of the peristyle and opens it symbolically, until Legba comes and mounts a dancer and rides him. This Legba is a lame old man with a crutch. Now that he is there, the others can come too.

Damballah is the loa of fertility. He lives in springs and swamps. His sign is the snake, and whoever is ridden by him hisses like a snake, creeps about on the ground in snake-like curves, climbs up the rafters, and hangs, head downward, from the beams of the roof. The name is compounded from 'Dan' (snake) or 'Dangbe', the cult of the snake of heaven, that is, the rainbow, and 'Allada', the name of that kingdom in South Dahomey from which came the dynasty of Abomey, founders of the kingdom of Dahomey. Dahomey itself means 'in the body of Dan' (Dan ho mê).[25] Damballah is identified with St. Peter or St. Patrick. His symbols are the snake and the egg. 'Because of him it was long believed that the Haitians practised ophiolatry',[26] that they were snake worshippers. His wife is *Ayida-Oueddo*, the goddess of the rainbow, that heavenly snake.

Agwé, 'the rolling one', is the ruler of the seas. Fish, boats and

* Pronunciation: vowels as in Italian, consonants as in English. é and è as in French. ~ means nasalization.

oars (*avirons*) are his symbols, above all *Lambi*, the giant conch which was the horn of the now extinct *Xemes* Indians and which called the slaves to rebel. Lambi (Haitian: ear), the 'conch horn of a new message'[27] called the slaves of Haiti to rise up against their masters and entered as a ceremonial instrument into the more revolutionary Petro rite. It calls up the storm, and the sailor blows on it when he needs a favourable wind. Agwé protects seafarers and loves the thunder of cannon and the salutes of ships before Port-au-Prince. His colour is blue. His choual sits on a chair and pretends to be rowing. From the boat a white sheep is sacrificed to him on the sea; then all turn quickly around and take care not to look back, for like the kings of Dahomey he does not like it if he is seen eating.

Zaka, also called Azaka-Tonnerre, that is, Thunder-Azaka, is the agricultural minister of the loas and also a real peasant: avaricious, suspicious, a lover of litigation, greedy for profit, and anything but affable with city people. The person who embodies him is always afraid someone will rob him. But in the country he is in his element. He darts lightning and thunder. 'The flashing axe on his altar reminds one of the thunderbolts which one finds used so often in rites in Africa, and which are supposed to invoke rain.'[28] Baskets are his symbols.

Ogun, the Yoruba divinity of iron and fire, who has already seven forms in Africa, has become in Haiti a whole group of loas, the *Ogou*, who are differentiated by their epithets. The most important are *Ogou Ferraille*, the god of the smiths, to whom fire is sacred, and *Ogou Badagri*, the loa of war. Both appear in military costume, wear a French cap, red robes or cloths, and are armed with sabre or machete. Whoever is possessed by either of them behaves very martially, brandishes his sabre, chews thick cigars, swears and demands rum. And while he swallows it down in huge gulps, the chorus sings: 'Mèt Ogu bué, li bué jamè su (= Maître Ogou boit, il boit, mais n'est jamais saoûl—Lord Ogun is drinking, is drinking, but is never drunk).' He is represented in uniform and is identified with Saint James the Elder.

The Goddess *Erzulie-Fréda-Dahomey* or Maîtresse Ezili has often been compared with Aphrodite. 'Like the Greek goddess, Erzulie belongs to the group of sea gods, but she has absented herself altogether from her original environment and has become almost exclusively the embodiment of feminine beauty and grace. She also has almost all the faults of a beautiful, spoiled woman: she is coquettish, sensual, loving adornment and amusement, extremely extravagant. A room is dedicated to Ezili in every shrine. There her white and rose-coloured garments are kept, and on a dressing table wash basin, soap, towel, comb, lipstick and nail file stand ready for her.'[29] Finery and toilet articles are her attributes, her device the heart, often pierced with an arrow or a sword. On pictures she appears as a white woman with a blue veil, and she is identified with the Blessed Virgin. Bedrooms are dedicated to her. 'If a possessed person, whether man or woman, appears in a silk robe, his or her fingers laden with jewellery, and perfumed from head to foot, then the spectators know that Lady Ezili is lingering among them. The "Goddess" strolls slowly along, swings her hips, throws seductive glances at the men or remains standing for the duration of a kiss or a tender gesture. Her whims are often costly. Does she not demand that the floor of the peristyle be sprinkled with perfume? She treats the women with disdain and extends to them only her little finger. It is an amusing detail that the believer who embodies her takes pains to speak French in a shrill voice, as this is considered elegant. When Ezili returns to her boudoir on the arm of two lovers the men hasten to accompany her.'[30] Damballah, Agwé and Ogou Badagri are among her lovers.

The loas of the *Guédé* group are gods of death; grotesque, absurd figures mostly, and very obscene. The most important among them is *Baron Samedi* or *Baron cimitière* or *Baron-la-Croix* or *Maître-Cimetière-Boumba*. On his black altar stands a black wooden cross ornamented with silver. It is the same one that, in connection with Legba, symbolizes life, for the kingdom of the invisible ones, of the life forces, is at the same time the cosmic graveyard, into which those who have died enter, and sink into the depth of the waters to rise again as loas. Thus the cross of the meeting of the visible with the invisible symbolizes at the same time the unity of life and death. Every Voodoo ceremony, therefore, begins with the invocation of Legba and closes with the salutation to the god of the dead Guédé.[31] The dancer whom Guédé mounts lets himself fall to the ground, holds his breath, and does not move again. Other loas of the Guédé group are symbolized by pickaxe, shovel, skull, crossbones or withered leaves—indicating clearly their functions in connection with death.

There are many more loas and groups of loas, of which we have mentioned only the most important. The loas receive the appropriate sacrifices—drink offerings or food offerings along with the slaughtering of living animals. These are mostly cocks, but sometimes pigs, goats, and now and then a bullock are slaughtered according to an exactly prescribed ritual.[32] Before they are slaughtered the sacrificial animals are offered food and drink, the acceptance of which declares the animal's consent to the sacrifice. Should an animal refuse these gifts, it is led away and another put in its place.

If even the animal that is to be sacrificed is asked, so to speak, for its consent, how improbable does the assertion sound, so often repeated by sensational authors, that in Voodoo children, even grown girls, are murdered. Hanns Heinz Ewers, for example, who in the year 1908 circled the island of Haiti on a Hamburg-America steamer and saw 'with his own eyes', gives as his authority some rogue of a Neapolitan who brews health-giving magic draughts out of tomato juice and claims to be married to a Voodoo priestess.[33] Williams, who quotes and investigates many reports with similar assertions, cannot adduce a single eyewitness. The only ostensible eyewitness account occurs in a letter from Sir Spencer St. John to the *New York World* of 5 December 1886. In this account the eyewitness remains anonymous, but Sir Spencer, who was British Consul-General in Haiti for twenty years, vouches for his reliability. Sir Spencer St. John himself wrote a book in which he describes the chapter 'Vaudoux-Worship and Cannibalism' as 'the most difficult chapter to write'.[34] The horrors collected there are said to come from Haitian documents, from reliable Haitian officials and their foreign colleagues. Certainly neither Sir Spencer nor his European colleagues nor the Haitian officials ever took part in a Voodoo ceremony. Sir Spencer is all the prouder when some years later he can produce his 'eyewitness account'. Here the anonymous witness, a European, declares that on 19 April 1886 he had taken part unrecognized, with blackened face, in a Voodoo ceremony and had sung with the others 'the deep and monotonous song'. After 'weird' dances in a 'horrible din', he says, when a strong Negro stabbed a young lad in the throat with a knife, he screamed and—still unrecognized—left the room, before they had slaughtered the girl who was destined for the same fate.[35]

'These legends,' Métraux comments, 'have their origin in folklore. They are not, as has often been said, slanders by the whites. The peasants live in dread of the sorcerers, whom they imagine as cannibals greedy for the blood of children. These folk tales are taken by the Haitian élite and the foreign journalists at their face value.'[36] To the same class belongs the belief in the *Zombis*, those soulless bodies, to which we shall return when we deal with magic.[37]

As proof of the reliability of all the undiscoverable 'eye-witnesses', we are given the repeated assertion that the person possessed by Voodoo, in his 'madness', in which he has lost all control over himself, can be credited with every wickedness. If someone is said to have seen for himself these dancers losing control and unleashing all their lowest passions, it must be more or less a matter of chance if he has not been an eye witness of murders and cannibal feasts.

IV. The Embodiment of the Gods

We have seen above how control is maintained in the so-called state of being 'out of one's senses'. Metraux writes: 'The interpretation of the trance as collective delirium or orgiastic frenzy cannot be applied to Voodoo. The state of possession is not produced in the midst of a crowd excited by mystical enthusiasm. The spectators, who are chatting on the sides of the peristyle, smoking cigarettes and chewing pralines, are not seized with any religious excitement. Even the dances, which are executed with rhythmic feeling and wonderful agility, have nothing dionysiac about them; on the contrary, they are difficult exercises, to which

47

one dedicates oneself with one's whole being, without letting them decline into disordered movements. The rite demands that the gods be there at certain moments of the ceremony, and they never fail to appear at the moment anticipated. The possession is therefore a controlled phenomenon, obeying exact rules.'[38]

The state of the dancers resembles, to all appearances, hypnosis more closely than trance. We know today that medicine includes hypnosis in its therapy, that a man can easily be guided through the exclusion of the foreground of consciousness. In this process consciousness is only narrowed, not removed, so that the dancer still finds himself at home in the external world. The rapport (the contact with the hypnotist) is maintained during hypnosis; in Voodoo it is the rapport with the orchestra, which is directed through the specific beats it introduces to the figure of the loa known to the dancer. So the dancer takes the loa up into himself and embodies it through his movements and his speech.

In all this we may doubt whether consciousness is as completely excluded as the spectators, and even the Voodoo worshippers themselves, assert. In a novel by Alexis we read: 'The departed Uncle Pierre had been the Cheval of Ti-Dangni, the child-Loa, the police chief of Olympus. Year after year, from Holy Water Saturday to Good Friday, Uncle Peter, possessed by Ti-Dangni, had cheerfully and happily pushed the *Loas-grenadiers* and *Loas-chasseurs* about in the court of the shrine.'[39] Thus it seems to be not uncommon for one person to be ridden repeatedly by the same loa, so that his appearance becomes a regular role. The costuming and the improvised dialogues also, of which Métraux[40] gives an example, point to the proximity of the theatre: 'Every act of becoming possessed has a theatrical side as well, which is apparent even in the careful contrivance of the costumes. These resemblances between possession and dramatic presentation should not permit us to forget that in the eyes of the public the possessed is not a proper actor. He is not playing the part of a personality: he *is* this personality for the whole duration of the trance. But how can we help describing as "theatre" those impromptu dialogues spontaneously produced when several divinities are manifested at the same time in differ-

3. Horse and rider. Yoruba, Nigeria. (Photo: Helmut Lander)

4a. Ancestral figure. Bakota, Gabon. (N. Städtisches Museum für Völkerkunde, Frankfurt-am-Main)

4b. Bronze figure. Ife, Nigeria. (Antiquities Service, Jos, Nigeria. Photo: U. Beier)

ent persons? These improvisations, the tone of which varies, are much appreciated by the public. They break out laughing, interrupt the dialogue, and noisily express their pleasure or dislike.'

In any case cult and theatre are here closely related. The longing for union with the creative ground of life and therewith the affirmation of life itself with all that it contains, may be at least *one* reason why the Voodoo worshippers like to surrender to possession. Added to this is the joy, for these poverty-stricken and necessitous farmers, of being allowed to play a role in the ceremony, of being allowed to be a god, of forgetting, in total self-surrender, their everyday world and their want. There are gods enough, and the worshipper will play the one who corresponds to his inmost desires. The poor farmer's daughter may, as Mistress Erzulie-Fréda, be a great lady; the smallholder, as Zaka, may show his avarice and greed and hold the great gods up to mockery. The coward may flourish his sword as Ogou Ferraille, and curse, and call for rum; the poor may give the gift of rain, the powerless thunder and lighten; the laughable may terrify the others as Baron Samedi. And yet all this occurs in regulated forms and within strictly defined limits—and to prevent hurt feelings or grudges a sacred agreement prevails to the effect that no one knows what he did or said during his possession, but that it was the god alone who spoke through him.

On the other hand, possession is by no means only acted. Let us look now at a ceremony already well in progress, which belongs to the Petro rite in contrast to the scene from the Arada rite already described. This material is selected from the account of Mme Odette Rigaud.[41]

Avotahi! The drummers beat the *kita-franc*, a different rhythm. One of the sons of the *houngan* has taken the place of the first drummer; his father comes now and then and shows him certain twirls, subtleties of drumming. Only an extremely practised ear can detect the nuances. Men carry past two enormous mortars, almost a man's height. Others bring huge pestles. The houngan draws vèvè-like signs with chalk on the mortars and pestles. Roots, herbs, consecrated and pointed to the four winds, are thrown into the mortar. The men beat the pestles in time. A woman is suddenly ridden by *Grand-Bois*, the god of fertility, a beautiful woman firmly shaped. She emits harsh cries, winds a red cloth around herself, pulls her blue woollen dress almost up to her hips and leaps upon the edge of the mortar with a single bound. Then she continues dancing, her hands on her hips, her legs spread apart on the edge of the mortar, a marvel of balance and perfect grace; the dance becomes quicker, and the men beat the pestle faster and faster. Then a second woman leaps onto the edge of the mortar, a young girl. She too is being ridden by Grand-Bois. And the dance grows faster and faster, the mortar shakes, two men hold it firmly to the floor. Suddenly the woman snatches with one hand at the rafter above their heads, lifts her feet high—shrieks pierce the room—and dances in the air. She is Grand-Bois, the god herself, through whom the magic powder that is being ground in the mortar under her gets its force. Then she leaps down—a whistle from the houngan, and the pestles stop. The magic powder is scraped out of the mortar, which is filled anew with fruits, herbs and roots.

The dance begins again, is intensified, more and more people are ridden, men as well as women. At regular intervals the houngan wipes the sweat from the trumpeters' brows. In the courtyard a great funeral pyre is erected. It is the night of the 24th of December. The man mounted by *Maloulou* watches over the fire, in the neighbourhood of which the drummers are also located. Those who are ridden by Maître-Cimitié-Boumba throw themselves into the fire and after they have bathed in it with shouts of joy they stand up again. They look impressive. Bits of rag project from their noses and mouths, their eyes move in terrifying restlessness or, by contrast, are much too static. From time to time they emit stifled laments like the howls of a dying dog.

This strange scene, played by firelight, lasts over two hours. The drums boom, the fire crackles, the hounsi, grouped about the drums, sing with full voices resounding far into the night. The gloomy sighs of Maître-Cimitié-Boumba are answered by the other loas with shrieks of joy while they throw themselves into the fire, toss themselves about and dance delightedly in it. The crowd press more and more tightly in on the free space, and keep having to withdraw again before the glow of the fire. But the loas keep dancing, their cry of *aaa-o-aaadié* grows constantly longer and infinitely modulated. But the man who has been transformed from Ogou to *Simbi* sits there with crossed legs and seems to be worshipping the fire. Suddenly he rises, breaks out laughing, and, stepping on burning timber, climbs up the huge bonfire. His naked feet tread firmly on glowing coals, before he takes the next step. Now he is at the summit, erect. With his hand he grasps the pair of tongs which has been glowing red-hot for two or three hours, lifts it up like a whip handle, and, his chin jutting forward, strides laughing down from his pedestal as slowly as he had climbed up. Meantime Maître-Cimité-Boumba, Baron-le-Croix and Zombi have introduced a dance. Their hands on their hips, with raised, quivering shoulders, as ruthlessly as death they push aside in blind movement all who come in the way of their sombre funeral march. On a sudden impulse Maître-Cimitié-Boumba stands still, turns around, and looks round the circle of people. He fixes, for example, on a six-year-old girl and grasps her. The little black body rests, supported by arms and legs, across the shoulder of the loa. Maître-Cimitié goes on dancing in this way and imperceptibly approaches the fire, turns around and dances and leaps into the flames. The child is by no means alarmed, but confidently lets herself be 'bathed'. Back on her own legs, she leaps back to her place and smiles, while Maître-Cimitié snatches other children in the same way. Mothers bring their sleeping babies; held by hands or feet, or often only by a single leg, the little brown bodies are rocked in the flames and given back to their mothers. *Soignage*, the magic bath, has been administered to them. . . .

V. RELIGION AND POLITICS

Voodoo also has a political side. The religious dances were all the slaves had to remind them of their home. For them these dances were Guinea. In their possession, surrendered to the old gods, for a short time they could feel themselves free once more. Where they could they came together to be near to Africa. Their enforced baptism after the most superficial instruction in the Catholic faith could not replace the old gods. And the more the slave-owners suppressed and punished the dancers, the dearer, the more sacred did they become to the slaves. The prohibitions forced them to secrecy, to the oaths that Moreau describes. Their religion became a secret cult, the faithful became sworn brothers, their secret meeting became the cell of the resistance. It needed only an efficient ringleader to drive their angered spirits to rebellion. Boukman, a Herculean slave, who came to Haiti via Jamaica, was a houngan. He caught the attention of his master, Turpin, who made him an overseer and a coachman. Thus Boukman came into contact with many slaves, swore them in, and at a Voodoo ceremony in the night of 14 August 1791 gave the signal to rebel, which after twelve years of war led to the liberty of Haiti. And when the war years were over the African cult and the African gods gave the fighters the courage, toughness and faith which were necessary to inflict upon the First Consul Napoleon Bonaparte his first defeat. The animal sacrificed in the ritual was not only a gift to the loas; its blood bound together those who made the sacrifice, it demanded of each individual who voluntarily entered this ritual group absolute confidence and complete reliability—otherwise the blood of the sacrificial animal would come over him and destroy him. That is the traditional blood pact of Dahomey,[42] which was assimilated to the Voodoo cult and which swore the former slaves to a community that was able, despite being badly armed, to oppose a drilled European army, and which, despite many defeats, repeatedly stirred the rebellion up anew. Thus the Haitians broke down the army which Napoleon had sent under the command of his brother-in-law Leclerc, 35,000 men, picked troops of the army of the Rhine, even though Napoleon, under the pretence of negotiating a peace, had lured the brilliant statesman of the rebels, Toussaint L'Ouverture, into a ship which took him off to France. Voodoo shares with other faiths, moreover, the custom of promising to fighters who die for their country privileges in the life to come. The bullets of the enemy were to fulfil for them in their death their most longed-for wish: to let them return to their kinsfolk in their homeland, Guinea.[43] Thus Voodoo is not an arbitrary cult, it is the true state religion of Haiti. Every hounfort is decorated with the coat of arms of the Republic.

The thin educated stratum very rapidly took possession of the offices of the new state, inevitably, since they could read and write; but they were entirely addicted to European doctrines and to a European, above all a French, style of living. This upper class considered itself immensely superior to the mass of former slaves, to whom they could scarcely give teachers or judges; they made no distinction between Voodoo and the widely current magical practices and persecuted both with intensity. In the constitution the country was declared to be Catholic, yet Rome had lost all its influence. The native divines came to an agreement with the magicians as well as with the priests, and participated in the lucrative trade in materials of magic. Thus Voodoo, in its time the only religion, acquired its Christian prerequisites, and the *pères savanes* or 'bush-fathers', mostly former bell-ringers and acolytes, who knew a couple of Latin prayers and could *croiciner* (=croix signer), cross themselves, travelled through the country, baptized, married, received confessions and saw to it that Voodoo and Christian practices were fused with one another. Thus we read in Jacques Roumain's famous novel, *Gouverneur de la Rosée*:

'La-place had placed a blood-red cock on a white cloth in the middle of the circle, all supernatural forces were meant to be drawn together in a living knot, in a burning bundle of fire and blood. Dorméus seized the cock and swung him over the heads of the participants in the sacrifice.

' "Hail Mary full of Grace"—the crowd voiced the thanksgiving, for this was the visible sign that Legba accepted the offering. With a violent twist Dorméus tore the head off the cock and held the body to all the four winds.

' "Abobo . . ." shouted the hounsi.

'The houngan repeated his movements and let three drops of blood fall to the earth. "Bleed, bleed, bleed . . ." said the worshippers. "Oh yes, one must serve the old Gods of Guinea," said Laurelien. "Our life lies in their hands," answered Lherisson.

'The carcass of the cock bled on the ground, it lay in a growing red circle. The houngan, the hounsi, Délira and Bienaimé dipped their fingers in the blood and wrote on their foreheads the sign of the cross.'[44]

Zealous in copying European methods the government in 1860

signed an agreement with Rome, imported French priests and outlawed Voodoo. But the country population continued to identify the practices of the *pères savanes* with Catholicism, conformed to its external forms and clung to its own faith. In the country the administration of law and justice, consolation, encouragement and instruction were all first and last in the hands of the houngans, who were not to be replaced by mere paper laws. The hounfort remained what it had always been: sanctuary, clubhouse, dance hall, hospital, theatre, chemist's shop, music hall, court and council chamber in one. Voodoo survived publicly or in secret, depending on whether a particular government proved to be tolerant or not. The ruling class often saw in the power of the papaloa and the houngan their own enemy, and spread further the rumours about the 'barbarous heathen cult', except when they ignored it out of national pride. On the other hand, the houngans were indispensable in their social function, and often had great influence on the government,[45] so that Bonsal could write: 'If he (President Simon) wishes to remain in the Black House and rule, he must share his sovereignty with the Voodoo priests. If he should exclude them from power and banish them from his presence, his term of office will be of short duration.'[46] During the unrest of 1957 the present president, François Duvallier, who as former Director of the Haitian Ethnographic Institute wrote several works on Voodoo and understands the religion, was accused of 'voodooism'. Thus the governments alternate between those who unwillingly tolerate the folk religion and those who want to stamp it out.

The Catholic priests, mostly Bretons, seeing their helplessness, made their peace with Voodoo and were happy if the farmers conformed at least externally with the commands of the Church. 'One must be a Catholic in order to serve the loas,' Métraux heard a farmer say.[47] He concludes from this that Catholicism and Voodoo have been fused into a kind of unity, since the farmer also ascribes magical efficacy to the sacraments, likes to have his children baptized, takes communion, and wants the priest at his death bed, and since Bon Dieu, Christ, Virgin, saints and loas all get on well together. Certainly the Haitian has built the Church into the Voodoo religion, since like the African he also respects other views of God and is only puzzled by the fanaticism of the Christians. Nevertheless Métraux misses the other point of the statement: one must also be a Catholic, that is, one must adapt oneself to the official religion, in order to be left alone by the state and so be free to serve the loas undisturbed.

Only in this century, under pressure from foreign powers, has it come to the point of extensive repressive measures against the national religion. While the governments in power at the time favoured these actions, the younger Haitian authors began in their novels to defend Voodoo. Edris Saint-Amand in his novel *Bon Dieu Rit* pictures the fate of a family which is faced with difficult conflicts through the pressure of a Protestant missionary. 'Formerly we served the loas, we danced the Voodoo, and went to the Catholic Church. The same saints who ornamented the altar watched over the hounfort. Every saint was also a loa. But now Pastor Henri has said strange things: "We must serve only Jesus. No man can serve God and Mammon." And since then, the people of Diguaran have been hating one another. Incessant quarrels have arisen among those who did not believe and those who were still "serving". There were two enemy camps. The village had two chiefs, pastor Henri and Docima the houngan.'[48]

The family of Uncle Prévilius is torn apart because one of the sons, Prévilien, the hero of the book, refuses to adopt the Protestant religion. Prévilius must disown his son, yet the Pastor makes still greater demands. Prévilius is to cut down the only tree in the courtyard, which gives it shade, because he once served the loa before this tree.[49] But he postpones it. When finally his other son, Plaisimond, is accidentally killed, old Prévilius sees himself persecuted by misfortune, Madame Erzulie appears to him in a dream and he returns penitently to his loas. 'We needn't worry about Pastor Henri. Are we supposed to be his servants? He is responsible for all our troubles, and yet when we need help is it on him that we can count?'[50] Prévilius is reconciled with his children and the family is again at peace.

'Protestantism,' writes Métraux, 'which wins numerous adherents, is also a formidable enemy of Voodoo, pursuing it with tenacious hatred and admitting none of the compromises with which the Catholic Church adapts itself.'[51]

In the long run, however, the Catholic clergy thought they ought not to lag behind the Protestant missionaries who had come to the country during the occupation by North American troops (1915–34). The opportunity presented itself during the Second World War, when a North American company to whom the government was indebted acquired territory for the development of plantations, from which the farmers, who had no official title, had first to be driven. It was therefore very convenient for the North Americans that the Breton priests should distract the people from this confiscation. The campaign against Voodoo was prosecuted with the greatest severity, the hounforts were destroyed, the faithful forced to 'renounce' their faith, the booty of sacred vessels were seized and destroyed on bonfires.

Jacques Stéphen Alexis has made this crusade the theme of his novel *Les Arbres Musiciens*. We see here the ambitious Léonie Osmin, a woman of the people, who herself believes in the loas. All her life she has worked and saved in order to give her sons a higher education. She has achieved this: Edgard is an army officer, Diogène a priest, Carlos a lawyer and a bohemian. Since church and state foresee difficulties in the district where land is to be expropriated, they send secret functionaries to Fonds-Parisien: Edgard Osmin is appointed commandant there, his brother Diogène is given the parish and begins his crusade. He seeks out, with his fanatical party of the faithful, one hounfort after another, destroys the altars, burns them down and forces the faithful to 'renounce'. His antagonist is the old sage Papaloa Bois-d'Orme Létiro of the old shrine Nan-Remembrance. Bois-d'Orme realizes that all the hostile forces are united against him: the church, the state and the wicked enchanter and mixer of poisons Danger Doussous, who has already subjected the captain Edgard Osmin and the local chief of police Joseph Boudin to his evil power. Bois-d'Orme recognizes the political background of the combination: 'What did our ancestors fight for? Why did Dessalines exist, if the whites were to come and take our land again? I remember the time, indeed, when the American whites, with the help of Haitian police, tore us from our hearths and drove us with their fists and their batons to forced labour on the roads. But one day the people of the cities heard us and together we all drove out the whites. But how can it be that the city police have now called in the whites to give them our land if they had not dared to take it themselves?'[52] His adherents press him to risk rebellion, but Bois-d'Orme continues to preach non-violence, in order not to stain the holy shrine La-Remembrance. Bois-d'Orme has the holy vessels buried and himself sets fire to the shrine. When Diogène Osmin enters with his procession, all the buildings are in flames and the High Priest of Voodoo says to the Catholic priest: 'The loas are immortal, priest! The loas have not allowed you to raise your sacrilegious hands against the ancient shrine of Remembrance. It is no longer anything but flames and ashes, but the loas live! Watch the light glowing on the ashes, La Remembrance lives! Bois-d'Orme can go to his death now, for the ancient shrine will rise one day, at the same place, greater, higher, more beautiful, eternal like the loas of eternal Africa. You, to your misfortune, you will survive, but no one will be more dead than you. When you look at the trees you will see in their symmetry the mystic and invisible body of the loas. When you hear the wind sighing over the land, it is their voice that will be cursing you. For you did not respect the right of men to believe according to their hearts. Go, son of no one! Man of no race! Man of no land! Man of no nation! The hands of the gods are upon you.'[53]

But Bois-d'Orme also sees the greater danger that threatens his loas, greater than the dangers of witchcraft, state and church. This danger is revealed to him in the third of the Osmin brothers, in Carlos, the Bohemian, who has come to him to warn him. 'All I know is that behind my brothers there are men of power, strangers, whites. I believe neither in God nor the devil, but I respect all that grows on the land. The loas grow on the land like the bananas, the manioc, the maize. Why does maize grow here and not wheat? Because our sun is hot, because our land contains just this, this and nothing else. The loas grow on our land because our land is wretched, because you have only your hands and poor primitive tools to cultivate the soil. They want you to renounce the loas for the religion of the whites, but your religion is maize and that of the whites is wheat. But they will not force their religion on you. The loas will die only on the day when electricity breaks into the country, the day when agricultural machines whinny in the fields, the day when the *habitants* learn to read and write . . .'[54]

Bois-d'Orme does not answer, although he could easily object that electricity and machines and reading and writing have altered even the religion of wheat but could destroy it as little as they can destroy the religion of manioc and maize. Instead Bois-d'Orme presents an allegory. 'Do you see this chain, child?' he asks young Gonaibo, who has grown up untaught among snakes and grass and trees, has married the priest's granddaughter and is to become the successor of the Papaloa. ' "Look!" Bois-d'Orme balanced the chain between his thumb and index finger. He lifted the little golden chain, took aim and hurled it into the waters of the lake. "Watch me," he said. Bois-d'Orme walked towards the water. He entered it and walked in deeper and deeper. Soon he disappeared from sight. Gonaibo held Harmonise's hand gripped tightly in his own. Did the old man want to drown himself before their eyes? Perhaps he was fulfilling a final secret rite, a last sacerdotal gesture? Incredible tales were told of Bois-d'Orme, they said he was endowed with magnetic powers that could even move stones. Gonaibo and Harmonise felt themselves rooted to the ground, unable to speak or stir. They saw his head reappear on the water, then his shoulders and his gaunt body. He was gasping and holding between his teeth a large grey fish, still flapping. When he came to the bank, the old man fell on his knees and dropped the fish in the grass. With one bite, without putting his hands on it, he opened the belly of the fish, searched feverishly through the entrails, still with his teeth, and rose; the little golden chain was hanging from his lips. He threw the fish back in the lake and walked up to Gonaibo and Harmonise, who stood as if turned to stone. He put the chain around Gonaibo's neck. "Go, Gonaibo," he said, "let me be." '[55]

The Papaloa is presenting an allegorical image of the power of his religion: a power which no persecution can break. But we must also understand the wrath of the Christian clergy. For the same misunderstandings have arisen wherever the emissaries of a monotheistic religion have come into conflict with the adherents of a polytheistic religion. As early as 1482 when Diego Cão came to the kingdom of the Congo, the missionaries were at first delighted that King Nzinga a Nkuwa, whom they found then in place of the legendary Christian priest and king John, allowed himself and his people to be baptized and took the name John the First. He exchanged embassies with the King of Portugal and was treated by him as his equal. But soon the missionaries discovered that the newly baptized Christians were continuing to honour their former gods as well. They were soon deeply disappointed and their descriptions lose their detached and impartial tone. 'The principal ground of their infamous false doctrine is this, that although God is one in himself and very great, yet beside him are many other lesser gods, who all deserved to be honoured and prayed to. To this end they set out a great horde of idolatrous images.'[56]

The misunderstanding is always the same and is inherent in the nature of both religions. The polytheists are gladly prepared to add an additional and obviously powerful divinity to their pantheon. They participate in the ceremonies required of them, allow themselves to be baptized and willingly learn the prayers and usages with which the new divinity is to be served. And from now on they serve all their divinities, old and new, each according to custom and propriety. The monotheists cannot understand this and are horrified by it, and the polythesists cannot understand why the monotheists are so distressed. For the latter the very foundation of their monotheistic world is at stake, so much the more so as their God now no longer opposes the others but —recognized alongside others—threatens to be transformed from the one and only God to just one more divinity among many others. Thus the polytheists seem to them apostates, heretics, who sin against the most sacred of all commandments, 'I am the Lord thy God, and thou shalt have no other Gods but me.' Everything the polytheists do appears in the light of the most terrible crime, and the more deeply their life is permeated by religion, the more does it appear false, idolatrous, abominable. The whole wrath of Jahweh and Moses against the apostates who danced before the golden calf comes to life in the disappointed missionaries; curses of banishment come to their lips and in their distress they become the images of their god and say: 'I am the Lord . . . and thou shalt!'

Even if the missionaries recognize that African polytheism has a monotheistic superstructure—or substructure—their battle against the 'false' Gods does not abate. And even if they notice that certain divinities do not count as full gods but as intermediate levels between the human and divine which are not so far removed from the Christian saints—even then the Old Testament prejudices are often too much for them and prevent their recognizing that the religion of the new dispensation with its Trinity, Mother of God and saints differs from the strict monotheism of the religion of the old dispensation. Instead of finding in this points of contact for an understanding of polytheistic peoples, they are inclined to condemn all they see.

Voodoo, like all things living, has changed. Voodoo has fused various African rites together and has assimilated Christian influences. Yet, as we have seen, Voodoo is no confused conglomerate, and Williams' assertion that the religion of the Africans has become a hocus-pocus is mistaken.

The process of fusion of the different African rites could be investigated by following back every individual loa, with its embodiments, its rhythms, its symbols, its significance, and so on, and comparing it, insofar as this is possible today, with its African original. For Haitian and West African culture have been developing for two hundred years without contact with one another, the West African presumably in a further process of fragmentation, while the Haitian shows a tendency towards synthesis. The process of fragmentation of West African cultures caused by slave hunts, foreign influence, colonization and missionary activity led to a loosening of relationships and favoured the retention of particular details, the higher relationship of which became increasingly less perceptible to the participants. Haiti, on the other hand, grew in its dearly bought freedom into a nation; the process of amalgamation obliterated particular variations, necessarily brought into the foreground the common denominator, and emphasized the comprehensive content.

Man is nowhere more conservative than in religion. In Christianity, also, every reformation has had the aim of restoring the original, the pure doctrine—or what was thought to be such. So we may perhaps conjecture that in Voodoo, precisely through the process of fusion, the religious core of African religion comes into view. From this point of view it also becomes apparent that the Christian influence in Voodoo is less than is usually thought. Maya Deren points explicitly to the fact that in translating Voodoo concepts into a European language one involuntarily calls up Christian associations, which are not really present.[57] Thus *pè*, the 'altar', has a different function from that suggested by the word 'altar', and the situation is similar with other concepts and symbols—we have only to think of the cross.

In the light of African philosophy,[58] the loas are forces, and in 'possession' man takes these forces into himself, intensifies his own nature, intensifies the force which he himself *is*. He experiences himself as universal force, strengthens his being, his vital force, through communication with superhuman forces, and experiences his ties (*religio*) with these forces.

Bon Dieu is only in name the Christian 'Good Lord' who is close to men and concerns Himself about the destiny of individuals. Like the African highest divinities, such as Olorun, Amma or Nyamurunga, he is infinitely distant from the world and unapproachable, while the Christian saints become deified ancestors, loas or Orishas. Voodoo is not christianized through these identifications, but Christianity is voodooized, assimilated to the residual-African religion. The identification of loas and saints has transformed the saints into forces.[59]

Chapter 3

RUMBA

The Meaning of the Dances

And Cuba has long known that she is a mulatto.
NICOLÁS GUILLÉN

I. THE SANTERÍA

In Cuba the *Santería* corresponds roughly to Voodoo. And the slaves who were long ago carried off to Cuba came for the most part from West Africa; the majority, however, came not from Dahomey, but from Yorubaland. Afro-Cubans who come from Yorubaland are called in Cuba *Lucumi*[1] or *Nago*.

The santería reflects the religion of Yorubaland, a religious system which Frobenius compares with that of the ancient world. He considers the Orisha system richer and more original, more rigorous and well-preserved than any of the forms that have come down to us from classical antiquity.[2] The same could be said of the Voodoo of Haiti, for Voodoo and santería spring from different, neighbouring and friendly sects of the same religion. The santería honours the orisha (Cuba: *orichas*), who correspond to the loas of Haiti. The ceremony is called *güemilere*, a word which contains the Yoruba word *ilé-ere*, 'house of images'. The 'house of images', corresponding to the hounfort, is also called *iléocha*, presumably a contraction of 'Ile Orisha', Orisha house. In it are the meeting hall, *eyá aránle* (from Yoruba: eyá = part + alá = group of persons + ilé = house), *igbodu*, the holy of holies (from Yoruba: igbo = forest + odù = oracle) and *ibà-baló*, the patio or court for the spectators. The priest is called *babalao* after the *babalawo*, the oracle priest of the *Ifa* cult in Yorubaland, from whom the Haitian high priest, the papaloa, also derives his name.

The rhythms in which the orisha are called to 'mount' (*subirse*) their 'children' (*hijos* and *hijas*) are called *oru*. But it is not our aim to elaborate a word list; the purpose of this chapter is to compare the orisha with their African models, with special attention to the dances.

In Cuba, as in Yorubaland, Bon Dieu is called *Olorun*. But since the absolute transcends all human understanding, no temples are built to Olorun either in Yorubaland or in Cuba, and no sacrifices made to him. On the other hand, the life force of the creator is thought to be present in all creatures and in all things, especially in the orisha, who in Yorubaland were originally human beings, important ancestors from whom the Yoruba people are descended. Their extensive spiritual and physical progeny demonstrates that they are forces, life forces, which share, just as you and I do, the primal life force. And the person who honours the orisha and serves them by letting them embody themselves in him, not only receives life forces into his own being, but in his turn strengthens the orisha too. The Yoruba word for prayer is 'She orisha': to 'make' the god.[3]

As is the case with Legba in Haiti, so in Cuba also the 'god of the roads', Ellégua or Echú, pronounced Eshú, is the first to be summoned when the ceremony begins. Among the Yoruba, Eshu is a very fragmented personality.* The missionaries identify him with the devil; Frobenius calls him the god of the world order;[4] Parrinder reports that in Ibadan he is identified with Jesus Christ;[5] Beier writes: 'He is full of mischief and can be deliberately malicious. Usually he is made responsible for all bad luck and all quarrels. Before a sacrifice is given to any other orisha, Eshu must receive his portion. Prayers and offerings are brought to him to prevent any kind of accident. Although he is cited as the originator of all quarrels, his social function is that of a peacemaker. A quarrel, which might otherwise never be made up, can often be blamed on the action of Eshu. Both parties can then unite in a sacrifice to Eshu and peace is restored without each side taking too much blame. To identify Eshu with evil is

* We have given the names of Orishas in English transcription. In order to distinguish the Cuban from the African orisha, the Yoruba orisha are printed without accents, the Cuban with accents. Thus in Africa: Eshu, Shango, Oshun, etc.; in Cuba, Eshú, Shangó, Oshún, etc.

to misunderstand the basic principles of Yoruba philosophy. Unlike the European, the Yoruba does not conceive the world as a conflict between good and evil, light and darkness, God and devil. He is realistic and recognizes that all forces—even divine forces—have destructive as well as constructive possibilities. The secret of life, then, and the purpose of orisha worship is to establish a constructive relationship with these powers.'[6]

In Cuba Eshú—with the epithet Eléggua or Elegbará, that is, the 'mighty one'[7]—is identified with the devil. His emblems are bits of iron, nails, chains and keys, for he 'opens'[8] gates and doors to good as well as to evil.

The dancer who is possessed or 'mounted' by Eshú wears a red and black jacket, a red and black cap as tall as a chief's, and knee breeches in the same colours decorated on the knee band and belt with shells, pearls and bells. His dance is grotesque. He makes faces, plays with a top or with marbles, steals the hats of the onlookers, takes the cigarettes out of their mouths, waggles his buttocks and his hips, swings his emblem—an iron hook 18 inches long, a gigantic picklock, like a machete, as if he were opening a path in an uncleared forest. At the same time he hops and turns around on one leg, improvises capriciously, and surprises and delights the spectators by his acrobatics and his virtuosity.[9]

Only now, as we know, are further orisha summoned by the chorus and orchestra, each by the appropriate beat—Fernando Ortiz has represented many of these beats in musical notation[10]—so that they may 'climb into their children's heads', '*suben en la cabeza*', or 'mount' them. Let us look at the most important of these orisha and above all at the dances, of which Ortiz writes: 'These pantomimic dances, their gestures, steps, costumes and symbols are as carefully planned as ballets. They were created by the Yoruba, an artistic people, said to be the best choreographers in Africa and possessing a highly dramatic mythology, as rich in narrative and as developed as the Graeco-Roman. Their allegorical movements are so highly stylized that the uninitiated are unable to understand them without interpretation. In fact, these religious dances of the Yoruba are much more than ballets, for there is always the singing as well, and in some cases the poetry of the songs is like a mythological parable which the faithful hear and which they find represented in the pantomime of the dance.'[11]

Ogun, the orisha of iron—we know him already, the lord of the smiths and of war, split into the Voodoo loas Ogou Badagri and Ogou Ferraille—the orisha of minerals, of mountains, or iron implements. He has as his emblem machetes, pickaxes, hammers and other tools, and recently in Cuba also trains, automobiles, tanks and planes. Because he is a locksmith he is identified with Saint Peter. His costume is like Eshú's, only purple. He dances in a stooping position, or hops along on one leg, and swings his machete as if he were cutting weeds, snatching up his other leg each time just out of reach of the blade. And then another time he swings his hammer like a smith.[12]

'*Yemayá*', writes Ramos,[13] 'is the goddess of rivers and springs.' But that is not true; Yemayá is the sea itself.[14] In Cuba she is the same as the *Virgen de Regla*, the protectress of Cuban sailors, whose shrine crowns the Bay of Havana. Ships and sea creatures are her emblems, and ducks, and also peacocks. She is the orisha of fertility, but of motherhood rather than of sexual love. In Africa she is the mother of all orisha, the Prime Mother of all things. She is a wifely person, fond of good company, and sometimes also of display. She wears fans, palm branches or peacock feathers; her colours are blue and white like the waves of the sea. In her white garment she appears full of virtue, she is the wife and mature woman, and yet she is sometimes wild and sensual, 'for the Africans do not consider virtue and sensuality incompatible'.[15]

Her dance is a dance of the waves, of the waves of the sea, to which the goddess surrenders herself, at first in large movements, slow and dignified. She steers back and forth over a large space, sometimes as far as the horizon, sometimes to the shore, where Oshún, the river, stands waiting for her. Her movements are soft at first, like those of the sea in a light breeze; then she begins to move more violently; she rumbles and rolls till she becomes a hurricane, and finally whirls raging through the room in the destructive fury of the tornado.[16]

Shango is Yemaya's second son.[17] He was the third ruler of

Oyo, the old capital city of Yorubaland, who ruled after his father *Oranyan* and his elder brother *Ajaka*. He was a powerful warrior, with a strong and generous character; but he was also quick tempered and often tyrannical. He seems to have been a most colourful personality who fascinated both his friends and enemies. He is the personification of the tragic hero, the great man, who brings calamity on himself through his own fault, but a calamity which is terrible out of all proportion to the fault. Different myths exist about his unfortunate end, some of which are told at length by Frobenius.[19] We shall follow here, with some supplementation, the exposition of Beier, which also interprets Shango's personality.[20] Shango was annoyed when two of his generals, Gbonka and Timi, became too proud and haughty. Shango incited them to a duel hoping that they would kill each other. But Gbonka killed Timi and then drove Shango out of the town. Shango was so bitterly disappointed when his people deserted him that he hanged himself.

Another version says that he had acquired the art of making thunder. One day when he tried out his secret art without taking proper precautions, he destroyed his entire palace with all his wives and children. In despair and remorse, he hanged himself.

But with all his faults, he inspired and continues to inspire loyalty in his close friends. To them Shango is not dead, and by continuing their loyalty to him they know they can strengthen both him and themselves. His friends and worshippers hold periodical festivals when they 'perform' for him. But with all their love they still remain aware of the dual nature of his character. He was married to three water goddesses, Oya, Oshun and Oba. He personifies masculinity with all its virtues and all its faults.

In Cuba he is lord of the lightning, of war, of virility. He is identified with St. Barbara, the saint of storms, the patron saint of gunners and mountaineers. 'Shango is a masculine Saint Barbara,' they say in Cuba.[21] He dances with weapons in a fashion compared by Ortiz with the Pyrrhic war dance of the Greeks and Cretans.[22] His dance also emphasizes the erotic element and his priapic potency.

Oshun, the wife of Shango, is identified in Cuba with the 'compassionate virgin', not to be confused with the 'gracious virgin', the 'Virgin de las Mercedes', who is identified with the Yoruba creator *Obatala*. Oshun also differs considerably from Yemayá, the maternal one. She is the Aphrodite goddess, and what we said earlier about Erzulie is true of her as well. Oshún rules over rivers and over all fresh waters.[23] Flowers are sacrificed to her and she drinks strained honey. Her colour is like the gold that is found in rivers; her emblem is the fan.

Her dance, with its tripartite choreography, follows in pantomime the legend of the goddess herself. The first part is a dance of the springs. She stretches out as if she were lying in the dry bed of a river, and calls the springs to her. They entwine themselves in spiral movement around her. She rises, and with outstretched arms, jingles her bracelets, moves her hands down along her body as if water were flowing over her, skips about gaily, uninhibited and youthful, like bright waters leaping over rapids, or then again rows as in a boat. But she is not only a river; she is also a maturing woman, who remembers her duties and grinds the maize with pestle and mortar to feed her ageing family. Then the rhythm changes; the second part represents the bath of Oshún. Tenderly she lets the water caress her, she bathes in it, cleans her body with seaweed, combs her hair, paddles through the waves, looks at herself in the still water of the pool and discovers her own beauty. She is the feminine goddess, the divine spouse, who welcomes the feast of life. In the third part, she adorns herself coquettishly and, with sensual swaying movements stretches out her arms with their golden bracelets to the rain, the water of heaven, the source of all fresh water. 'Honey! Honey!' she calls for the symbolic essence of love, her body is doubled up with passion as she awaits the mystic drops of conception.[24] 'Sometimes', writes Ortiz, 'Oshún meets the sensual Shangó, they recognize one another, and surrender themselves to a fervent dance of love in an unconcealed and incomparable imitation of carnal lust.'[25] 'Oshún used to dance naked, her body shining with honey,' Ortiz tells us further,[26] and he continues: 'Today the dance is no longer performed in its orthodox form, but perhaps we shall soon see it again, not in temples, but in cabarets and theatres as a great success of "white" civilization.'

In the Yoruba tradition in Africa, however, Oshun and Shango never meet. The Shangó-Oshún dance would be impossible in the country where the cult originated, since the embodiment of the orisha takes place one at a time, in strict serial order.

There are also other dances in the santería. *Agayú*, the orisha of those who carry burdens, who is identified with St. Christopher, dances stoutly, with large strides, lifting up his legs as if he were getting over obstacles, and picking up children and carrying them. *Obatala* is the creator orisha, who modelled man out of clay, and one day when he was drunk accidentally made cripples, albinos and blind men—since even the creative power produces a mixture of good and evil. Either a man or a woman may dance this double-sexed orisha, who is predominantly maternal and kind, but may also appear as a knight on a white steed, swinging his sabre, or as a frail old man,[27] a tottering cripple, or, again, as a wise man who is prophetically inspired. *Inle*, Erinle, the hunter-orisha of the Yoruba, is in his Cuban form a fisherman and gatherer. He dances zig-zag, searching everywhere, and pulls in nets and picks berries. *Oya*, the mistress of plant juices, dances at a furious speed, as if she wanted to purify the woods with the fire of the torch that she holds in her right hand. In Yorubaland she is the stormy wind and the river Niger. *Babalu-Aye*, who brings leprosy and also cures it, the god of infectious diseases in Yorubaland, walks slowly in, leading an imaginary mule; he is a sickly man, afraid of flies and insects, and whenever any one comes near him he warns him by shaking the little placard that hangs around his neck as a sign of infection. Thus there are countless dances, as many dances as orisha, each with its special songs and specific rhythm.* And with all this we must never lose sight of the fact that all these dancers dance 'possessed' embodying their particular orisha exactly as tradition prescribes. At the same time the steps are not specified in detail. For the control of the priest does not govern the movement of the feet; it is directed towards the correct embodiment, in that movement, of the spiritual reality.

* See pp. 38–9.

II. Ñañiguismo (The Secret Society)

In the santería, as distinct from Voodoo, the possessed are dressed and equipped with their emblems before the dance begins instead of during it. The participant in the santería does not simply suggest the apparel of his orisha; he wears a costume. Nevertheless, it is not a question of make-believe; he is not an actor representing the orisha; just as in Voodoo, he becomes the orisha. We can see this clearly if we compare the santería with *Ñañiguismo*.

'Ñañiguismo' is a term frequently used to include all expressions of Afro-Cuban religion. It is then, like Voodoo, a synonym for 'heathen superstition', 'idolatry', 'satanism', 'magic', and so on, including the santería as well as Ñañiguismo proper, and a great deal more. We are using the term here, however, in its narrow and correct sense, as the name of the secret society of the Ñáñigos. 'Ñañiguismo is not a religion,' writes Ortiz,[28] 'but a secret society, a kind of freemasonry, to which only the initiate, who have sworn their allegiance, may belong.' Women do not belong to it. In its religious ceremonies no one is 'ridden',[29] and Ortiz describes the ritual, in the temple or *fambá*, as a drama.[29]

In the santería the figure of death is absent; but nevertheless Baron Samedi and his train, the guédé, who are embodied by worshippers in Voodoo, have their own ritual in Cuba also. He and his macabre train have their ritual in Ñañiguismo, but they are not 'embodied'. Although this looks admittedly like secularization, it is based on Nigerian tradition. Thus Beier writes of the corresponding secret society of the Yoruba: 'Egungun is a secret society which has the social function of providing a link between the living and the dead. One duty is to comfort and instruct the bereaved after a funeral—and the Egunguns are no less subject to misrepresentation than the Eshu cult. The masquerades, it is said, "pretend to be spirits". They do not. They claim sometimes to become spirits and to lend the paraphernalia of human speech and movement to the departed . . . A man who is told by the Ifa oracle to worship one of his ancestors does not himself become an Egungun worshipper. Instead he has a mask made and presents it to the Alagba, the head of the Egungun, asking him to find a dancer. During the ceremony the ancestor will take possession of the dancer, and speak to his relatives whilst using the dancer as a medium.'[30] The difference is clear: a worshipper who dances an orisha becomes the orisha for the period of his 'possession', while the masked dancer, instead of becoming the dead man, remains a dancer and only 'lends' the dead man his voice and gestures. He *is* not the other person but represents him; he is an actor.

The Ñañiguismo of Cuba, however, is derived, not from the Egungun secret society of the Yoruba but from a very similar, also South Nigerian cult, the *Ekue* secret society of Efik or Ekoi at Calabar. Ortiz has compared the representation of a Ñáñigo masked dancer with the picture of an Ekue-dancer: the costumes are almost exactly alike. [31]

The secret ceremony of the Ñáñigos usually begins at about midnight with secret preparatory rites in the fambá or temple. There the initiate, who constitute a 'lodge' or 'potencia', sacrifice the blood of a cock to the 'Great Mystery', to *Ekué*. Ekué, the 'great mysterious one', remains invisible and permits only his voice—the voice of a leopard—to be heard. Ekué is death.[32]

The temple and everything in it are decorated with sacred emblems. Walls, floors, doors and altars, the participants and all the consecrated vessels, drums, calabashes, cauldrons, basins—everything has magic stripes and signs of yellow plaster. White plaster is used only for burials. The priests and the *okobios*, the 'brothers', put on the prescribed garments, which are also decorated with magic signs. When all the preparations are in order, three persons step out in front of the temple and the performance, the 'Juego', can begin. It is now broad daylight.

PROLOGUE

Participants

Ekueñón—the 'slave of Ekué', the 'helper of death', a sort of mystagogue, instructor, master of ceremonies and initiator.

Moruá Yuánsa—the priest.

Empegó—the 'scribe', an assistant to the priest.

Moruá Yuánsa, the priest, swings his *ekón*, the sacred bell,[33] Empegó beats the drum, 'the drum of command', and all three —Ekueñón, the 'helper', setting the key—sing the opening pledge. During the first act they remain on the scene as orchestra and chorus.

FIRST ACT: THE CONSECRATION

Participants
> *The above* and
> *Embákara*—'the help'.
> *Baroko*—the sacrifice (a he-goat).
> *Ekué*—Death (invisible).

Scene. Before the temple (fambá), on the Isaroko or place of sacrifice, where there is a silk-cotton tree.

The goat stands tied to the tree. While gourds and drums and choral voices sound, Embákara comes from the temple, unties the goat with ceremonial gestures, and turns it over to Ekueñón, the 'helper of death'. He in turn leads the sacrifice to the temple. There the animal is 'designated' with yellow plaster, is 'sworn in' and 'initiated' as if it were a 'brother', an *okobio* or *abanékue*. Then the sacrifice to death is introduced. Death is not visible, only his contented grunting can be heard.

SECOND ACT: THE SACRIFICE

Participants
> *Moruá Yuánsa*—the priest.
> *Enkrícamo*—the 'drummer'.
> *Ekueñón*—'the helper'.
> *Empegó*—the 'scribe'.
> *Nasakó*—the 'magician'.
> *Eribangandó*—the 'purifier'.
> *Aberisún*—the 'executioner'.
> *The novice* or 'candidate'.
> *Baroko*—the sacrifice (a he-goat).
> *Ekué*—Death (invisible).

Scene. Isaroko, the place of sacrifice before the famba (temple) where the silk-cotton tree stands.
Time. Noon.

The door of the temple opens. The actors enter in a solemn procession. The 'drummer' introduces them, and is followed by the 'helper', the 'scribe', the 'magician' and the 'executioner'. The 'executioner', however, acts as if he did not know this was his role. With them comes the novice, for whose sake the ceremony is taking place, and who is to be received into the circle of the Ñáñigos and ordained as a priest. He leads the goat on a line. The magician carries in his hand a vessel with some magic stuff in it. The 'purifier' is led by the priest. In this manner they march up to the silk-cotton tree and begin the story of invocation.

Meanwhile the 'scribe' begins his work. He decorates the tree with weapon-like shapes in yellow plaster. With the same material he draws on the ground at the foot of the tree complicated patterns and signs of the same sort as the vèvè.[34] These signs represent the holy place at the bank of that legendary river in Africa, where the secret society once practised its sacrificial ceremony. When the sacrifice has the purpose of increasing the stock of fish in a river, it takes place on the bank of an actual stream, on the bank of the Almendar or even in the Bay of Havana, where more than a century ago the oath to play the *Efik Butón* was taken. At the same time the drawings on the ground assign not only the place, but also the course of the action: it is the 'signature' of the programme, and corresponds to the magical drawings of the Efik in Africa.

Now the 'candidate', with bared torso and naked legs and arms, waits at the foot of the silk-cotton tree to be purified. The 'magician' or 'cleanser' approaches him with his vessel of magic medicine, smears him with it and purifies him with grandiose words and gestures. The 'purifier' helps him with this; he has a live cock in his hand, swings it over the body of the 'candidate', and thus dispels all evil from him. The 'scribe' draws magic symbols in yellow on his forehead, cheeks, neck, breast and back, arms and hands, ankles and feet. And then the 'magician' concludes the cleansing by mixing in his mouth brandy, wine and sacred smoke and spraying the 'candidate' with it in the manner of the Foulah.

During the cleansing ceremony the drums sound unceasingly, led by the priest and the 'drummer', and each particular action is accompanied by songs and oaths. Suddenly silence reigns, and out of the depths of the temple the fearful voice of Ekué, the invisible one, is heard like the rumbling of thunder, and the orchestra with its vegetable and animal instruments,—pan-pipes and goats' horns,—begins afresh.

The 'executioner' takes fright and stands up. He has heard the command of the 'drummer'—a frightening demand. Aberisún, who is wearing the dress of an executioner, must kill the sacrifice, he must become an 'executioner' in fact. But he does not want to. He has come to the temple with pure hands. He put on executioner's dress only in order to purify the temple, only to frighten the uninitiated by his dreadful appearance. So he hurries to and fro on the place of sacrifice, hurls imprecations, threatens his 'brothers' and runs away around the silk-cotton tree.

But the 'drummer' follows him and the rhythms become irresistible. The 'drummer' seizes the resisting 'executioner' and leads him up to the goat, who is being held in the prescribed manner at the foot of the silk-cotton tree by two other diablitos. The 'executioner' takes fright at the sacrifice, and again wants to run away. Then his brothers take pity on his despair; they kneel down with him and pray to *Abasi*, the invisible one up above, to spare the animal, who is after all a 'brother'.

But the invisible one is silent; he wants the sacrifice. As answer the 'executioner' hears once more the command of the 'drummer', and the 'helper' hands him the *itón*, the sacred staff. The command is irresistible. The 'executioner' looks at the sacrifice, decorated with the yellow signs of death; full of dread he goes trembling up to the goat, who turns his eyes and looks at his executioner. If the goat makes so much as a single sound, the ceremony stops short and the animal is released, for that would be the sign that the sacrifice had become a 'brother' and was pleading for his own life. But the animal does not make the slightest sound, for the 'magician' is holding his jaws tight together. Then the 'executioner' swings the staff and deals the animal a powerful blow on the skull, which either kills him at once or stuns him. Then the 'executioner' runs away in horror.

An assistant thrusts a dagger into the animal's throat, cuts the jugular, and lets the blood run into the vessel that is held in readiness for it. The goat's head is cut off and he is skinned and disjointed. During all this songs have been announcing the death of the sacrifice, threnodic plaints alternating with songs of thanksgiving for the successful sacrifice.

INTERLUDE

Scene. Within the fambá.
Persons. All *Abanékue,* 'diablitos' or 'brothers', *Ekué*—Death (invisible).

The 'brothers' return to the interior of the temple. There the blood of the sacrifice is offered as a drink to Ekué. The invisible one lets his voice sound, uncanny as the snarling of a leopard. The voice of the invisible one consecrates the blood-drink (*macuba*), which now passes in a special jug from mouth to mouth. The 'candidate' drinks of it in common with the abanékue, the 'brothers in death', to whom he now belongs and whose life force vitalizes them all anew through this communion. The head of the sacrificial beast is handed to *Ekueñón,* the 'helper of death', on *Eribó,* the sacred drum.

In this connection Ortiz points to the parallel with the Eleusinian mysteries. There, in the initiation of a novice, we find the statement:

> *I have eaten on the drum,*
> *I have drunk out of the cymbal,*
> *I have carried the sacred vessel,*
> *I have stepped under the canopy.*

In Eleusis as in Cuba the testicles of the sacrifice are presented to the divinity, and only then is the blindfold removed from the eyes of the novice. Only then is he a 'purified' one, one who is reborn, to whom one can now show the sacred utensils.[35]

THIRD ACT: THE PROCESSION (*Beremo*)
Scene. In front of the temple, on the place of sacrifice.
Participants
    Enkoboró—the 'head-diablito'.
    Moruá Yuánsi—the priest.
    Isué—the 'high priest' or 'bishop'.

Mkongo, Mosongo, Abasongo—three chief priests.
Abasí—the crucifix.
Sukubakariongo—a goatskin.
Ekoko—the skin of the sacrifice (the he-goat).
Eribo—the drum.
and as above.

From the temple a solemn procession moves to the place of sacrifice. Accompanied by the priest, the 'head diablito' dances ahead and at the same time 'purifies' the path by leaping to frighten off imaginary intruders. Behind them both walks the 'bishop', the 'high priest', who carries the head of the cock that has been sacrificed, holding it between his teeth by the comb. In his hands he carries the sacred drum on which the body of the cock is lying. This sacred drum, Eribó, is decorated with skins, shells, and feathers, and the 'high priest' swings it up and down and makes it bow as if it were alive and were greeting the spectators. It represents a supernatural power, divinity itself.

Three chief priests follow the drum, each one carrying his sacred staff, the itón, as a sceptre which embodies the magical power of the ancestors. Behind them comes Abasí, the crucifix, carried by an official and flanked by two further officials. One of them sprays holy water about with a feather duster made of basil leaves, and the other swings the basin of sacred smoke and sings a song of praise. The officials carry large altar candles—although it is said that they used to carry torches.

After the group with the crucifix and the candles comes a goatskin, stretched out like a flag, carried by a Ñáñigo in women's dress. The goatskin and its bearer are meant to represent *Sikanega*, according to legend a woman who once, back in Africa, discovered the secret of the founders of the cult, and was therefore condemned to death and sacrificed under the silk-cotton tree.

Seven musicians accompany the procession, which walks several times around the place of sacrifice, while the choir sings dithyrambs:

Ekué! Ekué! Chabiaka Mokongo Ma Cheberé! ...

Finally the procession comes to a standstill in front of the silk-cotton tree, where the skin of the he-goat that has been sacrificed is lying on the altar. The 'assistant' lifts the skin of the goat, salutes the sacred drum with it and, accompanied by singing, wraps the drum in the skin. Then the newly received Ñáñigo, who is thus to be ordained a priest, is wrapped in the skin of the sacrifice, and it is he who now carries the sacred drum back into the temple. So, while the choir strikes up the hymn of offering, the procession dances back into the temple.

Here the new priest is anointed, and the procession comes once more out of the temple, this time in a different rhythm and with slow, grave steps. Nasako, the magician, strides ahead, the 'head diablito' follows him, led by the 'drummer'. Behind them comes the 'high priest' or 'bishop', on his right the 'scribe', striking his 'drum of command', on his left the 'helper' with the sacred drum, on which now, not the cock, but the head of the beast of sacrifice is lying. Behind them, between the candles, comes the crucifix with the hymn-singer and the holy water sprinkler and then, finally, the new priest. While the hymns continue, the procession moves once around the place of sacrifice and then back once more into the temple.

FOURTH ACT: THE SUPPER

Participants
   Empegó—the 'scribe'.
   Nasakó—the 'magician'.
   Enkandemo—the 'cook'.
   Eribangando—the 'purifier'.
   and the remaining 'diablitos'.

The 'scribe' enters and draws new yellow signs under the silk-cotton tree, as the ritual prescribes. Then comes the 'magician' and dusts the signs with a black powder of great magical power. The 'cook' comes out of the temple with a steaming cauldron and announces that he has offered Ekué, death, his share of the flesh of the sacrifice. Now in his verses he presents the sacrifice to the supernatural powers, just as his ancestors in Africa once for the first time held their sacrificial meal on the bank of the legendary river Usagaré. Then he puts the cauldron with the roasted flesh into the prescribed magic circle and a small empty pot in its place, which is also prescribed.

The 'purifier' leaps from the temple, dances about the cauldron, invites the invisible powers, and while the other diablitos dance forth from the temple, he snatches the cauldron and with grotesque leaps throws bits of meat in all directions. Some pieces he brings into the temple, so that the high dignitaries who do not show themselves can also begin the ceremonial meal.

When he returns from the temple the other diablitos surround him dancing and singing. While the 'magician' is busied with the magic powder and all attention is fixed on him, the 'purifier' snatches a few pieces of meat out of the cauldron and puts them into the small pot which is off to one side—but the 'brothers' know that the 'purifier' is not allowed to eat this meat, they tease him, while they are dancing, and keep him from getting a single bit into his mouth. Suddenly the 'magician' lights the magic powder and in the comic confusion that folllows a 'brother' steals his pot from the 'purifier' and runs with it around the silk-cotton tree—the cheated 'purifier' behind him, yet unable to catch the 'brother', who finally gets away and brings the pot of meat to the ancestors.

Now all the others surround the cauldron, each one takes from it his bit of sacred meat of the 'brother' who has been sacrificed, the consumption of which gives new life and energy. While they dance round the cauldron with the pieces of meat in their hands they sing the great song of joy:

> *Bambá ekón mamá ñanga eriké*
> *ndiagame efik obón ekué . . .*

FIFTH ACT: FINALE

Participants

The whole group.

Now all make their appearance, apart from the dignitaries, the guardians of the shrine, who never show themselves. The 'magician' opens the final procession, cleansing its path of foreign magic. He is dressed in rags and carries bright bits of stuff, skins of wild beasts and feathers of birds of ill omen. His head and wig are covered with crowns of feathers, and his hands and feet garishly painted with magic signs. In his mouth he has a pipe, his breast is hung with chains, at his waist hang magic horns and a case of gunpowder. The 'purifier' carries the cock and 'sweeps' the path clean with it. All the actors appear: 'scribe' and 'drummer', 'cook' and 'head diablito', each led by his ékon-ringing priest; the 'high priest', who now beats the sacred drum, Abasí; the crucifix, with its trains and even some diablitos whom we have not yet met and who now draw attention to themselves by extremely grotesque dances. The procession circles the place of sacrifice and the silk-cotton tree, and to the beating of the drums hymns are sung celebrating Ekué and his marvels as the power of nature, which is revealed in the secret utensils, the bells, the magic powder, the signs, the symbols and the sound of the drums.

Then the 'scribe' steps forward with his 'drum of command', and while the procession withdraws into the temple, he remains in front of the door and concludes the ceremony with a recitative of thanks to heaven. The music stops. The sun has set. In the temple Ekué is silent, the mystery is at an end.[36]

Ekué, death, is identified with Jesus Christ.[37]

III. The Origins of Rumba

The dances of the Santería are religious, the dances of the Ñáñigo drama are cultic. But Ñañiguismo has another side as well. It is not the cult drama that has made the Ñáñigos so famous, but their appearance here and there in public, in small groups, on the 'Dia de Reyes', that is, Epiphany, at the carnival season or even on ordinary days. In such cases a Ñáñigo group, a *potencia* (power), a *juego* (game) appears, the individual members of which call one another *ekobio*, 'friend' or 'brother', but are called *diablitos* (little devils) by the people: hobgoblins, the terror of women and children. Each in turn dances with his staff, the itón, a dance that is neither acrobatic nor graceful, but only strange and inhuman, for the diablitos act the parts of dead who have come back, creatures of the other, invisible side of the world. While one gives his performance the other diablitos look on contentedly.

These dances were soon incorporated into the carnival, until in 1880, when slavery was abolished, they were forbidden. Secretly, however, these profane dances continued, the diablitos occasionally terrified women or children, but without violence or malice. 'In 1908', writes Ortiz, 'they were once more forbidden, since they were in danger of being lost in the folk culture of the people. Repression and secrecy help to preserve these esoteric rites.'[38]

Ñañiguismo has a cheerful side as well; alongside high tragedy there is buffoonery. Secularization of the cult? Scarcely. The diablitos are indeed pranksters, but 'terrible' too—nobody forgets that they are acting the parts of dead men. Nor are those who have died 'dead' in the European sense: they continue to exist and to associate with the living. But in Cuba the distinction is not strictly observed.

'The Egungun society in Africa provides a link between the living and the dead *and* it also represents living characters. But in this case they use "profane" masks which are only meant to entertain people. This secret society produces social plays in which they imitate Hausa, Nupe and Europeans. They have other masks satirizing policemen and prostitutes, and others again imitating animals.'[39] Thus in Africa the masks are clearly divided into bazimu- and bazima-masks[40] but in Cuba the distinction is obscured.

Alongside the religious dances and the masked dance there are in Africa as well as the Antilles secular dances also, 'socials' if you like, although the cult dance itself is social and the most secular work dance of farmers tilling the fields or work teams building roads never disavows the relation of the cult to the growth of the corn or the strength of the iron.

Ortiz assumes that the rumba derives from the *yuka*, the yuka possibly from the *calinda* of the days of slavery 'which the moralists of the colonies so abominated'.[41] Father Labat, who travelled in the Antilles in the seventeenth century, describes a calinda of 1698 as follows: 'The commonest dance and the one the slaves enjoy most is called calenda. It came from the coast of Guinea, probably from Ardra. The Spaniards have learned it from the Negroes and they dance it all over America just as the Negroes do.

'Since the postures and movements of this dance are highly obscene, decent masters forbid their slaves to practise it and watch out to see that they give it up. Yet the slaves love it so that even children who can hardly toddle try to imitate their parents when they see them dancing and spend whole days practising. The dancers are drawn up in two lines, one opposite the other, the men on one side and on the other the women. The spectators and those who are waiting their turn form a circle around the dancers and the drums. Some specially talented person among them sings a song which he composes on the spur of the moment on some theme that he considers appropriate, and the refrain, sung by all the spectators, is accompanied by hand-clapping. The dancers themselves hold their arms somewhat after the fashion of people who dance while playing castanets. They hop, turn to right and left, approach one another until they are two or three feet apart, and withdraw in the same step, until the sound of the drums indicates that they should come together and touch thighs. This is done by each pair, that is, a man and a woman. It looks as if the bodies meet, although in fact it is only the thighs that make contact. They at once pirouette back again, and repeat the same movements with lascivious gestures from the beginning, as often as the drum gives the signal, which it does several times in succession. Occasionally they fold their arms and turn two or three times in a circle, each time striking thighs and kissing. It is easy to see from this brief description how extremely this dance offends against the proprieties.'[42]

Moreau de Saint-Méry describes the calenda somewhat differently, but afterwards describes the *chica*, which, as we shall see, corresponds to Labat's calenda: 'A Negro dance came with them from Africa. . . . They call it the Calenda. The Negresses, drawn up in a circle, mark time with handclapping and answer in chorus one or two singers whose penetrating voices repeat or improvize little songs. For the Negroes possess the talent of improvization, and this gives them an opportunity to indulge their love of satire.

'The dancers, both men and women, advance repeatedly in the same number to the centre of a circle formed on a flat place in the open, and begin to dance. Each one turns to a partner and executes a figure before her. This dance, which originated on Mt. Atlas and offers little variety, consists of a movement in which each foot is raised and lowered in succession and first the toes,

5. Head of a Queen Mother, from Benin, West
Nigeria. (British Museum, London)

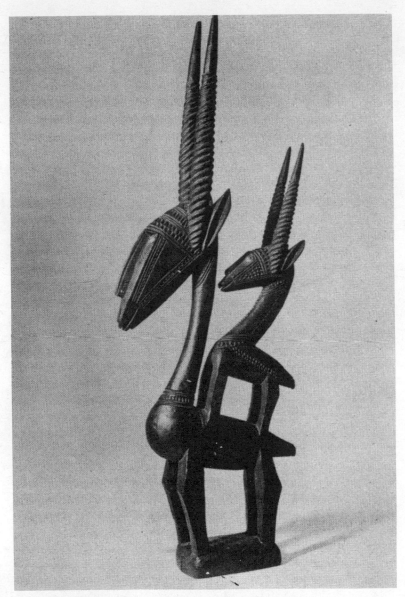

6. Woodcarving of antelopes for a head-dress.
Bambara, West Sudan. (N. Städtisches Museum
für Völkerkunde, Frankfurt-am-Main)

then the heel stamped energetically on the ground in a way that closely resembles the English step. The dancer revolves or turns around his partner, who also turns, changes her place and waves the two ends of a cloth which they both hold. The dancer alternately lowers and raises his arms, holding his elbows close to his body and his hands tight shut. This dance, in which the play of the eyes is nothing short of extraordinary, is lively and gay and the precision with which the step is kept gives it true charm.

Another dance of African origin is the *chica*, which is simply called calenda in the Windward islands and in the Congo and Cayenne, and which the Spaniards call the *Fandango*. This dance has its own melody and a sharply marked rhythm. The accomplishment in this dance consists of the degree to which the dancer is able to move her hips and the lower part of her back, while the rest of her body remains in a kind of immobility which persists even when she moves her arms ever so slightly, swinging both ends of a cloth or her skirt. A dancer approaches her, leaps suddenly into the air and comes down at a precise moment so close to her that he nearly touches her. He withdraws, leaps again and excites her with the most seductive play. The dance becomes livelier and soon takes on an appearance the whole import of which is at first voluptuous and finally obscene. It would be impossible to describe the chica in its true character, and I shall confine myself to saying that the impression evoked by it is so powerful that an African or Creole of any colour who comes and dances it without excitement is looked on as a man who has lost the last spark of vitality.'[43]

Of the present non-sacred dances the *yuka* is closest to the rumba. Its rhythm is beaten by the yuka-drum, a secular drum which has not been consecrated although a sacred drum of the Ekué secret society of the Efik, which is perpetuated in the Cuban Ñañiguismo, has the same name. The drummer of the Yuka, the *yukero* (yuquero) has a pair of tiny *maracas* on his wrists in order to protect himself and his drum from hostile magic powers.[44]

The Yuka is danced in 2/4 or 6/8 time. The strongly marked rhythm is rapid. In the first part the dancer importunes his partner in a courtship which she coyly resists. The second part is quicker, she flees, he follows and tries to stand opposite her when the music 'marks the beat' (*marca el golpe*). At this moment exactly he gives her the '*golpe de frente*', the 'blow on the front', the *vacunao*, which also occurs in other dances, and which in Brazil is called *ombligada*, 'umbilic', and by the Congo-Cubans *Nkúmba*, that is, navel (from which the Creole words *cumba*, *cumbe*, *cumbancha*, and so on are derived). The *vacunao*, in which the body of the dancer meets that of his partner, concludes the dance with the symbolic union of the two.[45]

However, the choreography of the yuka permits some variations. The woman may resist. As the dancer stands opposite her, she covers her genitals with a corner of her skirt and turns around with lightning speed at the very moment when the orchestra 'marks the beat'. This turn is called *botao* (from *botar*: to change the rudder, to recoil, to leap) and is the opposite of the vacunao. The dancer tries again. In order to 'force' her he lays a cloth or his hat on the ground and so narrows the space of the dance. She tries to pick up the object from the ground and is thus forced to dance very close to it, while he tries to stand just beside her when the beat is marked. If she succeeds, still turning and covering herself, in substituting botao for vacunao, snatching the 'booty' on the ground and appropriating it for herself, then she is the victor, the forfeit belongs to her, and the man must 'redeem the booty' by a gift of money.[46]

The yuka is obviously the secular equivalent of the dances of Oshún when she meets Shangó. The symbolism of the two dances is identical, although the dance of Oshún is infinitely richer. But how do Shangó and Oshún come to meet in Cuba, although in Africa this is impossible? It is generally assumed that European influence is to blame, but the gesture of vacunao, so characteristic of the yuka, is not derivable from Europe. It is to be found in Africa, among the Sara who live in the vicinity of Lake Chad. There the boys and girls gather under the 'dancing tree', the boys dancing in a row approach the group of seated girls, some of the girls stand up and form a corresponding row, slowly boy and girl approach one another, still dancing, closer and closer, their bodies touch, their eyes meet for a moment—and at once the partners move off again in opposite directions. The women once more become onlookers, while other women take their places and in their turn obey the call of the tom-tom.[47] The photographs used to illustrate Keita Fodeba's account demonstrate even more clearly the similarity of this dance to the yuka. (See Plate 7.)

But now the question arises: can a dance of the Sara of Lake Chad have come to Cuba? It is at any rate not impossible. Among the Africans the Sara are especially tall, powerful and handsome men who would certainly bring a high price to a slave dealer. Kano, in present-day Northern Nigeria, is a former slave-trading centre, from which traders undertook extensive raids, and the Sara live not too far away from Kano. From Kano old commercial roads lead south to Badagry, or to the Niger and along the Niger to Benin, from where the Yoruba slaves who imprinted their culture on Cuba were shipped to the Antilles. Even though one cannot assume that Sara in any large number were sent on this journey and came through it alive, we may nevertheless imagine that even a small group among the Cuban slaves might loosen the strict ties of the Yoruba in the new social situation and in contact with many other ethnic groups and might find their dance drawing attention and readily imitated. The dance of the Sara may have stimulated the meeting of Oshún and Shangó; it may also be the immediate ancestor of the calenda and so have begotten the characteristic vacunao symbolism all the way to the yuka and the rumba.

Is yuka a secularized religious dance or have religious and secular dances always existed side by side? To this we must answer that the question is falsely put. On the basis of African philosophy there can be no strict separation of sacred and profane. Since everything is force or energy, the orisha as well as the human being, the sacred drum as well as the profane, and all force is the embodiment of a single universal life force, the boundary between sacred and profane cannot be drawn as it is in Europe. Everything sacred has, as we have shown, a secular component, and everything secular a relevance to religion. There are infinitely many gradations, depending on whether a dance symbolizes more or less of the universal life force, whether it contains more or less *nommo*.[48] The dance of Oshun contains more than the yuka, but the latter is equally unthinkable without the universal life force, and is therefore not secular in the European sense. An African or Afro-American dance is secularized only when it is Europeanized, as has happened to the rumba. Ortiz writes: 'To the extent to which the yuka is Creolized in Cuba, ombligada and botao disappear and the vacunao is replaced by a simple gesture in the direction of the female sex organ which the dancer executes with his hand or foot. Finally the yuka fades and disappears and is transformed into *rumba brava* then into *rumba picaresca* and at length into the "salon-rumba" which can be danced in "society". The last is altogether modest yet it still retains a minimum of its inexhaustible grace and therefore also something of its original character.'[49]

The rumba is a dance of the nature of a pantomime and like the yuka is the representation of courtship up to the achievement of orgasm: highly stylized however and executed with subtle courtesy.[50] In Cuba it was not danced without embarrassment until in 1932 it was presented, though with a certain reticence, at the World Fair in Chicago and became a great success. Since then it has spread over the whole globe and has become a regular ballroom dance. It became everywhere a tolerated and often much-loved dance, with no enemies but its rival dances which come from the same source.'[51]

In all the works of Fernando Ortiz we can feel a kind of sadness because the rumba alone has spread over the whole world, and not one of the many other dances which the Cuban musicologist describes. Only the Oshún and the Shangó dance of the santería, as an expression of the fertility rite, has erotic character, he says; the dances of the Ñáñigos have nothing to do with eroticism,[52] nor have the dances of the societies of labourers—in Haiti the *corvée* or *coumbite* (combite), with its introductory singer, the *simidor* or *samba*. We must observe, however, that Ortiz is speaking here from the point of view of Christian and Western concepts. Since the African dance always manifests the life force, since the work dance is a function of an unceasing process of growth, it can never be other than erotic, nor can it ever be obscene. Ortiz is clearly distressed because it was the very dance which had nearly altogether lost its liturgical significance[53] and which is the poorest in expression among all the secularized dances, that achieved world fame. But that is surely no accident.

Only a dance which had largely sacrificed its sacred and pantomimic character and which could satisfy individualized erotic needs would be suitable for assimilation by European culture.

For what is the difference between Western and African dancing? When does a dance belong to African and when to Western culture? The difference lies first in the rhythm—it is almost impossible to dance in the European fashion to African rhythms—but also in posture, steps and gestures: both steps and gestures can be taken over, but only singly and superficially. But the difference lies above all in the sense, in the meaning of the dance. In all African art the meaning flows plainly from the sign used to express it: no gesture in the dance stands by itself, every one is a symbol. The yuka dancer woos his partner and presents the battle of the sexes and their union—not his personal wooing, not his personal battle, but wooing, battle and union as such. His dance is paradigmatic, illustrative.

For this reason most African and Afro-American dances are dances of display even when the spectators are also taking part in the performance. European dancing always has a purpose: to move one's partner, to express the mood of the dancers, to satisfy their love of movement, to entertain them, to intoxicate them and so on. African dance, on the other hand, always has a meaning, a sense. It holds the world order on its course (we shall see later how); and therefore it is necessary, in fact indispensable.

In Cuba there is a sort of rumba especially applauded by the tourists which is called 'Herrar le Mula', 'shoeing the hinny'. The female dancer, on all fours, respresents the she-ass, the male dancer represents the smith who is shoeing her 'hoofs'. 'This dance', writes Ortiz, 'is one of the many common degenerations of the Afro-Cuban dance, created only for the entertainment and exploitation of foreign tourists. It has lost all its charming music, which is typical of the true Cuban rumba.'[54]

But Ortiz has not got to the heart of the matter. It is not the loss of 'charming music' that constitutes the falsification. 'Shoeing the hinny' is not an Afro-Cuban dance even though it is presented in Cuba with Afro-Cuban rhythms, by Afro-Cuban dancers, and even though it seems to have a 'sense'. 'Shoeing the hinny' is not an Afro-Cuban dance, for one thing because it has fallen prey to a purpose—that of taking dollars from foreign tourists—and further because its 'sense' is not a sense, but nonsense. An Afro-Cuban fertility dance even, and especially, in its greatest extreme of sexual realism, symbolizes the sense, the meaning of the world. It is in order, within the unique and valid African world order; only in the European sense is it 'obscene'. But to place a woman on all fours as a she-ass, and thus to put her into a lower species, is to confuse the hierarchy of forces, to destroy the cosmic world order and is therefore, even if the lady is wearing brassière and panties, highly obscene.

A dance belongs to African culture so long as it has its specific meaning and so long as this meaning remains evident. The rumba is still an Afro-Cuban dance, even in Europe, for its meaning remains evident, though who knows for how long. 'Ever since 1930,' writes Helmut Günther, 'and more extensively since 1945, new dances have been surging in from Latin America. *Rumba, samba, mambo, cha cha cha, merinque,* and so on, express a new sense of life. They are once more action, not only movement. They express something. It is a question—the new cha cha cha demonstrates this quite plainly—of the age-old game of courtship and coyness, that is, of a pantomime. The English style is pure form, it no longer expresses anything, it is pure beauty, *l'art pour l'art,* absolute style.'[55] But the Latin-American dances still come from life, they have something to say, something to express.'[55] What they express, we have already explained. It is the only thing that a dance of couples can express if it is to have a non-religious meaning.

And since Europe for its part, because of its tradition as well as its social structure, adopts foreign dances only in the form of dances for couples, it has never taken over a dance directly from Africa. Dancing in couples, which is conceivable in Africa only as the fulfilment of the fertility dance and is therefore very unusual, had to be considerably altered in America. Its symbolism necessarily lost clarity and was adapted to the norms of European morality. In Europe the dance was further and completely emptied of meaning and became the expression of abstract movement.

This process has been repeated over and over again, beginning

with the *sarabanda* in the sixteenth century. Giambattista
Marino, the Italian Baroque poet, reports:

> Chiama questo suo gioco empio e profano
> Saravanda e Ciaccona il novo Ispano.

> Sarabanda, Ciaccona: that is the name
> The New Spaniard gives to his impious game.

'New Spain' was at that time the name for Mexico, and Curt
Sachs conjectures therefore that the dance comes from Yucatan
and is thus of Indian origin.[56] We should rather assume, however,
that the Italian is making no distinction between New Spain
(Mexico) and Cuba, both of which lay in the 'New Indies'. The
Jesuit Juan de Mariana (1526–1623) considers the dance a
Spanish invention, yet, as Sachs says, 'this contradiction is
hardly to be wondered at, for dances from the colonies are first
adopted by the dance-mad Andalusians and brought to their
home province. From there they spread over the whole peninsula,
and may easily come to be considered Andalusian.'[57] The *Lexikon
der Frau*[58] considers the dance to be of Moorish origin, and says
that Spanish women have danced it with bells and castanets since
the twelfth century. But the sarabanda was a dance for couples
which appeared in Spain about 1565 and was so 'godless' and
'obscene' that it was forbidden in 1583. On the other hand, the
Enciclopedia Universal writes: 'It is thought that the dance was
introduced into Spain by the Arab conquerors, who in their turn
owed its rhythmic elements to the chica or danza of the African
Negroes.'[59] The reference to the chica is far from foolish, but the
agency of the Arabs in view of temporal as well as sociological
considerations is highly improbable. Any one who sang or danced
the sarabanda was punished with two hundred stripes, and in
addition the men got six years on the galleys, and the girls were
banished from the kingdom.[60] 'The devilish noise of the sarabanda' (Cervantes) was something new, and since all ships from
'New Spain' sailed to Spain via Havana, we may assume with
Ortiz that the sarabanda was already of Cuban origin. 'It is
doubtless the characteristic Cuban music that even then as
always found a world-wide echo. Springing from the streams of
the African nature, and mixed in this melting pot under the

tropical sun, it has been a mixture of black and white cultures from long ago in the time of the sarabanda and the cumbé up until the present day.'[61] Ortiz also points out that there is no Indian influence of any sort in Cuba and that even the dance later called '*areíto de Anacaona*' is apocryphal and has nothing to do either with the *areíto* of the Indians described by Las Casas, nor with the Indian queen Anacaona, but derives from Voodoo.[62]

The sarabanda has been danced with castanets only since 1593, 'in order to enliven its deep melancholy sound'.[63] The castanets are always a Spanish addition and despite the centuries-old association of Spain with Cuba have never become a Cuban folk instrument, for Cuba has always kept the *claves*. On the other hand the *maracas*, the gourd rattles,[64] which belong among the most sacred Afro-Cuban instruments, have been adopted as rumba rattles by dance orchestras.

The sarabanda crossed the Pyrenees into France where it became the *sarabande*, a society dance cultivated at the French court in the seventeenth and eighteenth centuries. Its origin and meaning were forgotten.

The same fate overtook the *chacona*, which was originally identical with the sarabanda.[65] It is described by Cervantes as '*Indiana amulatada*' (the mulatto-ized Indian) and by Quevedo as '*chacona mulata*' (the mulatto chacona), and according to verses of Lope de Vaga dated 1618 it 'came by post from the Indies':

De las Indias a Sevilla
Ha venido por la posta.

'Las Indias' in this case too we must take as a purely geographical designation for America. The chacona also became, as the *chaconne*, a dance of the French court. *Pasacalle*, *folía* and *cumbé* are subspecies of sarabanda and chacona and have the same Afro-Cuban origin.

A good century later the *fandango* came to Spain, also from the '*Reinos de las Indias*', the 'kingdoms of the Indies'. For this reason Sachs again conjectures that it is of Indian origin, with the limitation that even on Spanish soil it preserves a two thousand year old phonetic heritage of the castanet rhythm.[66] But in all these dances it was only in Spain that the castanets were added, and as far as the 'Reinos de las Indias' are concerned, we have already made the acquaintance of this dance there as calinda and chica. As a Haitian religious dance it is called *loaloachi* (loiloichi), and Moreau explicitly says that the Spanish call it 'fandango'. Again it is an 'immodest' dance; even a Casanova marvels at its lasciviousness.[67] Yet thanks to the 'natural modesty of the Spaniard', without which 'the symbolism of the dance would far exceed all the limits of moral censure',[68] the fandango became the Spanish national dance. The *madagueña*, the *randeña*, the *grenadina*, the *murciana* and still other dances are derived from it, all the way to the *bolero* and the *seguidilla*, which made their appearance about 1780.

The nineteenth century, with its bourgeois prudery, did not import any Afro-American dances, but adopted European folk dances like the Ecossaise, the quick waltz, the Bohemian polka, the Polish mazurka and the Alpine country waltz into 'society'. Just before the turn of the century, however, to the horror of the bourgeoisie, a new and tardy invasion of Afro-American dances took place, no longer by the traditional road from Cuba to Spain but by the more circuitous route via South America to France or North America to England. There was the *Maxixe* in 1890, the *Cakewalk* in 1903, the *One Step* or *Turkey Trot* in 1900. About this time Havana society was dancing the *habanera*, an Afro-Cuban dance already tamed in its birthplace, but which, as Friedenthal writes, 'was not only danced by the well-bred Creoles but was also popular in the West Indies among the coloured populace'. He continues: 'Then indeed there is nothing more of grace to be discovered in it; on the contrary, in the way of unambiguous obscenity the movements of the dancers leave nothing to be desired. It is this vulgar dance (in the West Indies usually called *tango* after an African word *tangana*) that people have been trying in vain to introduce into our salons, via Argentina, as the "Tango Argentino". Be it said, at the same time, to the honour of the great city on the silver stream, that the Habanera is danced there exclusively in its most modest form.'[69] In 1912 came the *Foxtrot*, in 1920 the *Shimmy*, in 1926 the *Charleston* and *Black Bottom* and finally the *rumba, samba, conga, mambo, baiao, merinque, cha cha cha* and so on. Other Afro-Cuban dances such as *bembé, són* and *danzón* may possibly follow. All of them, from sarabanda to cha cha cha are, as far as their meaning goes, one and the same dance, in rhythm the 'partly stylized and thus somewhat lamed, direct imitation of West African percussion rhythm',[70] in choreography fragments of the African religious fertility pantomime reduced and stylized to the point of unrecognisability.

Thus the dance of Oshún and Shangó lost, in the European sense, its obscenity, became 'respectable' and so spread over the whole world. According to the African view, however, the contact of the bodies symbolizes the act of copulation and the climax of the dance should last only the briefest possible time; to Africans, therefore, almost all these 'respectable' dances are intolerably obscene.

IV. Rumba Rhythm in Lyric Poetry

In the course of the enthusiasm for American folklore which arose in the United States in the twenties and spread to the Antilles, the folklore theme was discovered by Cuban authors of the post-modernist school. Alejo Carpentier, a Cuban poet and novelist of Franco-Russian origin, put together in 1928 the ballet 'La Rebambaramba'. In the same year appeared Ramón Guirao's poem 'Bailadora de Rumba'[71] and the rumba poem of José Zacharías Tallet.[72] Here for the first time the rhythm of the rumba was adopted for language.

The rhythm gives these poems, for their whole length, tension, it goes beyond pure description and allows the hearer to see the dance even without the help of instrumentalization. The poet tries to achieve precision in the onomatopoeic reproduction of the instrumental sounds of the differently pitched drums. The theme is soon expanded to scenes from folklore; exclamations and dialect expressions are introduced.

The first anthology of Afro-Cuban lyric poetry, by Ramón Guirao,[73] was a transcript of the existing material and a stimulus to elevate popular material to the level of art. And just as in Germany Wilhelm Müller, Eichendorff and Heine shaped the folk song into a work of art, so Nicholás Guillén, Emilio Ballagas and Marcelino Arozarena raised Afro-Cuban folklore to the sphere of world-wide validity. [74]

Significantly, it was not the santería which at first stimulated these poets, but Ñañiguismo, above all in its more secular forms, which had been assimilated to the carnival. The attempt was even made to put Ñañiguismo on the stage. In 1928 in the civic theatre of Guanabacoa a piece with the title 'Apapa Efí' was to have been performed, a one-act play, which was to be given as an interlude. The public were newly enthusiastic for folklore and a group of Ñáñigos who wanted money were going to show them some sacred objects and some of their picturesque rites. Nothing secret was to be made public and no sacrifice was to be undertaken. Nevertheless the actors were 'suspended'. It was not, however, the church that interfered; the Ñáñigos were punished by their own adherents, for such a performance would have been sacrilege. 'As if priests were to sing the *Te deum laudamus* in a cabaret,' remarks Ortiz, [75] and he goes on to say, 'The ancient art of the dance has sunk to the level of buffoonery which today poisons everything.' [76]

Soon, however, Afro-Cuban lyric poetry went further than superficialities. In Guillén's famous poem 'Sensemayá', with the subtitle 'Song on how to kill a snake', it is not just a question of instructions for killing a snake. At Epiphany a 'snake' of people has long wound its way through Havana and has invoked with its singing the snake-divinity. For Cubans the text of the sacred song

> *And see her eyes, they look like candles . . .*
> *And see her teeth, they look like needles . . .* [77]

comes to life again in Guillén's verses:

> *Sensemayá with the eyes . . .*
> *Sensemayá with the mouth . . .* [78]

Guillén's poem closes, like the traditional dancing song, with the line:

> *Sensemayá is dead!* [79]

This snake dance was celebrated as a great popular festivity with lanterns and images of saints and in a special step that imitated the motion of the snake, its irregular and yet rhythmical advance. The 'Procession of masks with the lantern' of Emilio Ballaga plays on the theme of the snake dance:

> *With its long snake's tail walking it goes*
> *with its long snake's tail dying it goes*
> *the black troupe of the Guaricandá.*[80]

The Conga with its special step, the *arrollao*, is derived from the snake dance:

> *And the Conga line is moving*
> *to the beat of the kettle-drum.*[81]

Ballagas reproduces the rhythm in his verses:

> *The procession with the light*
> *rattles on and rattles by.*
> *Rattling the procession dances*
> *as the rattling drum goes by!*[82]

Arozarena pictures the same step:

> *Tus hombros vienen y van*
> *con el ritmo de las ancas:*
> *arrancas,*
> *mides el paso*
> *y cuando a mi te aproximas me vas haciendo bagazo.*[83]

What are passing in the procession, for Ballagos, are not so much the Christian saints as the orisha of the santería—and the 'diablitos', the little devils in blood. 'I am possessed by the spirit of Shangó.' And Arozarena plays in almost every poem, now on the Ñáñigos, now on the orisha: Shangó, Ogun, Babalú Ayé and Obatala.

These are by no means stage-properties, but they are essential elements in a lyric poetry which is carrying on African traditions in a European language.

The authors of Afro-Cuban lyric poetry are black and white and hybrids of all shades. It is not the skin colour of the authors, but their style and content which permit us to reckon them with neo-African culture. First, there is their rhythm. The poets present the rhythms through onamatopoeic sound groupings, sometimes taken from African languages, which are varied and repeated as major themes and which determine the basic rhythm of a poem. This is also frequently broken by a counter-rhythm, entirely in the tradition of African antiphony:

> *Amalia dances and whirls.*
> *Si, Señor.*
> *Amalia whirls and dances.*
> *—Como no.*[84]

The rhythmic stylistic devices of traditional African poetry are also the devices of Afro-Cuban lyric poetry. Not the alternation of short and long syllables, but of stressed and unstressed syllables, of strong and weak measures, which, however, cannot be counted with the help of European metres such as iambs, trochees, dactyls, and so on. For even the pauses have rhythmical weight. The accented syllables are emphasized by rhyme or position and are sharply scanned; but the unstressed syllables in between— one, two, or often three in number—are so articulated that a tension arises between the basic rhythm, whether thought or beaten on the drums, and the secondary rhythm, and the accents frequently fall in the syncope. 'The essential rhythm is not the verbal rhythm, but the rhythm of the percussion instruments accompanying the human voice, more particularly the rhythm of those percussion instruments which carry the basic rhythm. It is a question of a polyrhythm, a sort of rhythmic counterpoint. And this prevents, in the words, that mechanical regularity which so easily becomes monotonous. Thus the poem appears as a work of architecture, as a mathematical formula founded on unity in plurality. In addition we must also notice certain forms of the diction: alliterations, assonances and repetitions. With the repetition of the phonemes or sounds they constitute soothing secondary rhythms and strengthen the effect of the whole.'[85] What Senghor is saying about the style of African poetry, is true without reservation also of Afro-Cuban poetry.

Cuban lyric poetry has borrowed from the Spanish tradition the *copla*, the short verse of popular poetry, although not without interruption. The classical Spanish verse, the eleven-syllable line, does not occur, although it sometimes echoes so to speak in the counterpoint, where its metres and unities are constantly broken through and rearranged.

Thanks to its wealth of short-sounding vowels, the Spanish language has been able to assimilate African words and phrases without marking them off as foreign. Thanks to the possibility of sharp accents, in contrast to French, African rhythm has been able to make itself at home in Spanish. Thus there has grown up perfect harmony between Spanish language and African rhythm, Spanish and African poetic art, in a lyric poetry that can be grasped only by those who hear it. The poems can be recited to the drum, some lines are even sung to the drum in the Cuban recitative style. Afro-Cuban lyric poetry has taught a European language to dance once more in an elemental way[86] and in this way it fulfils one of the demands of Léopold Sédar Senghor: 'I insist that the poem is perfect only when it becomes a song: words and music at once. It is time to stop the decay of the modern world and especially the decay of poetry. Poetry must find its way back to its origins, to the times when it was sung and danced. As it was in Greece, in Israel, above all in the Egypt of the Pharaohs. And as it is still today in black Africa.'[87]

Afro-Cuban lyric poetry, the 'lyric in rumba time' has, like the rumba itself, spread far beyond the island; its influence is perceptible in the whole of Latin America, its popularity unique. Through absorbing its African heritage, Cuban lyric poetry found itself; to that heritage it owes its efficacy and originality.

As long as Cuban lyric poetry was 'white', it remained sentimental and decadent. In the great Cuban anthology of 1904, *Arpas Cubanas*, we find in the foreword an indication of the models for the poems included there. From Homer to d'Annunzio, from Goethe through Daudet, Victor Hugo, Schopenhauer, Rostand, Sainte-Beuve to Heine European literature is involved, and the taste of the anthologist is revealed in the statement: 'The "Ofélidas" of Pichardo rise to the same height as the equally exquisite poetic garland of the "Bonheur Manqué" of Georges de Porto-Riche. The trouble is that the poem of Porto-Riche seems to me just as wonderful as, if not even more wonderful

than, the "Intermezzo" of Heine.'[88] It was a poetry at second
or third hand, homeless, purposeless, styleless, meaningless.

In Afro-Cuban lyric poetry, on the other hand, Cuba found
her own expression. Like the African or Afro-American dance,
this dancing poetry preserves its symbolic force, its relation to an
order, and so every poem is a paradigm. 'The events become
images and so acquire the value of examples.'[89] Arozarena's poem
'Caridá' portrays for the onlooker in the foreground the sensual
dance of a mulatto woman who 'threshes the floorboards with
battering boots',[90] becomes more and more ecstatic, and finally
'tears off her girdle'. But the raging dancer is not just any one,
not any mulatto woman who happens to let herself go in the
ecstasies of the rumba. She is the 'daughter of Yemayá', the
daughter of the sea-goddess, an orisha, a goddess of the santería.
She is Oshún in the sacred fertility dance which we have described
above. 'Why does the daughter of Yemayá not come to the
dance,' asks the poet, and he describes how she would dance if
she were there. A demand, a claim is contained in this: not to
forget the symbolic content of the dance, to keep its meaning.
Folklore may turn into carnival, the santería may be amalga-
mated with the ritual of the church, Ñañiguismo may become a
Cuban Oberammergau—but so long as the meaning of the symbols is not forgotten, the style maintained, the rhythm preserved,
so long does African culture succeed in surviving its entry into
the modern world. It is transformed and reborn, as Afro-Cuban
lyric poetry demonstrates, in a new form.

In the rumba, wherever it is danced all over the world, it is
Yemayá's daughter dancing: Oshún, life unfolding, becoming
fertile, the opposite to Ekué; Yemayá's daughter with the Christianized but still primitive Latin name Caridá—*caritas*—Love.

Chapter 4

N T U

African Philosophy

The age-old times return, the rediscovered unity . . .
LÉOPOLD SÉDAR SENGHOR

I. THE BASIC PRINCIPLES

When we say that the traditional African view of the world is one of extraordinary harmony, then except for the word 'African' every single word in the sentence is both right and wrong. For in the first place the traditional world view is still alive today; secondly it is a question not of a world view in the European sense, since things that are contemplated, experienced and lived are not separable in it; thirdly it can be called extraordinary only in the European sense, while for the African it is entirely commonplace; and fourth, the expression 'harmony' is entirely inadequate, since it does not indicate what parts are being harmonized in what whole. And if we say 'everything' is harmonized, that tells us less than ever. 'Everything' cannot be imagined, nor can we say in a few words what it means.

Adebayo Adesanya, a Yoruba writer, has found a pretty formulation to characterize briefly the harmony of African conceptions.

'This is not simply a coherence of fact and faith,' he writes, 'nor of reason and traditional beliefs, nor of reason and contingent facts, but a coherence or compatibility among all the disciplines. A medical theory, e.g., which contradicted a theological conclusion was rejected as absurd and vice versa. This demand of mutual compatibility among all the disciplines considered as a

96

7. Sara dancers, Republic of Chad. (From *Les Hommes de la Danse*, Editions Clairefontaine. Photo: Michel Huet)

8. Christ carrying the cross. Panel of door of Catholic chapel, University College, Ibadan, Nigeria. (Photo: U. Beier)

system was the main weapon of Yoruba thinking. God might be banished from Greek thought without any harm being done to the logical architecture of it, but this cannot be done in the case of the Yoruba. In medieval thought, science could be dismissed at pleasure, but this is impossible in the case of Yoruba thought, since faith and reason are mutually dependent. In modern times, God even has no place in scientific thinking. This was impossible to the Yorubas since from the Olodumare[1] an architectonic of knowledge was built in which the finger of God is manifest in the most rudimentary elements of nature. Philosophy, theology, politics, social theory, land law, medicine, psychology, birth and burial, all find themselves logically concatenated in a system so tight that to subtract one item from the whole is to paralyse the structure of the whole.'[2]

The unity of which Adesanya is speaking here holds not only for Yoruba thought, but presumably also for the whole of traditional thinking in Africa, for African philosophy as such.

This systematic unity of views and attitudes that often appear irreconcilable in European terms has indeed been observed by European scholars, but has led to serious misunderstandings. Since it could not be accommodated to European systems of thought, the African way of thinking was considered non-logical. Lévy-Bruhl called the attitude of the primitives 'pre-logical', a term by which he meant to characterize a kind of thought which does not refrain from inner self-contradiction, a kind of thought in consequence of which 'objects, beings, phenomena can be, in a fashion unintelligible to us, both themselves and at the same time something other than themselves'.[3] At the end of his life Lévy-Bruhl renounced his theory of 'prelogicism' and thus furnished a rare example of scholarly integrity. In his posthumous notes he asks himself how he could ever have conceived so ill-founded an hypothesis,[4] and he comes to the conclusion that 'the logical structure of the human mind is the same in all men'.[5]

Lévy-Bruhl's insight and recantation, however, left a gap. Till then Europeans had been able to subsume whatever was unintelligible to them under such vague headings as 'pre-logical' or 'mystical'; now there was no longer any system at their disposal to make the unintelligible intelligible to the non-African. So research workers buried themselves in useful investigations of special subjects and avoided every sort of generalization. But now there have appeared a small series of systematic presentations from particular, strictly limited areas, each of which reveals to us the material for and the possibility of seeking their common denominator.

There are five such works, all of which have appeared since the close of the Second World War. First there was the *Bantoe-Filosophie* of Father Placied Tempels, which was published in 1945 and 1946 in French translation, in 1946 in the Flemish original, and in 1956 also in German. Tempels, a Franciscan who had been active as a missionary in the Congo since 1933, owes his knowledge to the observations of many years. He analysed the conceptions of the Baluba from their statements and their behaviour, and with an alert mind and a sensitive imagination felt his way into the thought of the Bantu, tracked out their system of thought and finally presented it as an integrated whole.

The second book results from an unusual and happy incident. The French ethnologist Marcel Griaule had spent many years studying the Dogon, a people who live in the great bend of the Niger. In October 1946 Ogotommêli, an old but vigorous sage and hunter who had been accidentally blinded, summoned the ethnographer and expounded to him, in conversations which lasted thirty-three days, the world system, metaphysics and religion of the Dogon: 'a world-system, the knowledge of which completely invalidated all the conceptions we had formed about the mentality of the Negroes or the mentality of the primitives in general.'[6] Ogotommêli set forth his knowledge systematically, in a poetic language rich in images; the ethnographer had only to write down what was dictated to him and translate it into French.

Encouraged by his success, Griaule's collaborator Germaine Dieterlen investigated the religion of the Bambara and was able to exhibit a similar system in her 'Essay on the Bambara Religion'.

In 1949 an Afro-American actress travelled from the United States to Haiti to take some films of the Voodoo cult. Maya Deren was soon so gripped by this religion that she stopped her film-making, had herself initiated, and finally gave a systematic exposition of Voodoo. In the chapter on Voodoo we have already made use of her book *The Living Gods of Haiti*, which appeared in London and New York in 1953.

The fifth book is called *La philosophie băntu-rwandaise de l'Être*. Alexis Kagame, himself a Bantu, compiled this extensive work, which was published by the Royal Academy of Sciences in Brussels and won for him the degree of Doctor of Philosophy at the Gregorian University at Rome. The study of western philosophy impelled him to analyse the system of thought which the priests who initiated him—'*nos vieux initiateurs*'—had taught him and to define each concept in comparison with Western conceptions.

Five entirely different authors—a Belgian monk, a French ethnographer, a North American actress, an African sage who can neither read nor write, and an African scholar who speaks several European languages—these five, from different motives, have presented the philosophical systems of five different peoples—Baluba, Ruandese, Dogon, Bambara and Haitians—who live far apart from one another. And for all the differences in detail these systems agree basically with one another.

It cannot be the task of this book to spread before the reader the agreements and differences of the five systems. And it would take several hundred pages to give an adequate presentation of any one of them. All we can try to do here is to make the reader familiar with some of the basic concepts that are indispensable for an understanding of neo-African culture.

II. THE FOUR CATEGORIES

In his exposition of the philosophy of the Bantu of Ruanda, Kagame starts from his mother tongue, Kinyaruanda. Like all Bantu languages, it is a language of classification, that is, the substantives are not divided as they are in German into grammatical genders, but are grouped into kinds or classes. There are classes for human beings, for things animated by magic, including trees, for tools, fluids, animals, places, abstractions and so on. The class of a word can be recognized by a sound or group of sounds which precedes the stem and which European grammarians call a 'prefix', but which Kagame with good reason calls a 'determinative'. For when a prefix like 'un' in 'unpleasant' or 'im' in 'impossible' is separated from the stem, a meaningful word, 'pleasant' or 'possible', remains. In the Bantu languages, on the other hand, the stem without the determinative does not give a word; the stem cannot stand alone, but loses all concreteness and in fact does not occur in speech.

In order to keep the concepts we are borrowing from Kagame's mother tongue as simple and easy to remember as possible, we shall suppress the tones as well as their true prefixes which, in this language, precede the determinatives. So we get in simplified form four basic concepts which are to be explained in what follows:

    I Muntu='human being' (plural: Bantu);
    II Kintu='thing' (plural: Bintu);
    III Hantu='place and time';
    IV Kuntu='modality'.

Muntu, Kintu, Hantu and Kuntu are the four categories of African philosophy. All being, all essence, in whatever form it is conceived, can be subsumed under one of these categories. Nothing can be conceived outside them.

Since there are ten classes in Kagame's mother tongue, the determinatives of the words do not necessarily agree with the determinatives of the four categories. But all words can be subsumed under one category or another. Thus 'muhanga'= 'scholar' (first class) belongs to the category Muntu ('human being'); 'ruhanga'='forehead' (third class) to the category Kintu ('thing'); 'mahanga'='foreign lands' (fifth class) to the category Hantu ('place') and 'buhanga' = '(specialized-) knowledge' (eighth class) to the category Kuntu ('modality').

Everything there is must necessarily belong to one of these four categories and must be conceived of not as substance but as force. Man is a force, all things are forces, place and time are forces and the 'modalities' are forces. Man and woman (category Muntu), dog and stone (category Kintu), east and yesterday (category Hantu), beauty and laughter (category Kuntu) are forces and as such are all related to one another. The relationship of these forces is expressed in their very names, for if we remove the determinative the stem NTU is the same for all the categories.

NTU is the universal force as such, which, however, never occurs apart from its manifestations: Muntu, Kintu, Hantu and Kuntu. NTU is Being itself, the cosmic universal force, which only modern, rationalizing thought can abstract from its manifestations. NTU is that force in which Being and beings coalesce. NTU is—so we may say by way of suggestion—that Something which Breton probably had in mind when he wrote: 'Everything leads us to believe that there exists a central point of thought at which living and dead, real and imaginary, past and future, communicable and incommunicable, high and low, are no longer conceived of as contradictory.'[7] NTU is that 'point from which creation flows' that Klee was seeking: 'I am seeking a far off point from which creation flows, where I suspect there is a formula for man, beast, plant, earth, fire, water, air and all circling forces at once.'[8]

But in NTU Breton's contradictions have never existed, nor is it something 'far away'. If we said that NTU was a force manifesting itself in man, beast, thing, place, time, beauty, ugliness, laughter, tears, and so on, this statement would be false, for it would imply that NTU was something independent beyond all these things. NTU is what Muntu, Kintu, Hantu and Kuntu all equally *are*. Force and matter are not being united in this conception; on the contrary, they have never been apart.

NTU expresses, not the effect of these forces, but their being. But the forces act continually, and are constantly effective. Only if one could call a halt to the whole universe, if life suddenly stood still, would NTU be revealed. The driving power, however, that gives life and efficacy to all things is Nommo, the 'word', of which for the moment we can only say that it is word and water and seed and blood in one.

First, however, we must distinguish more clearly between the four categories. We have given translations above for Bantu concepts, but have carefully put them in quotation marks. For the concepts *Muntu* and *human beings* are not coterminous, since Muntu includes the living and the dead, orishas, loas and Bon

Dieu. Muntu is therefore 'a force endowed with intelligence', or better: Muntu is an entity which is a force which has control over Nommo.

The second category *Kintu* embraces those forces which cannot act for themselves and which can become active only on the command of a Muntu, whether living man, dead man, orisha or Bon Dieu. In the category Kintu belong plants, animals, minerals, tools, objects of customary usage, and so on. They are all *Bintu*, as the plural of Kintu is expressed. None of these bintu have any will of their own, unless, like animals, they are given a drive by the command of Bon Dieu. The bintu are 'frozen' forces, which await the command of a Muntu. They stand at the disposal of muntu, or at 'at hand' for him. The only exceptions are certain trees, which, like the poteau-mitan in Voodoo, are the 'street of the loas'. In them the water of the depths, the primal Nommo, the word of the ancestors, surges up spontaneously; they are the road travelled by the dead, the loas, to living men; they are the repository of the deified. In many Bantu languages, therefore, trees belong, linguistically speaking, in the Muntu class. Yet when a sacrifice is made to a 'tree', it is never the plant for whom the sacrifice is meant, but the loas or ancestors, that is, the Muntu forces, that are journeying along it. As part of such trees, the wood from which sculptures are carved also has a special quality: the Nommo of the ancestors has given it a special consecration.

Space and time fall together into the category *Hantu*. Hantu is the force which localizes spatially and temporally every event and every 'motion', for since all beings are force, everything is constantly in motion. To the question, '*Where* did you see it?' the answer may be, 'Where did I see it? Why, in the reign of King X.'[9] That is, a question of place can be answered in terms of time. To the question, '*When* did you see it?' the answer may be: 'In the boat, under the liana bridge after Y.' Here the question of time is answered by an allocation of place. This is by no means unusual; everyone who looks at a clock reads time by the position of the hands—a determination of place; and the mathematician who wants to represent motion indicates the distance on one axis of his co-ordinates and the time on the other. How the unity of space and time is conceived in traditional African thought without clocks or Cartesian co-ordinates is not important for our exposition. Kagame takes thirty-one pages to deal with this extremely complicated problem.[10]

That Muntu, Kintu and Hantu are forces may be to some extent intelligible to the Western reader. It is more difficult to explain the modal force *Kuntu*. A modal force such as 'beauty' is hard to imagine as an independently acting force. It is similar with a kuntu like 'laugh'. Laughing is an action that somebody performs—but how is 'laughing' to be understood as an independent force, without anybody being there to laugh?

In order to clarify *Kuntu*, we shall quote an African author, Amos Tutuola. We could of course also quote traditional verses, proverbs and stories. But we have purposely chosen a modern author, who writes in English, in order to show that African philosophy is not destroyed by contact with European culture, but rises up again, whether consciously or unconsciously, in neo-African literature and art. Tutuola is not a Bantu but a Yoruba, which shows, incidentally, how far our 'Bantu' concepts can be generalized.

In Tutuola's *Palm Wine Drinkard* there is a passage in which 'laughter' as Kuntu, as a modal force, is portrayed. '. . . we knew "Laugh" personally on that night, because as every one of them stopped laughing at us, "Laugh" did not stop for two hours. As "Laugh" was laughing at us on that night, my wife and myself forgot our pains and laughed with him, because he was laughing with curious voices that we never heard before in our life. We did not know the time that we fell into this laugh, but when we were only laughing at "Laugh's" laugh and nobody who heard him when laughing would not laugh, so if somebody continue to laugh with "Laugh" himself, he or she would die or faint at once for long laughing, because laugh was his profession and he was feeding on it. Then they began to beg "Laugh" to stop, but he could not . . .'[11]

Another passage in Tutuola's *Palm Wine Drinkard* shows how 'beauty' is manifested as a force: '. . . if this gentleman went to the battle field, surely, the enemy would not kill him or capture him and if bombers saw him in a town which was to be bombed, they would not throw bombs on his presence, and if they did throw it, the bomb itself would not explode until this gentleman would leave that town, because of his beauty . . .'[12]

III. GOD

For Father Tempels God is the 'great Muntu', the 'great person', the 'great, powerful, Life Force'.[13] But in another passage Tempels describes God as 'the supreme wise man, who knows all things, who established at the deepest level the kind and nature of their forces. He is force itself, which has force within itself, has made all other beings, and knows all forces . . .'[14] God—or Bon Dieu as we shall tentatively call this being—seems according to this description very similar indeed to the Christian creator. On the other hand, according to Tempels, the earliest ancestors are *descended* from God, he must have *begotten* rather than created them. Sartre emphasizes this difference between European and African creation in his analysis of neo-African lyric poetry: 'For the white technician, God is first of all an engineer. Jupiter introduces order into chaos and gives it laws; the Christian God conceives the world by his intellect and realizes it by his will: the relation of creature to Creator is never carnal, except for certain mysteries on which the Church looks askance. Even mystical eroticism has nothing in common with fertility: it is wholly passive expectation of a sterile penetration. We are lumps of clay: little statues issuing from the hands of the divine sculptor! For our black poets, on the contrary, creation is an immense and unceasing confinement; the world is flesh and son of the flesh; on the sea and in the sky, on the dunes, on the rocks, in the wind, the Negro finds again the velvet of the human skin; in the belly of the sand, in the thighs of heaven, it is himself he is caressing; he is "flesh of the flesh of the world",[15] "porous to every breeze",[16] he is alternately the female of Nature and her male; and when he makes love to a woman of his own race, the sexual act seems to him the celebration of the mystery of being. This spermatic religion is like a tension of the soul balancing two complementary tendencies: the dynamic sense of being an erected phallus and the heavier, more patient, more feminine sense of being a growing plant.'[17]

When I pointed out Sartre's analysis to Tempels, he quoted to me several proverbs confirming the idea that the Balubas consider God to be a spiritual creator rather than a begetter. On the other hand, we find in Kagame turns of phrase which seem to justify Sartre's interpretation: 'We should not boast: "I have begotten", for it is God who begets.'[18] 'God alone begets, men only bring up the children.'[19]

Thus we have three theses. In Bantu philosophy God is either a creator, a planner; or he is a universal begetter, the pure force of procreation, the primal phallus of a spermatic religion, as Sartre affirms, or he is, as the philosophy itself would suggest, NTU itself, and that would mean: that Being which is at once force and matter, unseparated and undivided, sleeping primal force, yet without Nommo, without 'life'.

According to Kagame, the highest divinity in Ruanda is Nya-Murunga,* and this name means 'the true, the great begetter'. It looks then as if Sartre were right. But Ogotommêli shows that spiritual and physical interpenetrate. In the creation myth of the Dogon, Amma, the only God, created the earth as a woman, and then married her. His seed, Nommo, is water and fire and blood and *word*. Nommo is the physical-spiritual life force which awakens all 'sleeping' forces and gives physical and spiritual life.

It is neither a question of a 'spermatic religion' nor of a 'spiritual religion' nor is God NTU itself. God is, as Tempels says, the 'Great Muntu', First Creator and First Begetter in one.

IV. LIFE AND DEATH

According to Tempels, the Bantu distinguish between what one can see with the sense organs in visible being and the 'thing itself'. 'By the thing they mean the peculiar inner kind, the

---

* The 'divinity recognized in Ruanda' is called Immana, but Kagame shows that this divinity—Mana—is imported. The original god of these Bantus is hidden in the eighth epithet of Immana: Nya-Muranga (cf. Kagame 2, pp. 328–38).

nature of the essential being or the force. In their picture language they express this as follows. In every essential being there is another essential being: in a man another little man is sitting, all unseen.'[20] Tempels considers this formulation to be a circumlocution for the concept of 'soul'. 'I always heard the old men say that man himself goes on existing, he-himself, the little man, who sits in hiding behind the outwardly visible form, the muntu that went away from the living ones. It seems to me, therefore, that Muntu cannot be translated by "man" or "human being". Muntu has naturally a visible body but that is not Muntu itself. An educated Negro once said to me: "By Muntu we mean rather what you call in French *la personne* and not so much *l'homme*." '[21]

Tempels then goes at length into the problem of the strengthening and weakening of life, and explains that the dead live on in a diminished condition of life, as *lessened* life forces, while nevertheless retaining their *higher*, strengthening, fathering life force. The departed must therefore have gained in deeper knowledge of the forces of life and nature and their lessening of force must be 'less extensive than we might at first believe'.[22]

Tempels' information comes from 'the mouth of the people'; it is not false, but on the other hand it is not particularly exact. In his account, above all, the boundary between living and dead is obscured in such a way that one begins to wonder what death really could be.

Kagame goes in detail into the question of life and death.

There are three words meaning 'life' in Kinyaruanda: *bugingo*, *buzima* and *magara*. Bugingo means the duration of life and is unimportant for our inquiry.

Buzima, characterized by the determinative BU as an abstraction, means the union of a 'shadow' with a body. As an abstraction the word buzima belongs to the category Kuntu, the category of way or manner. It is a principle which specifies *how* life originates and it 'operates' as a principle. This principle asserts: if a shadow unites with a body, life originates and lasts till shadow and body are separated—which is death.

When, however, for example, an animal is born, that is itself not an abstract but a concrete event. An *animal* body unites with an *animal* shadow, and the result is a living animal, a *kizima*, which belongs to the category *Kintu*.

Now let us assume that the life of this animal has run its course and death comes. Then buzima, the union of body and shadow, ceases, and kizima, the concrete, living animal, is no more, its body decays and its shadow vanishes. Nothing is left of an animal after death.

The origin of a human being, however, is represented as a double process. On the one hand it is the purely biological union of shadow and body according to the principle buzima. But at the same time something spiritual, Nommo-force, if we may say so, unites with the body, for the production of a human being is a process of body and spirit. The principle which designates the union of Nommo-force with a body is called *magara*: life. Magara is a Kuntu force, a principle which assists in every beginning of a human creature.

Biological life (buzima) and spiritual life (magara) meet in the human being. In a concrete human life neither the one nor the other can be present alone. It is not pure biological life that is embodied in man, nor is the living human person ever without a 'shadow'. In fact just this is the essence of the living human person: that he partakes of both principles; only in this way is he a *muzima*, a living human individual, who belongs to the category Muntu. Biological life (buzima) he shares with the animal, but spiritual life (magara) divides him from the animal.

When a man dies, therefore, his biological life (buzima) is in fact over, and his spiritual *life* (magara) also ceases—but something remains, namely that 'life force' Nommo which formed his 'personality'—what Tempels calls the 'genuine Muntu'. *Muzima*, a living human being, becomes *muzimu*, a 'human being without life'.

Muzimu is a person who has died, and bazimu are the dead—a regular plural, like Bantu, the plural of Muntu. And now it is clear also why muzima, the living human being, and Muntu, 'man', are not identical and why we had at the beginning to put 'man' in inverted commas. Muntu='man' includes the dead. Bantu, 'men' or 'human beings', are *bazima*, the living, and also *bazimu*, the dead.

Bazim*a* and bazim*u* are distinguished only by a single letter. The *u* is the negative ending which changes the positive ending *a* to its opposite. If we compare the two words we may guess why Kagame emphasizes that in his language life and existence are not identical.[23] The dead are not alive, but they do exist. The root ZIM designates existence.

The continued existence of the dead is expressed by Birago Diop, a Senegambian poet writing in French, in the following verses:

> *Hear more often things than beings,*
> *the voice of the fire listening,*
> *hear the voice of the water.*
> *Hear in the wind*
> *the bushes sobbing,*
> *it is the sigh of our forebears.*
>
> *Those who are dead are never gone:*
> *they are there in the thickening shadow.*
> *The dead are not under the earth:*
> *they are in the tree that rustles,*
> *they are in the wood that groans,*
> *they are in the water that runs,*
> *they are in the water that sleeps,*
> *they are in the hut, they are in the crowd,*
> *the dead are not dead.*
>
> *Those who are dead are never gone,*
> *they are in the breast of the woman,*
> *they are in the child who is wailing*
> *and in the firebrand that flames.*
> *The dead are not under the earth:*
> *they are in the fire that is dying,*
> *they are in the grasses that weep,*
> *they are in the whimpering rocks,*
> *they are in the forest, they are in the house,*
> *the dead are not dead.*[24]

V. DEATH AND RE-BIRTH

In African philosophy, the human soul, so long as a person is living, has not even a name of its own. 'It is true, therefore,' writes Kagame, 'to say that our old initiating priests did not "dissect" man. The intelligent living creature is in their eyes indeed a composite, but during his lifetime an undivided entity. Only when the principle of intelligence is separated from the body, does it become muzimu, an intelligent being without life. And if it has needs, it can only turn to the living.'[25]

Strictly speaking, therefore, it is false to say that the dead 'live'. They do not 'live', but exist as spiritual forces. As spiritual force, the dead man, the ancestor, is in communication with his descendants. He can, as Tempels expresses it, 'let his "life force" work on his descendants'. Only when he has no further living descendants is he 'entirely dead'. But Kagame is more exact about this. 'Our philosophy', he writes, 'knows the problem of immortality and deathlessness (*éviternité*) and has recognized and solved it long ago.'[26] The living person has the 'innate wish to exist for ever'. But since death is inevitable, he prolongs his existence as a living person in his descendants. And as a dead man he is concerned about his living descendants. Traditional African philosophy starts from the living person and recognizes in him an obvious finality: the living individual is either male or female. Man, therefore, is constructed for reproduction, he is put into the world in order to perpetuate himself by reproduction.[27]

To leave no living heirs behind him is the worst evil that can befall a man, and there is no curse more terrible to put on a man than to wish him to die childless. But the whole weight of an extinct race lies on the dead. 'The worst of evils, the irremediable catastrophe falls on the dead ancestors who came before him.'[28] For they have all, for the whole time of their infinite deathlessness, 'missed the goal of their existence', that is, 'to perpetuate themselves through reproduction' in the living person. Thus everything is concentrated on the precious existence of the living, in whom the life that was transmitted to them from their ancestors is carried on.[28]

How the living come into contact with the dead, with their ancestors, and how the dead influence the living, Kagame does not explain. He pushes these questions aside into the realms of mythology and ethnology. Adesanya also draws a sharp line between philosophy and mythology: 'Yoruba philosophy is a taught philosophy, since from it, man and women, old and young sought and obtained guide to their daily life and conduct. Hence it was necessary to make it accessible to them in the easiest way. But when one approaches an Ifa professor,* one sees the entire absence of myth and one is carried to the realm of pure thought, where pure being is contemplated under the category of spatio-temporal changelessness. Myths are a way of solving the problem of making intelligible to the market-place conclusions arrived at in the ivory tower.'[29]

We cannot follow Adesanya, however, when he puts the myths of his people on the same level as the legend of the stork, which grown-ups who know better palm off on naive children. In his effort to interpret everything rationally, Adesanya clearly goes several long steps too far. But it is significant that this idea should occur to him. For the relation between African mythology and philosophy is in fact amazing. This is nowhere clearer than in the exposition of the blind sage Ogotommêli. Here myth follows myth, each fits in logically with the next, and from the whole arises a clear, non-contradictory cosmology, which is mirrored in the ritual, in the social order, in house-building and even the design of everyday utensils. And at the basis of all this we find philosophical principles which agree with the analyses of Tempels, Deren, Dieterlen and Kagame.

According to African philosophy, the departed are spiritual forces which can influence their living descendants. In this their only purpose is to increase the life force of their descendants. When a child is born to one of the living, he gives thanks to his ancestors, to whose helpful influence he owes the child. In this process the physical birth arises from the union of body and shadow, but spiritual birth from the magara-principle, the union of body and Nommo. Thus the force that goes on existing in the

* Ifa-priests are the oracle priests of Yorubaland. They are the guardians of traditional philosophy.

ancestors becomes active again in a living person. This has, however, nothing to do with transmigration, that Pythagorean and
Buddhist doctrine of the circle of births, in which the soul is
separated from the body and is born again in another body. For
in Africa, in contrast to that doctrine, a dead person can be born
again in several different individuals, for example in his grand-
children. This possibility of the rebirth of a dead person in different descendants seem to Lévy-Bruhl and others proof of their
assertion that the Africans were not logical in their thinking. But
in fact this result is a strict consequence of the magara principle.
The system of 'life-strengthening' and 'life-weakening' is founded
on it also; the system in which one force can inwardly strengthen
or weaken another[30] and in which individual growth can take
place only in and with the growth of human nature.

What is 'growing' here is magara, that 'life force' which is
expressed in the living human being in contentment and happiness, and which increases in him thanks to the influence of his
dead forebears. But this force, the wisdom that gives happiness,
intelligence, the principle which distinguishes man from all other
living things, exists in 'pure' form only in the dead: it is a force
from their kingdom. In this sense the wise man is 'nearer to the
dead' and has already a 'share in their nature'. On the other
hand, man is able to strengthen his ancestors, to let magara flow
upon them through honour, prayer and sacrifice. 'As to ritual,
which is religion in action,' writes Senghor, 'it is expressed in
black Africa by sacrifice. It is the head of the family who offers
the sacrifice. It is the priest, who is such purely by virtue of being
the oldest descendant of the common ancestor. He is the natural
mediator between the living and the dead. Closer to them than
others, he lives in intimacy with them. His flesh is less fleshly, his
spirit is more liberated, his speech more powerfully persuasive;
he already partakes of the nature of the dead. Sacrifice is above
all a way of entry into relations with the Ancestor, the dialogue
of Thee and Me. Food is shared with him; its existential force is
to give him the sense of life. And this communion extends to
identification, in such a way that, by an inverse movement,
the force of the Ancestor flows into the sacrifices and into
the community which he embodies. Sacrifice is the most typical

illustration of the interaction of the vital forces of the universe.'[31]

The individual dead are therefore of different 'strengths', according as they have many or few living descendants who honour them and sacrifice to them. Thus an ancestor, who is an aggregate of magara, can transfer to many new-born individuals the small share of magara that they need to begin their lives. This 'quantity' is not great, and it must be constantly 'strengthened' in the course of the individual's development, and even as an adult he will always beg the ancestors to 'strengthen' him further. This 'strength' is not to be understood as physical; it is not strength of the buzima principle, otherwise the 'old men', aged and often physically infirm, could not occupy the first place in the hierarchy of the living. But they, the 'wise men', are the most powerful forces. Buzima and magara are both 'life force', but buzima is constant: one cannot 'have' buzima, but only 'be' it. Magara, on the other hand, the living person can 'have', receive or lose, but he cannot 'be' it. To 'be' magara means to live as one of the dead, as muzimu.

The magara principle, which makes the living and the dead, bazima and bazimu, close kin, who can mutually 'strengthen' one another, seems to us characteristic of African culture. Senghor calls Africa 'the land where dead men and kings were my kinsmen'.[32] Here, however, we must stop and ask whether we ought really to apply so generally the principles which we have taken or derived from the sources mentioned. But there are countless examples in the traditional literature of the African peoples which confirm the principles we have been describing. They occur just as frequently, also, in neo-African poetry. The poets do not, admittedly, distinguish between the 'dead' and the 'departed' or between 'living' and 'existing'. For them the dead 'live'. Birago Diop of Senegal calls the ancestors the 'gay souls'.[33] Lettie Grace Nomakhosi Tayedzerhwa, a Xhosa from South Africa who is influenced by Christian conceptions, permits the dead Xhosa poet Samuel Edward Krune Mqhayi to go to heaven, but at the same time she says of him:

> To and fro he waves in the leopard's skin,
> that cloak of enchantment and courage.[34]

Amos Tutuola from Yorubaland lets his 'palm wine drinkard' look for the dead palm wine tapster in the city of the dead,[35] and in *My Life in the Bush of Ghosts*, the hero of the story is initiated in the 'Tenth Town of Ghosts' into muzimu existence: 'In the evening my cousin would be teaching me how to be acting as a dead man and within six months I had qualified as a full dead man.'[36]

The inward relation to the dead is clearest in the verses of Senghor: 'Then I returned from Fa'oye, after drinking at the solemn tomb. And it was the hour when the Spirits are visible, when the light is transparent.'[37] There is 'the purple city of the living and the blue city of the dead'.[38] 'Of those who are hungry,' he says, 'their smile is so gentle. It is the smile of our dead, who dance in the blue village of the mirages.'[39] To his beloved, the poet says: 'With my head on your breast . . . I would breathe the scent of our dead, that I might receive their life-giving voices and learn to live.'[40] One afternoon 'the troubles of the day come to visit, the dead of the year', and the heaven is 'weakened by hidden beings; it is the heaven that all men fear who are in debt to the dead. And suddenly my dead approach me.'[41] And he says to the dead: 'You dead, who have always refused to die, who oppose death, protect, from Sin[42] to the Seine, and in my fragile veins, my imperishable blood, protect my dreams like your sons, the birds of passage . . . Oh you dead, protect the roofs of Paris!'[43]

At the end of the initiation ceremony Senghor makes the new initiate speak to the lion: 'And let me die suddenly, to be born again in the revelation of beauty',[44] for initiation is a rebirth, in which new magara forces are made available to men through contact with the ancestors and their wisdom. And the revelation of beauty is the wisdom of the ancestors. Africa, as Césaire writes, is 'there where death is lovely in my hand like a bird in the season of milk'.[45]

Yet Césaire has never seen Africa; he is from the island of Martinique to which his ancestors were shipped. This intimate relation to 'death' and 'the dead' occurs in many Afro-American poets. 'That is the broad path to Guinea, death leads you there,' writes the Haitian Jacques Roumain; 'your fathers await you

without impatience.'[46] The Jamaican writer Philip M. Sherlock
makes the 'spirit' of a dead man appear in a magic dance,[47]
and his compatriot Basil McFarlane writes: 'To know birth and
to know death in one emotion. . . In this time that is no time, to be
and to be free, that is the final man.'[48] Even in the North American Paul Vesey we find once more the African conception of
death: '. . . I could tell better where my shadow's father groans
tonight. I could tell better where he groans . . .'[49] On the other
hand, in the poem 'Drum' of the North American Negro
Langston Hughes we find the passage:

> *Bear in mind*
> *that death is a drum*
> *beating for ever*
> *till the last worms come*
> *to answer its call,*
> *till the last stars fall,*
> *until the last atom at all*
> *until time is lost*
> *and there is no air*
> *and space itself*
> *is nothing nowhere.*[50]

Death as destroyer is a Western conception. We may therefore
risk the assertion that the philosophical system we have been
sketching is valid not only for the Bantu and the Dogon and the
Bambara, and not only for Africa, but for African culture in
general, both traditional and modern. And we can take it as a
touchstone in our further investigations, when we want to know
how far African culture extends, what works of art, poems and
novels belong to it and what do not.

VI. RELIGION AND ETHICS

NTU is the universe of forces; it is not fitted to be the object
of worship. And neither can the mythological representative of
this universe, 'God' as Nya-Murunga, 'the great begetter', as
Olorun, Amma, Vidye, Immana, Bon Dieu or whatever the repre-

sentative of the world order happens to be called, be brought into a personal relationship with man. Complaints and wishes are not directed to the world order itself; a woman who pleads to have a child does not want any change in the fundamental laws of the cosmos. With one's personal cares and wishes one turns to the ancestors, above all to those who are strongest among them, founders of whole lines or special, famous ancestors, whose life, embroidered with legends, already has supernatural splendour. And these privileged ancestors, to whom a special cult is devoted, and who acquire increased force through the worship of many people—these ancestors become gods, 'orishas', as the Yoruba expression calls them. 'An orisha', writes Beier, 'is honoured not for his virtue but for his vitality. It is the intensity of life that attracts men to Shango. When they pray to him, they share in his life force, it helps them to achieve a higher life. At the same time the forces of the orisha are rejuvenated by the prayers, and so the community helps to build up and enlarge his powers; the Yoruba word for prayer is "She orisha", to "make" the God.'[51]

Thus there arose the specific gods, the whole systems of gods, which make African religion polytheistic. Thus if we separate philosophy and religion, we have at the top, as representative of the philosophical system, the absolute godhead, always one, uniform, all-embracing, which bears different names in different regions; and at the top of the religious system we have a number of gods, ancestors strengthened by worship: laos or orishas. The orisha systems also concentrate on the living person; there is no contradiction between religion and philosophy; religion is the practical application of philosophy in the daily life of man.

Thus the relations of men to one another are governed by the magara principle. Tempels has formulated the following laws for them:

1. The living or dead man (muzima or muzimu) can directly strengthen or weaken another man in his being.

2. Human, and therefore spiritual life force (magara) can directly influence lower (Kintu-) forces in their being.

3. A rational being (muzima or muzimu) can indirectly influence another rational being, by practising its life influence (magara) on a lower (Kintu-) force, and letting this force influ-

ence other rational beings. This influence too must necessarily be effective, unless the other rational being himself is stronger, or is strengthened by a stronger rational being or protects himself in his turn by means of lower life forces which are stronger than those used by his enemy.[52] This is where the so-called magic and witchcraft belong, the influences of medicine men, talismans and so on, which we shall deal with in the next chapter. Here we may simply emphasize that it is always a question of forces of the magara principle, of the force of intelligence which flows into the living man from his ancestors (or orishas) without whose help there is little he can do. 'The living man is happier than the departed,' writes Kagame, 'because he is alive. But the bazimu are more powerful.'[53]

Their ethics is also derived from the philosophical system. The bazimu, the departed, are the guardians of morals. In the life of the community each person has his place and each has his right to magara, to well-being and happiness. If the magara of one person is weakened by the fault or neglect of another, then the latter must reinstate the former's well-being. Tempels relates a striking story which clarifies the magara principle in African law and which we reproduce here in abbreviated form.

The village chief Kapundwe was entrusted by a man from the neighbouring village of Busangu with a young sheep. One day Kapundwe's dog was found eating the sheep. This dog had never attacked a sheep, and nobody had seen whether the dog had killed the sheep, which had probably died a natural death. And yet Kapundwe gave his friend a sheep in compensation, then another, finally a third, and for good measure a hundred francs as well.

Why did he do this? 'The sheep was at Kapundwe's house, that is, under his life influence. Everything that happened to the sheep, for good or ill, can, according to the Bantu conception, be ascribed to the life influence, whether conscious or unconscious.' Kapundwe gave what according to the European view was such an enormous compensation because the man from Busangu said: 'The loss of my sheep pains me, it gives me sorrow.' After the reparation by one sheep he was still suffering. Only after he had had three sheep and a hundred francs could he forget his sorrow, and feel himself once more a living, happy man, only then was his life force, his magara, restored.[54]

In contrast to the European sense of justice, which measures liability by material damage, it is according to African philosophy the loss in force, in joy of life, that is evaluated, independently of material considerations.

Thus we can see already from these few examples that it is the merit of African philosophy, as Senghor says, 'to have given shape to an harmonious civilization'.[55]

But the harmony of this system of thought and belief does not prevent it from adjusting itself to new situations, especially since, as Adesanya reports, it includes a tradition of assimilating foreign influences: '. . . at the approach of foreigners, possibly the Europeans, it was reasoned out that the newcomers were really different from the Yorubas, it meant that they had something by which the Yorubas could benefit and vice-versa. Hence it was decided that the foreigner should be welcome. This is the rationale of the Yoruba attitude to foreigners. It is just remarkable that in no other country of the world, except perhaps Hausaland, are strangers, whether white or black or brown, and new ideas, however strange they may appear at first, accepted and assimilated as in Yorubaland.'[56]

Out of local patriotism Adesanya may be giving special emphasis to the readiness of his own people to assimilate foreign culture. The reports of the first Europeans to come to Africa agree that they were received *everywhere* with friendliness and good will, beginning with Diego Cão. King Nzinga a Nkuwa readily let himself be baptized and, as we have already explained, incorporated the Christian God in his own pantheon. The Christian doctrine, however, did not have the success the missionaries hoped for. Far from throwing off their own philosophy and religion and subjecting themselves to the foreign view, the Africans have again and again assimilated the foreign religion to their philosophy and stitched it seamlessly into their own system of thought. The missionaries, in their effort to bring God as close as possible to the 'childish Africans', have always stressed his presence, his fatherly relation to suffering humanity who need his help, and have thus put him in his place among the orishas.

And where the Roman Catholic church was more effective in its missionary work, the Christian God, as in Haiti for example, became, as Bon Dieu, a name for the far-off Olorun, Amma or Nyamurunga, while his saints were identified with the orishas. It seems to us worth emphasizing that in both cases the system of African philosophy remains intact and where hybrid forms arise, Christian belief is adapted to African rather than the other way around.

This ought to give those authors in Europe and Africa something to think about who consider traditional African culture worthless, and who assert that its destruction is the necessary prerequisite for the entry of Africa into the family of free nations. We have been able to find in the African philosophy of NTU nothing that would contradict, in principle, the modern naturalistic view of the world or the structure of a society based on the division of labour, for modern science does in fact conceive the world as a world of forces, although it still grossly underrates the forces of the spirit. And the society of specialized labour sees man, just as African society does, rather as function than as individual. Perhaps African philosophy could even add something of its own to this conception, by enlivening and making meaningful once more its one-sided materialistic orientation in human relationships.

Kagame does not conceal the fact that in his analysis he has rationalized to a considerable extent principles which are not so precisely stated in the priestly tradition but are preformed in the language itself. But this very fact demonstrates our thesis. That NTU philosophy can be thus rationalized shows that it does not stand in opposition to a rationally ordered world and that it has that power of assimilation of which Adesanya speaks.

The future intellectual leaders of Africa, poets and politicians like Professor Léopold Sédar Senghor, who was minister in the French government in 1955 and who is now President of the Republic of Senegal, and Aimé Césaire, who was a deputy in the French National Assembly, and who won the election in Martinique in 1957 against all parties, and all the poets of 'Négritude' confess that they owe the sweep of their arguments and the force of their self-awareness to the rediscovery of African philosophy. Senghor celebrates this 'rediscovered unity' in his verses:

118

The age-old times return, the re-discovered unity,
  reconciliation of the lion, the bull and the tree,
The thought bound to the act, the ear to the heart,
  the sign to the sense.[57]

And no poet has expressed more beautifully the NTU philosophy of the total relationship of all things and beings than Aimé Césaire in his poem 'The body lost':

I who Kra-Katoa
I who open breast
I who maelstrom
I would wish to be ever humbler and lower
ever heavier without vertigo or vestige
to lose myself falling
into the living grain of a well-opened earth.

outside replacing atmosphere a lovely mist
not dirty
each drop of water making a sun there
the name of which the same for all things
would be COMPLETE ENCOUNTER,
complete: one would not know what was passing
whether a star or a hope
or a petal of the flame tree
or a submarine procession
run by the flames of aurelia medusas
then life I imagine would bathe me altogether
I would know it better when it touches or bites me
stretched I would see the odours approaching released at
    long last
like helping hands
finding their way through me
to weigh there their long hair
longer than the past I no longer await.

scatter things make room among you
for my terrible rest whose wave
hides in itself my terrible comb of anchor roots

that seek a place where they can cling
things I probe I probe
I the burden-bearer, I the root-bearer
I weigh I press I hide
                    I navel.[58]

Chapter 5

NOMMO

The Magic Power of the Word

Words out of fresh blood,
words that are spring-tides
and swine-fevers and swamp fevers
and lavas and bush fires and
flames of flesh and flames of villages.

AIMÉ CÉSAIRE

I. MAN IS MASTER OF 'THINGS'

Ape, cock and snake, iron, copper and gold, tree, grass and stone all belong to the category Kintu = 'thing'. They are all bintu, 'things', forces without intelligence, which stand at the disposal of man. Of themselves they are without activity. Only through the effect of a muntu, a man, living or dead—and that includes the ancestors, the orishas and even God —can 'things' become active and in their turn influence other 'things' and also rational creatures, according to the laws specified by Tempels.[1] What 'things' lack that is needed for activity is 'intelligence', that abstract modality *ubwenge*, which constitutes one component of the concept magara ('the life of intelligence').

Only man can possess *ubwenge* or intellect. Animals cannot have ubwenge; they can only 'show' it or 'know' it, since what takes place in their brains is passive, purely receptive. Animals possess only 'memory'.[2] Only creatures of the category Muntu, to which man belongs, possess active intelligence.

Men and animals have in common the five senses: sight, hearing, feeling, smell and taste.* But in Bantu philosophy these five

* In Kinyaruanda: *kubona, kwumwa, gukora, kunirkirwa, kuly oherwa*.

121

senses are not of equal value; the last three are subsumed under hearing. Thus one says, for example, 'The dog *hears* the track of the wild beast.'³ 'Hearing' in the wider sense is a concept that includes hearing, feeling, smell and taste, so that perception is thought of in two main groups: vision and contact; for perception through contact can be divided into chemical contact through the organs of taste and smell, the indirect physical contact of hearing carried out by vibration, and the immediate physical contact of touch.⁴ All forms of perception are passive and excite in the animal only his memory or his 'innate instinct', his drive, his greed, his lust. In man, however, they assist in knowledge. The animal hears and reacts, but man hears and understands.

Ubwenge as human, active intelligence has two levels, depending on whether it is a question of a 'practical' or a 'habitual'⁵ intelligence. Practical intelligence is nothing more than slyness, cunning, intellectual grasp or cleverness. Habitual intelligence, on the other hand, means active knowledge, ability, understanding, wisdom. Recently, however, this habitual intelligence or wisdom has again been subdivided. 'Since we have come into contact with European culture,' writes Kagame, 'the fact of studying has suggested a conception formerly unknown, from which has arisen another ubwenge. Ask about a child: "Does that child have intelligence?" And hear the reply: "He has the intelligence of books, but he does not have intelligence."⁶ The person answering means by this that although the child understands readily what he learns in school, he is wanting in the wisdom of life, in the knowledge of relationships, of situations in life in which he is placed by the play of actual circumstance. In other words: the child has a lively intelligence, but no wisdom; he cannot apply his theoretical knowledge to the practical situations of life.' Kagame reports that an old Ruandese woman who cannot read and write will say with the most complete conviction: ' "White men are really disarmingly naive! They have no intelligence." Dare to reply: "How can you say something so stupid? Have you been able, like them, to invent so many marvels that exceed our imagination?"; and she will reply with a pitying smile: "Listen, my child! They have learned all that, but they have no intelligence! They understand nothing!" [7]

That active, habitual wisdom or intelligence which constitutes true understanding is in fact the knowledge of the nature and relationships of the world, as we have presented them in the preceding chapter. And this includes the knowledge of the manner in which muntu, the being with human intelligence, makes use of the bintu or 'things' and activates the forces asleep in them. The European-Christian conception ascribes the growth of the corn, the flow of milk from the cows, the malleability of gold to the agency of God. 'Give us this day our daily bread,' the Christian prays, and he thanks God for all the earthly goods that he obtains. On the other hand, European materialism ascribes all events and effects in nature to the laws of nature, without, however, being able to explain why the corn grows, or *what* life really is. The African conception corresponds neither to the Christian nor to the materialistic, and it has seldom been understood by Europeans. Their misunderstanding is already apparent in one of the earliest reports on Africa, a German report from the year 1603. The Dutch told African inhabitants of the Gold Coast about the works of God and mentioned that they owed everything to God. The report continues: 'When they heard such a thing they marvelled and said: "Why doth not our God to us likewise? Why sayeth he and giveth he not to us also all things as your God doeth to you? Why giveth he not to us also Linen Cloth, ironware, basins or copperware and such like goods even as ye receive from your God?" To which they were answered by the Hollanders, "Indeed all such came to us from our Lord God and were meted out unto us but neither had our Lord God forgotten them although they knew Him not. For verily they had from our Lord God received their gold and He bestowed upon them also the wine of the palm trees and fruit and grain of all sorts, fowl, oxen and goats. Item: bananas, iniamas and such like, such as were needful for the preserving of their life." But this they would in no way confess to nor could they believe it that such things would come from God and would be bestowed upon them by the grace of God, and then they said that God did give unto them no gold but the earth did give it unto them wherein they did seek it and find it. Nor did God give unto them neither millet nor maize nor corn but the earth did give it unto them when they did sow it and afterward at the right time did reap and garner it. And for the fruits, these the trees did give unto them which they themselves had planted. Item, the young goats or lambs did come from the old ones. The sea did give unto them fishes and they needs must catch them therein. So they would not allow that these and such like things did come from God but were brought forth from the earth and from the water and were gained by their labour.'[8]

Thus it is the earth, not God, that bears fruit. And it is not only manual labour that puts the fruits of the field at man's disposal. Sowing and reaping are only parts of human activity. Man must do much more than sow and reap, for the seed corn has of itself no activity of its own, it does nothing without the influence of man, it would not grow but would remain lying in the ground without his help, without the influence of human *ubwenge*, active reason. How does man accomplish this? Through *Nommo*, the life force, which produces all life, which influences 'things' in the shape of the *word*.

'The Nommo', says Ogotommêli, 'is water and heat. The vital force that carries the word issues from the mouth in a water vapour which is both water and word.'[9] Thus Nommo is water and the glow of fire and seed and word in one. Nommo, the life force, is the fluid as such, a unity of spiritual-physical fluidity, giving life to everything, penetrating everything, causing everything. 'The vital force of the earth', says Ogotommêli, 'is water. God has solidified the earth with water. Again, he makes blood with water. Even in stone there is that force, for dampness is everywhere.'[10] And since man has power over the word, it is he who directs the life force. Through the word he receives it, shares it with other beings, and so fulfils the meaning of life. Therefore Ogotommêli says: 'The word is for all in this world; it must be exchanged, so that it goes and comes, for it is good to give and to receive the forces of life.'[11] Even the act of conception which produces a human being, who is not only a physical, but also a spiritual creature—muzima[12]—is a conception not only through the seed, but at the same time through the word. Ogotommêli formulates this in his picturesque language: 'The good word, as soon as it is received by the ear,* goes directly to the sex organs where it rolls about the uterus just as the copper spiral rolls about the sun. That word of water brings and maintains the moisture necessary to procreation and by this means Nommo brings about the penetration of the uterus by a germ of water. It transforms into a germ the water of the word and gives it the appearance of a human person through the essence of a Nommo.'[13] Yet this Nommo, which effects conception and then *calls* forth birth, is not sufficient to produce a *complete human being, a personality, a muntu.* For the new-born child becomes a *muntu* only when the father or the 'sorcerer' gives him a *name* and *pronounces* it. Before this the little body is a kintu, a thing; if it dies, it is not even mourned. Only the giving of a name adds the magara principle to the buzima principle. A creature which is sharply distinguished from the animal and has its place in the community of men is produced, not by the act of birth, but by the word-seed: it is designated. To this giving of a name, the *designation of the human being*, corresponds the designation of images, and even the designation of the gods, of which we shall speak in the chapters KUNTU and BLUES.

Thus the magara principle is actualized through the life force which is the word. Senghor writes of 'the power of the word in black Africa'.[14] All change, all production and generation are effected through the word. 'I sow through the world,' writes the poet Bernard B. Dadié of the Ivory Coast.[15] Sowing alone is not sufficient to make the maize germinate and grow; speech and song must be added, for it is the word that makes the grasses germinate, the fruits grow, the cows go in calf and give milk. Even handicrafts need the word if they are to succeed. In his novel *The Dark Child* Camara Laye tells how his father makes a golden ornament. While the gold sizzles and the bellows cough, the goldsmith is silent, but the author emphasizes: 'Although my father spoke no word aloud, I know very well that he was thinking them within. I read it from his lips, which were moving while he bent over the vessel. He kept mixing gold and coal with a wooden stick which would blaze up every now and then and

---

* Even the ear is a sex organ, as Ogotommêli explains in another passage, for it receives the fruitful seed of the word.

constantly had to be replaced. What sort of words were those that my father was silently forming? I don't know—at least I don't know exactly. Nothing was ever confided to me about that. But what could these words be but incantations?'[16] Yet the incantations of the goldsmith were not sufficient to bring about the marvel of the transformation of the gold into a fluid and again to a solid state. So the sorcerer was also there. 'Throughout the whole process his speech became more and more rapid, his rhythms more urgent, and as the ornament took shape, his panegyrics and flatteries increased in vehemence and raised my father's skill to all the heavens. In a peculiar, I would almost say immediate and effective, way the sorcerer did in truth take part in the work. He too was drunk with the joy of creation, and loudly proclaimed his joy; enthusiastically he snatched the strings, became inflamed, as if he himself were the craftsman, as if he himself were my father, as if the ornament were coming from his own hands.'[17] Senghor comments on this passage: 'The prayer, or rather the poem that the goldsmith recites, the hymn of praise sung by the sorcerer while the goldsmith is working the gold, the dance of the smith at the close of the operation, it is all this— poem, song, dance—which, in addition to the movement of the artisan, completes the work and makes it a masterpiece.'[18]

Thus all the activities of men, and all the movement in nature, rest on the word, on the productive power of the word, which is water and heat and seed and Nommo, that is, life force itself. The word frees the 'frozen' forces of minerals, brings activity to plants and animals, and so guides bintu, the 'things', to meaningful behaviour. The word of the muntu—and 'muntu', once more, includes living men and the dead and the gods—is an active force which causes and maintains all movements of 'things'. All other events are only appended to these. Amma, 'the great begetter'; produced the world through the seed of the word.

Thus for everything that happens in the world, for fertility and drought, for sickness and its cure, for happiness and unhappiness, some muntu or other is responsible, whether living man, departed or orisha. The soothsayer says where the word that produced the evil originated and the 'medicine man' knows the counter-word, which is stronger and can prevent the evil or illness. All the practices of magic, so much despised, rest on the practice of the Nommo.

No 'medicines', 'talismans', 'magic horns', no, not even poisons are effective without the word. If they are not 'conjured', they are of no use in themselves. They have no activity at all. Only the intelligence of the word frees these forces and makes them effective. All substances, minerals, juices are only 'vessels' of the word, of the Nommo. Nommo is the concrete entity through which the abstract principle magara[19] is realized.

II. African Medicine

No aspect of African culture has so much alienated Europeans and Americans as the so-called practices of magic. In them, so it was and is still believed, all the 'superstitions' of the Africans were concentrated, and all their backwardness was made manifest. Magic was therefore attacked with all possible weapons, and so successfully that even modern Africans explicitly keep their distance from African medicine and, for fear of being taken for backward savages, scarcely dare breathe a word in its defence.

The fundamental objections to the therapy of the 'medicine men' came from the circles of pragmatic European medicine—arguments which were appropriated also by the missionaries. In ignorance of African philosophy, its body of knowledge and its principles, Europeans asserted that the cures offered by the 'sorcerer' had in most cases no connection with the illness that was being treated. A 'medicine man' who treated an asthmatic with incantations and 'prescribed' for him a secret extract of herbs which the patient was not even to swallow, but was perhaps to carry under his arm in the hollow tooth of a beast, was, they said, deceiving the patient and dispensing hocus-pocus in place of medicine. There was no relationship between the medicament and the disease, therefore the 'medicine' was ineffective and the mysterious mumbo-jumbo nonsensical. Its only point was to conceal from the patient the incapacity of the physician. A real medicament, on the other hand, they believed, as manufactured by European and American industry, was distinguished by the following criteria: firstly, the remedy is effective only for a strictly defined malady; secondly, the effect of it is so reliable that its success can be predicted with great certainty; a failure leads to doubt of the diagnosis. In the third place, given the same malady, the result is reproducible by all doctors all over the world.[20] With these ideas of the efficacy and quality of the western pharmacoepia, African 'magic' was attacked and held up to ridicule.

Recently, however, we have become more modest in our claims. Above all, the 'placebo experiments' in America have led to surprising results. 'Placebo' is the name for a wholly indifferent substance which contains no remedy but looks and tastes and is packaged like the medicine it is imitating. In these experiments the patient, without knowing it, is given the placebo instead of the medicine. In the 'doubly-blind experiment', the doctor himself does not know whether he is offering the patient an effective remedy or a placebo. The outcome of the experiments was that with many patients the expected cure took place in either case: whether an effective remedy or only a placebo was given to the patient above all, when the doctor himself was convinced that he had dispensed the genuine remedy. 'Thus Jellinek and his collaborators established that 60 per cent of all people with headaches respond to a placebo, and in 30–40 per cent of the cases the pain can be relieved by a solution of common salt. Approximately the same number of asthmatic patients were relieved of their attack.'[21] Thus Professor Jores, the Director of the university clinic in Hamburg, draws the conclusion: 'Even in the field of medicine, which is striving for objectivity and scientific accuracy, the magical effect plays an uncontrollable part which is frequently overlooked. We cannot remind ourselves often enough, that a least 40 per cent of all individuals respond positively to a remedy no matter what it contains. Only in this way is the ever astonishing number of medicines explicable, as well as the fact that the pharmaceutical industry can live on them. The subtle compounding of many medicaments is probably "magic" and without any objective value. It is not an exaggeration to assert that the pharmaceutical industry is really producing placebos on the grand style.'[22]

9. Cement grave sculpture. Ibibio, East Nigeria.
(Photo: U. Beier)

10. Woodcarving by Felix Ídubor of Benin. Door of
Co-operative Bank of Ibadan, West Nigeria.
(Photo: U. Beier)

If, then, even in the critical west, the restoration of health depends in large part on the personality of the physician, his persuasive power and the faith of the patient, so much the more is this true of traditional African medicine, in which the patient, in view of his own philosophical convictions, does not expect to be cured by the medicine alone. In the light of African philosophy all medicines are 'placebos', that is, powerless in themselves and effective only in connection with the genuine power of the Nommo. If, for example, a patient refuses, after successful treatment' to honour the medicine man, the latter casts a spell which takes the force out of the medicine and the patient falls sick again.[23] The 'stronger' the 'medicine man', the mightier his word, the more effective is his 'placebo', whether one has to swallow it, rub it in, or carry it on a string around one's neck. Through exact, western medicine, which was once its severest opponent, the African art of healing has been given a belated vindication.

Admittedly, it is not only placebos that western medicine has dispensed in Africa. When it introduced hygiene and battled sleeping sickness, malaria and many other causes of disease (which Europeans had also brought into Africa) it did perform a service for Africa. On the other hand, it is true, not every remedy in African medicine consisted in a 'placebo'. 'The medicine men', writes the English ethnographer Leakey, who grew up among the Kikuyus and was initiated by them, 'were always of outstanding ability and great wisdom. As a medical practitioner, the medicine man often became somewhat of a specialist, and so it was common to find that one was renowned for his knowledge of herbs and his treatment for special types of illness, while another might be sought out more often to diagnose obscure maladies and treat them by the method of discovering what form of "spiritual uncleanliness" the patient was suffering from and then conduct a suitable purification ceremony to remove the cause of ill. The herbal specialists certainly had a considerable knowledge of the healing properties of various plants and their juices and fruits, some of which would undoubtedly repay a careful study by our own medicine research workers. The man who specialized in tracing the causes of malaise to supernatural events and then bringing about a cure by cleansing was really a very clever practitioner in psychotherapy.'[24]

Under European rule the African doctors lost much of their influence. The African healing herbs were replaced to a large extent by placebos from Europe. And even European medicaments which are by no means placebos, were and are used as placebos. For, since according to the African conception the substance as such has no force or effect, any and every medicine is used, in connection with the appropriate 'words', for any and every illness. Thus African chemists, and above all the many illegal purveyors of medicines, may for example dispense three spoonfuls of plaster of Paris for a cough or penicillin for worms. Since European poisons are considered just as harmless as the healing herbs of the medicine men, every misuse is made of them, and since the African has more faith in the power of the word than in the power of the substance, unscrupulous firms and dealers provide their analgesics, antibiotics, and inoculations with effective slogans and get stupendous results.

The attack of Europeans of all camps against the 'magical nuisance' was directed in the first instance against the 'wizards', those destroyers of life, with their obscure practices. But European zeal in fact struck the wrong victims, namely the doctors, and only gave an impetus to the 'wizards'.

A 'wizard' is a 'sorcerer' who fails to use his knowledge, his verbal power, in the service of the community, but misuses it maliciously and for his own gain. A 'wizard' has succumbed to the lust for power, he disturbs and destroys the life force of his fellow men, and spreads terror for its own sake. In Haiti, for example, it is thought that there are 'wizards' who have the power to draw every drop of Nommo-force out of a person, so that he can only run about as a *zombi*, a living corpse, a will-less dummy obeying the wizard's word. This goes on as long as his diet contains no salt—for salt is the Nommo of nourishment. To conceal his crime, the wizard makes his victim play dead; he is buried by his family with all honour, but in the night the wizard fetches his zombi out of his grave and makes him work for him. Hence the notion that the wizard 'wakens' the corpse. But a wizard does not awaken; he only destroys. Thus he twists the meaning of the Nommo into its opposite, purposely disturbs the harmony and frame of the world order, and if he is known and unmasked, is sure of the most terrible punishment. 'The wizard', writes Jomo Kenyatta, who was imprisoned in 1952 as the alleged leader of the Mau-Mau, 'practices his works of darkness alone. And when a man has been convicted of the crime of anti-social wizardry, his offence is against the whole society, but it is only one of his own kinsmen who has to pass final judgement against him by lighting the fire of his execution.'[25] In contrast to all others condemned to death, the wizard is either burned or thrown to the hyenas. For he is not to go on existing as one departed; he is destroyed. Thus in a poem of the Nyasa writer Alfred David Mbeba a wizard says:

> . . . *My course relentless and my work of death* . . .
> *those things were all unlawful.*
> *That which waits me now:*
> *my grandchildren the hyenas.*
> *Death thus, self-brought, is rightful recompense.*
> *Animal death, as beasts die in the bush.*[26]

The wizard is the only muntu who is not permitted to survive death. He is therefore considered the same as an animal and is cast into nothingness. *Ubusa*, nothing, is in Bantu philosophy the 'absence of any firm or perceptible corporeality'.[27] 'Nothing is opposed, first, to substance in general, and to material substance in particular. Air is something and occurs in nothing. It is thanks to this nothing that all distinct bodies are separated, its absence would cause them to press tightly together, without the possibility of finding an empty space to mark their boundaries.'[28] 'In our philosophy', Kagame says further, 'nothing is the negation of the determinate being realized in nature. It signifies neither non-essence nor non-existence. It serves as a universal receptacle, a void which is at one and the same time a divider and incapable of opposing any resistance to the movement of determinate beings.'[29]

The destruction of the wizard casts him, therefore, into the empty space of things, it provides for him the death of an animal, a bintu, and excludes him from the deathlessness of a muntu.

Cast into the void of ubusa, he is robbed of spiritual existence, of buzimu. His magara is dissolved and can no longer exercise any sort of Nommo in the universe of forces.

Thus in traditional African society the person who misused the power of the Nommo, or word seed, was threatened with the most terrible metaphysical punishment, the only possible annihilation, the only real death, since normal death represents only the transition to another form of existence.

It was only through the disruption of the traditional order that the practices of the wizard lost their terror and, where foreign rule drove the masses to despair, became the only remaining means of resisting a lawless oppression in an equally lawless fashion. Thus wizardry or illegal witchcraft became the source for the power of the Mau-Mau.

III. The Words and Exorcism

All magic is word magic, incantation and exorcism, blessing and curse. Through Nommo, the word, man establishes his mastery over things. 'In the beginning was the Word, and the Word was with God, and the Word was God',[30] so begins the gospel according to St. John, and it looks as if Nommo and the *logos* of St. John agreed. Yet the apostle continues: 'The same (i.e. the word) was in the beginning with God. All things were made by it and without it was not anything made that was made.'* In the gospels the word remains with God, and man has to testify to it and proclaim it. Nommo, on the other hand, was also, admittedly, with Amma, or God, in the beginning, but beyond that everything comes into being only through the word, and as there is Muntu, the word is with the muntu. Nommo does not stand above and beyond the earthly world. *Logos* becomes flesh only in Christ, but Nommo becomes 'flesh' everywhere. According to the apostle, *Logos* has made all things, once for all, to become as they are, and since then all generated things remain as they are, and undergo no further transformation. Nommo, on the other hand, goes on unceasingly creating and procreating, creating even gods.

* In the German Gospel.

The God of Israel said, 'Let there be light', and there was light. In Africa every muntu is capable of such an utterance. Every muntu, even the least of them, is by the force of his word lord over every thing, over animal and plant, stone and hammer, moon and stars. If he says, 'Let the sun fall from the sky!' then it falls, unless a more powerful muntu than he has already, by the force of his word, commanded the sun to stay in the sky. Thus the word force of one muntu is different from the word force of another: the Nommo of Amma or Olorun or Bon Dieu is more powerful than the word of a living individual, or the Nommo of an orisha more powerful than that of one's dead father. The hierarchy of the *Bantu* ('men' both living and dead) is ordered according to the force of each one's word. The word itself is force.

If there were no word, all forces would be frozen, there would be no procreation, no change, no life. 'There is nothing that there is not; whatever we have a name for, that is'; so speaks the wisdom of the Yoruba priests.[31] The proverb signifies that the naming, the enunciation produces what it names. Naming is an incantation, a creative act. What we cannot conceive of is unreal; it does not exist. But every human thought, once expressed, becomes reality. For the word holds the course of things in train and changes and transforms them. And since the word has this power, every word is an effective word, every word is binding. There is no 'harmless', noncommittal word. Every word has consequences. Therefore the word binds the muntu. And the muntu is responsible for his word.

The force, responsibility, and commitment of the word, and the awareness that the word alone alters the world; these are characteristics of African culture. When, after long agony, in the middle of this century, poets began to speak African words in European languages, the world began to listen. 'Natives' who had been taught in missionary schools to repeat European words and descendants of the generations of slaves shipped to the New World who had learned the words of Europe from their fathers and mothers, and who had scarcely heard a word of an African language, spoke the first *free* word that they were allowed to speak in their acquired or inherited European languages with that same degree of commitment proper to the word in African culture, and so transformed the European word into an African word. The Europeans could not recognize their own words, for they were different. At first it was only the reproach, the attack that was heard and this strange sound was interpreted in terms of the situation. 'What did you expect when you took away the muzzle closing those black lips?' asked Sartre. 'Did you think they would sing your praises? Those heads that our fathers ground into the dust, did you think when they raised themselves again, you would read adoration in their eyes?'[32] Unrest, reproach, rebellion—that was what Europe expected; that was to be understood. What was not understood was interpreted as surrealism. In his well-known essay 'Orphée Noir', the introduction to Senghor's *Anthologie de la nouvelle poésie nègre et malgache*, Sartre analysed this new type of poetry with all the skills of psychology and sociology. He brought to light much that was correct and worth reading, yet the heart of the matter eluded him, for he writes in conclusion: 'What will happen when the Negro, throwing off his negritude for the sake of the Revolution, no longer wants to be considered as anything but a member of the proletariat? . . . What if, in order to fight white capitalism, he has to assimilate white techniques? Will the source of the poetry dry up? Or will the great black river colour, in spite of everything, the whole sea into which it flows? No matter: in every age, the circumstances of history choose a nation, a race, a class to take up the torch, by creating situations which only poetry can express or overcome.'[33]

In other words, Sartre is interpreting this poetry out of the historical situation. A particular combination of circumstances and relationships has made this poetry possible at a particular time; yesterday there was no such thing, tomorrow it may no longer exist: 'Let us salute today,' he writes, 'the chance given by history which allows the Negroes to fill the air so loudly with the great Negro cry, that it rocks the layers of the earth.'[34] But the 'cry' which 'rocks the layers of the earth' is Nommo, the function of which does in fact consist in rocking the layers of the earth. For the central significance of the word in African culture is not a phenomenon of one particular time. It was always there, an age-old tradition which has recently—and here only is the 'situation'—been carried on in European languages and will be carried on so long as and wherever African poetry makes its influence felt.

According to African philosophy man has, by the force of his word, dominion over 'things'; he can change them, make them work for him, and command them. But to command things with words is to practise 'magic'. And to practise word magic is to write poetry—that holds not only for Africa. Thus African philosophy ascribes to the word a significance which it has also in many other cultures, but there in poetry only. That is why African poetry made such a world-wide impression the moment it was heard beyond the bounds of Africa. African poetry is never a game, never *l'art pour l'art*, never irresponsible. 'To practise magic' is therefore a weak expression; the African poet is not 'an artist using magic', but a 'magician', a 'sorcerer' in the African sense. He is the *muntu* on the captain's bridge of the world. Out of the great coherence of all things he calls 'things' individually and then they are there. As Césaire writes: 'I would find again the secret of the great communications, of the great conflagrations. I would speak storm. I would speak river. I would speak tornado. I would speak tree.'[35] And in another passage: 'Let come the colibri! Let come the sparrow hawk! Let come the break of the horizon! Let come the dog-faced baboon! Let come the lotus, the bearer of the world!'[36] The word of the poet has not only called the 'things', it has *produced* them, it is Nommo, word seed. We *see* the 'things' when we read the verse. The poet *made* them in the word; 'I say, deeply cut river, huge, constrained, in the smallest swamps, dammed water, spilling over the sluices for with new blades, I *made* you a river.'[37] And what man creates through the word is 'at hand' for him and serves him. Thus Césaire writes: '. . . who draws me back toward the harpoons—I am very weak—I whistle, I whistle old, old things, serpents, cavernous things',[38] the tree has 'helpful hands',[39] things are allies of him who invokes them and so places them under his command. 'My northern lights, my sisters, my good friends,' calls Césaire, 'oh you my marvellous friendships, my friend, my love, my death, my calm, my cholera, my lunar rhymes.'⁴⁰ Since through NTU, Muntu, Kintu Hantu and Kuntu are closely related one to another, man stands in a fraternal relation to all these forces which he creates: 'The shooting star is my sister,' Césaire proclaims, 'my brother is the shattered glass, my brother is the blood kiss of the cut head on the plate of silver, and my sister the epizooty and my sister the epilepsy, and my friend is the chicken hawk, my beloved the fire's lust. My brother is the volcano in the belly of the pistol . . .'⁴¹ And the muntu, the poet, tells all the 'things' that his words created what they are now to do. Thus Césaire writes: '. . . let come a dolphin's pearly insurrection breaking the shell of the sea! Let come a plunging of islands! Let come the disappearance of the days of dead flesh in the quicklime of the rapacious! Let come the ovaries of the water where the future moves its little head! Let come the wolves who graze in the savage orifices of the body at the hour when, at the inn of the ecliptic, my moon and your sun meet.'⁴² 'Come here, our grass is fat, come here, you deer,' commands Tchicaya U Tam'si, a Congo poet, 'This way the soft fruits, that way the infected blood.'⁴³ 'Lord of the three roads,' Césaire prays to his orisha *Legba*,⁴⁴ the protector of the crossroads, 'May it please you that for once I move ahead, with my little *sorcerer's step*, through the dead lives, there where the *inexhaustible command of man* threatens triumphantly . . .'⁴⁵

Since the word produces, commands and conjures, this poetry speaks in imperatives. Its basic form is the form of command. The future and the present, even the imperfect appear as imperatives. When the Ivory Coast poet Bernard B. Dadié writes: 'Stars in profusion, pure as the eyes of Sages, will be as brilliant as the destiny of men',⁴⁶ this is not a description of a future occurrence, but an invocation of it. The stars *are* to shine. The event is created in the vision. The vision is always an imperative addressed to time; the future is commanded how it is to be. For 'time-and-place-in-one', *Hantu*,⁴⁷ constitutes a force of its own and is as such, like all forces, subject to the command of the muntu. Thus when he puts his vision even back into the past, the poet is commanding time, as if the order were already executed and irrevocably accomplished. In the alternation of future, imperfect and present, the incantation acquires its greatest force and becomes a single imperative:

> *Farmer strike the soil with your daba:*
> *in the soil there is haste that the syllable of the*
>   *event be not disentangled.*
> *I remember the famous plague which will happen*
>   *in the year* 3000
> *there was no announcing star*
> *but only the earth in a flood without*
> *stony pebbles of space*
> *a bread of grass and of prison*
> *strike farmer strike*
> *the first day the birds will die*
> *the second day the fishes were grounded*
> *the third day the animals came out of the woods.*[48]

Even where there is a pure present, it is not a question of narration or description but of incantation. The word makes concrete reality of the vision, as in the lines of Césaire: 'Oh I listen through the cracks of my skull. It rises, it rises, the black flood rises. It rises out of the depths of the earth. Waves I hear of shrieking, swamps I smell of animal odours, and storm foams from naked feet. And there is a swarm of ever new feet climbing from the mountains . . .'[49]

The incantation is at the same time transformation. Just as Camara Laye's father, the goldsmith, transforms the gold into an ornament with the help of Nommo, so in poetry the word transforms every 'thing'-force that it produces by placing it in a relationship of tension with other forces it has also produced. The line 'I am listening through the cracks of my skull' has just been quoted. The transformation takes place in the sequence of images. 'I am listening'—we see the listening poet. 'Through the cracks'—we see, how the poet puts his ear to a crack in the rock to listen, '. . . of my skull'—the poet changes, he has a skull on his shoulders, the cracks become the cracks of this skull, which the poet splits by his incantation, and the listening becomes his own activity from the inside of the skull. Space and time—that is Hantu—are also transformed, for the listening is, as the following lines show, not the listening to a reality which is taking place outside the skull, but the listening to an imperative which the poet both projects and makes happen. 'And the Negroes', writes Césaire, 'go seeking in the dust the splinters to make mica to make moons and the flaky slates from which the sorcerers make the intimate ferocity of the stars.'[50]

Thus the magic of metamorphosis never stops. Nommo, the word, creates images upon images and transforms them and the poet with them. For he himself never approaches things unchanging; since he too is in his nature a force among forces, he changes with them and from them. The 'things' are of his kind and he of theirs. He too, therefore, is subject to the same magic of constant transformation. 'Open my flesh to the ripe blood of the tumult,' writes Tchicaya U Tam'si, 'the true sperm adds me as breath to the ferment of the leaves and the tornadoes.'[51] 'The weakness of many men is', writes Césaire, 'that they do not know how to become a stone or a tree.'[52] Thus one must be able to transform oneself. It brings pleasure: 'As for me, I sometimes put lighters between my fingers, in order to have the pleasure of setting myself afire all evening in fresh poinsettia leaves.'[53] 'I sprout like a plant,' he writes elsewhere, 'without remorse and without bending toward the disentangled hours of the day pure and sure like a plant without crucifixion toward the disentangled hours of the evening.'[54] Even in drowning, the forces of men only change to other forces: 'that my wave may devour itself in her wave and lead us back to the sand as drowned men as the flesh of shredded guavas as a cleansing hand as lovely algae as flying grain as a bubble as remembrance as a prophetic tree.'[55] The certainty that by the force of Nommo one can transform everything, even oneself, permeates the revolutionary art of a Césaire as much as it does the profound irony of an Amos Tutuola. The catastrophes which Césaire conjures up lose their terror, in the last analysis, because he and his are among 'those whose survival goes its way in the germination of the grass',[56] and Tutuola's comic sorcerers' competition appears in the last analysis as the deepest metaphysics:

'. . . I went to a village which is near this 18th. town, luckily I met a ghost magician who was displaying his magical power for the head chief of that village at that time. Then I joined him to display my own as well before these chiefs, as a competition. But when I changed the day to the night, so every place became dark at once, then I told him to change it back to the day as usual, but he was unable. After this I changed him to a dog and he started to bark at everybody, then as my power was above his own the chief with all the scene-lookers gave me all the gifts which were to be shared for both of us. After that I changed him from the dog to a ghost as usual. Then I packed all these gifts and kept going to the 18th. town where I came to that village, I did not give him any of the gifts.

'Having left this village to a distance of a mile this ghost magician came to me on the way, he asked me to let both of us share the gifts, but when I refused he changed to a poisonous snake, he wanted to bite me to death, so I myself used my magical power and changed to a long stick at the same moment and started to beat him repeatedly. When he felt much pain and near to die, then he changed from the snake to a great fire and burnt this stick to ashes, after that he started to burn me too. Without hesitation I myself changed to rain, so I quenched him at once. Again he controlled the place that I stood to become a deep well in which I found myself unexpectedly and without any ado he controlled this rain to be raining into the well while I was inside. Within a second the well was full with water. But when he wanted to close the door of the well so that I might not be able to come out again or to die inside it, I myself changed to a big fish to swim out. But at the same moment he himself changed to a crocodile, he jumped into the well and came to swallow me, but before he could swallow me I changed to a bird and also changed the gifts to a single palm fruit, I held it with my beak and then flew out of the well straight to the 18th. town. Without any ado he changed himself again to a big hawk . . .'[57]

All change reveals the flowing of forces; Nommo, the word itself is moisture, fluidity; word and seed and blood and water, as Ogotommêli says. And laughter itself, this special *Kuntu* force, is closely related to the word, to Nommo, for 'man' has not only the power of the word, but also the power of laughter. Laughter is a special kind of flowing; in neo-African poetry it is repeatedly associated with a river. Senghor equates it with Nommo; he speaks of God 'who created heaven and earth out of the laughter of a saxophone'.[58] Laughter is a special word, it liberates and throws off one's bonds, it is unbound like a river. 'A river rises in the heights,' writes the Ecuadorian Adalberto Ortiz in his novel *Juyungo*, 'and goes into the depths. It carries gold and silver and mud and glass, always different, never tiring, full of goodness. It is a prolonged Negro laugh on the dark face of the forest.'[59] And the Cuban Nicolás Guillén writes: 'To you, tropics, I owe that childlike enthusiasm of running, laughing over mountains and clouds, while an ocean of sky is shattered in innumerable star-waves at my feet!'[60] And his countryman Marcelino Arozarena sings: 'Laughs, river, not of water, river of teeth, not a boat road, but warm laughter seasoned with peppers and water teeth, as we do it at home, as my wit is seasoned with the salt of your tears.'[61] Laughter becomes Nommo, the power word itself, in the verse of the North American poet Paul Vesey: 'and my raining laughter beats down the fury . . .'[62] And in the revolutionary verses of Césaire: 'Yes, friends, your untamed laughter, your lizard laughter in their walls, your heretics' laughter in their dogmas, your incorrigible laughter, your whirlpool laughter, into which their cities fall spellbound, your time bomb laughter under their lordly feet, your laughter will conquer them! Laugh, laugh, till the world, conquered by your laughter, falls at your naked feet!'[63]

IV. Négritude and Surrealism

Aimé Césaire's poem 'Cahier d'un retour au pays natal' appeared in Paris in 1939 in the journal *Volonté* and was ignored. The first *free* word that the Martiniquian spoke, an African word, which inaugurated neo-African poetry, was understood only by Africans and West Indians. Only two years later, when Hitler's tanks overran France, did André Breton, the pope of the surrealists, leave Paris to follow the path of Columbus. In Martinique he 'discovered' the 'great black poet', and taking Césaire's revaluations and reinterpretations of French words for surrealistic techniques, received him proudly into the ranks of his dis-

ciples and began to beat the drum for him. Thus after the war
Césaire became famous for the revival of surrealism. And not
only his poems but those also of Senghor, Damas, Roumain,
Birago Diop, Rabéarivelo and many others, the whole poetry of
'Négritude' was celebrated as the consummation of surrealism
and thus classified in one of the transient periods of European
literature. Sartre then interprets it out of the historical situation,
and inquires anxiously what will happen to it under altered circumstances.

The surrealists wanted to open to art new areas of consciousness. According to a saying of Rimbaud, the poet, through the
consciously practised separation of the senses, is to become a
seer. Thus Breton and his followers, influenced by Freudian
psycho-analysis, turn hallucinations, dream states and ecstasies to
literary account. Inspiration is said to come from the subconscious. 'All men are poets once they meet the unconscious,'[64]
writes Breton. Groups of authors were formed who wrote 'automatic' texts; sunk in a half-sleep in sofas and armchairs, they
fixed with paper and pencil the messages of their unconscious.[65]
Thus they tried to penetrate as far as possible into the subconscious, where, beneath the individual unconscious, the collective
unconscious was supposed to lie, a treasure of myths and images.
Objects, reason and reality were despised, and the images of true
poetry were supposed to spring from the unreal, a-logical and
absurd.

Surrealism did indeed extend the sphere of experience of its
authors, and in among the Freudian sexual symbols it dug out of
the depths of the soul some images with magic iridescence. But
in the light of an acquaintance with African philosophy it is
difficult to see what neo-African poetry could have to do with all
this. The surrealist renounces his command of words and waits
in a trance for the words to overwhelm him; but for the African
poet, on the other hand, dominion over the word is inalienable.
It alone gives him dominion over the world of things, it alone
makes him human. Sartre did indeed see that the poets of
'Négritude' hold to their domination over the word and control
it, but unfortunately he fails to dissent enough from Breton's
assertions, using this unintelligible formulation: 'One may speak

here of committed, even directed automatic writing (*écriture automatique engagée, et même dirigée*)—not because there is any intervention of reflection, but because the words and images are constantly translating the same torrid obsession. In his own depths, the white surrealist finds relaxation; in his, Césaire finds the fixed inflexibility of the demand for vindication and revenge.'[66] It sounds as if Sartre is contradicting himself, because either one writes automatically or one controls one's writing. But in Sartre the contradiction is resolved, because according to his philosophy every man remains responsible even for his automatic gestures, and because the existential project of his being reveals itself very clearly in his automatic actions, especially as Sartre does not acknowledge any subconscious. But everyone who is not fully acquainted with Sartre's philosophy will think it to be an attempt to interpret neo-African lyric poetry through psychology and depth psychology when Sartre writes that the African poet descends 'untiringly into his own self' and experiences there 'an exceptional poetic good fortune:* falling into trances, threshing about on the ground like one possessed of himself, singing his wrath, his pain, his revulsion, displaying his wounds, his life torn between "civilization" and his ancient black heritage, in brief, behaving lyrically to the highest degree.'[67] By this emphasis on the ego, Sartre believes, he is surest to produce collective poetry. By the very process of speaking only of himself he speaks for all Negroes.[68] The theory of surrealism appears to demonstrate that the collective is revealed in the deepest layer of the individual unconscious.

Moreover, Sartre discovers in Césaire's soul above all else 'inflexibility' and 'desire for revenge', individual feelings. But in reality the neo-African poet is not primarily concerned about his own ego. He is Muntu, man, who speaks and through the word conquers the world of things; directs it and uses it to change the world. His word is the more powerful the more he speaks in the

* (V/67: . . . descente inlassablement en soi-même . . . un bonheur poétique exceptionel: en s'abandonnant aux transes, en se roulant par terre comme un possédé en proie de soi-même, en chantant ses colères, ses regrets, ou ses détestations, en exhibant ses plaies, sa vie déchirée entre la 'civilisation' et le vieux fond noir, bref en se montrant le plus lyrique . . .)

name of his people, living as well as dead. As a poet he is the representative of all, and as representative he is a poet. And in order to achieve his goal, namely freedom, he makes use of all the powers at his command. 'Inflexibility' and 'hate' are nothing but forces which he uses, which he throws into the battle as he does pearls, islands, plants, trees, weeping and laughter. In this context his own personal sensations, which Sartre puts in the foreground, are unimportant.

Sartre himself recognized that neo-African lyric poetry could be only with difficulty classified as surrealism. 'Surrealism,' he writes, 'a European poetic movement, has been stolen from the Europeans by a black who turns it against them and assigns to it a vigorously defined function.'[69] Surrealism, however, is by definition 'l'art pour l'art', and if one tries to assign it a function, one is bound to fail, just as 'Elouard and Aragon failed to give a political content to their verse.'[70] But neo-African poetry is Nommo, that is, it is function above all else, and thus the very opposite of surrealism. 'African Negro surrealism', writes Senghor, 'differs from European surrealism.'[71] But why not drop the concept of surrealism altogether in connection with African poetry? The poetry of *Les Armes Miraculeuses*,[72] Hubert Juin believes, 'made surrealism ineffective, completed it by destroying it, enriched it by engulfing it. The tragedy *Et les Chiens se taisaient*,'[73] he says, '. . . supported surrealism in its articles of faith, but at the same time reduced it, annihilated and restored it in the form of a stutter.'[74]

In what articles of faith was surrealism supported? There is in the first place the attack on reason. Breton had declared war against the logic of the intellect. And he found in Césaire verses which also declare war on reason. 'Reason, I sacrifice you to the evening breeze. You call yourself the language of order? For me it is the lash of the whip. But oh, there is the hoarse contraband of my laughter, my treasure of saltpetre! For we hate you, you and your reason, for we appeal to the dementia praecox of the flowering absurdity of a stubborn cannibalism. Our treasures, then, are the madness that remembers, the madness that roars, the madness that sees, the madness that breaks loose. And besides, you know that two and two are five, that the forest miaows, that the tree fetches the chestnuts out of the fire, that the sky strokes its beard, et cetera et cetera.'[75] But the attack here, as we can see, is against a special reason, against that pseudo-reason of some Europeans, who misjudge African customs and beliefs. It is the reason of the whip that Césaire hates. 'Dementia praecox', 'flowering absurdity' and 'stubborn cannibalism' are the labels that a certain sort of unreason had fastened on the Africans. And conversely, the 'madness' that Césaire celebrates is madness only in the eyes of the same unreason; in reality it is the traditional African wisdom. 'The madness that remembers' is the memory in which the images of the past rise up—and at the same time memory itself is a madness, for it is madness to remember the time of the slave hunts. 'The madness that roars' means the loud, ecstatic religious festivals—and at the same time the madness of an injustice that cries to heaven. 'The madness that sees' is the art of the African seer—and at the same time knowledge as the stimulus to rebellion. 'The madness that breaks loose' is the ecstasy of freedom; it is revolution.

Thus it is no absurdity that Césaire is stating, nor unreason that he is preaching; on the contrary, he is expressing the most reasonable indignation, which is disguised as madness only through the retention of the language of prejudice. The next lines do indeed appear to European reason altogether foolish, but they are none the less logical. 'And besides, you know that two and two are five', is: 'that your calculation doesn't come out right'.* 'That the forest miaows': escaped slaves in the woods, giving prearranged signals to their brothers, used to imitate the voices of animals in order to deceive their masters. 'That the tree fetches the chestnuts out of the fire': 'chestnuts' (*marrons*) was the name given to runaway slaves; and whoever got to a tree at the edge of the plantation could climb up and get away. Thus the

---

* In addition Césaire is playing here on the marassa-symbol. In Voodoo the marrassas are the twins (in Cuba: Imaguas; in Yorubaland and Brazil: Ibeji), symbols of the eternity of man. Their vévé is mirrored, like the pattern of playing cards: this horizontal division signifies that man is half mortal and half deathless (buzima principle and magara principle); the vertical division splits them into male and female, from which there results a third: marassa—three. Twins two and two give *five*, literally as *quint*-essence of life. [76].

11. Painting by Ben Enwonwu, Nigeria. (Federal Information Service, Lagos, Nigeria)

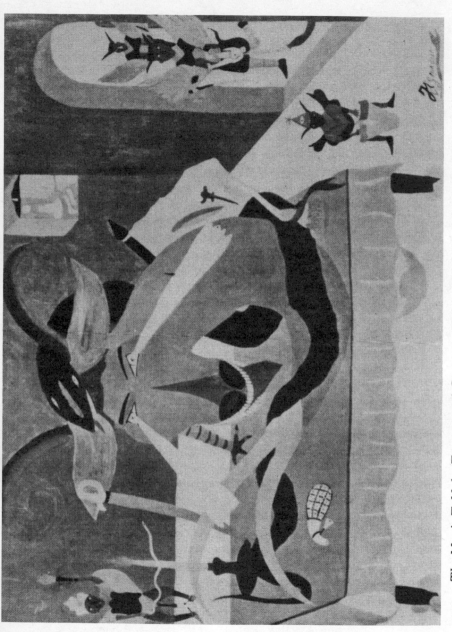

12. *The Magic Table* by Enguerrand Gourgue, Haiti. (Stedelijke Museum, Amsterdam)

line means that the tree helps runaways to escape the fire of slavery. 'That heaven strokes its beard': that God looks on helplessly as a priest might do and can take no action against the runaways. In other words Césaire has said simply:'I hate and despise that reason which calls us mad. But our treasures are memory, faith, knowledge and revolt. You know yourselves that your calculations go wrong, that we help one another, that even nature helps us and God cannot help you.'

Thus images taken from a real milieu, in this case the plantations under slavery, are evoked and used as weapons. Every image used by Césaire has in itself a precise meaning and stands in a precise context. Nowhere do we find the magic of the absurd, that decisive symptom of surrealism. There are, indeed, images which appear absurd or surrealistic in the European view. This begins even with the relation of black and white. Sartre writes: 'The Negro learns to say "white as snow" to signify innocence, and to speak of the blackness of a look, a soul, a misdeed. As soon as he opens his mouth, he is accusing himself, at least so long as he makes no effort to reverse the hierarchy. And if he reverses it in French he is already speaking poetically; imagine how strange such phrases would sound to us as the "blackness of innocence" or "the shadows of virtue",'[77] In Senghor there is 'black milk',[78] in Attuly 'milk of ebony',[79] in Césaire 'the abyss of innocence'.[80] But if we consider this reversal absurd or surrealistic, we are retaining the perspective of white superiority, in consequence of which innocence has to be white and guilt black. For the neo-African poet the reversal is nothing but the establishment of a reality and by no means surrealistically inspired. Such a reversal had already occurred to the German dramatist Grabbe, who wrote his horror play *Duke Theodore of Gothland* in 1822. There Berdoa, the Finnish General, who is an African, speaking to Gustav, the son of the Duke of Gothland, praises his one-time African beloved: 'Never, Ella! shall I forget thee, thou purest of African women; how noble was her heart! How woolly was her hair! Two feet long her bosom! And oh she was so black, as black as innocence!' Gustav: 'What? Is innocence black?' Berdoa: 'Well, we Negroes have a different taste from yours: for us the beautiful is black, but the devils are all white!'[81]

Of course there are admittedly in Césaire, as in all Neo-African poets, images which are not clear at first sight: 'the stars of the rim of their unseen ring will cut the pipes of the glass organ of evening and then spread out upon the rich extremity of my fatigue.'[82] Here it is once more a question of a vision that proclaims what *is* to happen. In the great revolution about which Césaire is always concerned and which is always at the same time a cosmic revolution, the stars are to be brought into their unseen ring: in this transformation the cosmic order will become visible. These stars, adjusted to the cosmic order, are to break apart the glass organ pipes of the evening. The organ playing and piping of the evening, already fragile, is to stop. Cosmic rest is to arise, in which the ring of stars spreads itself over the end of the poet's fatigue: over his awakening in the new world order.[83]

'The image', writes Senghor, 'is not a simile but a symbol, an ideogram.' While Breton emphasizes that the *European* surrealistic analogy differs fundamentally from the mystical analogy, because it never presupposes, behind the web of the visible world, an invisible universe that wants to show itself, Senghor emphasizes that in the African more-than-real analogy it is indeed a universe of hierarchically ordered life forces that is being presupposed and constantly revealed.[84] We may go a step further and say: in African poetry the poetic process itself is a continuous revelation of this order, since it is only the word in its function as Nommo that can activate the life forces in question. The word conjures up what it names. If this named and invoked object, which the word has created, occurs not in the real, but in the more than real world, then it has been named, conjured up and created in order that it should become a reality. To write poetry means here: to create new reality.

V. Négritude and Expressionism

The power of expression of Césaire's verse and that of other neo-African poets suggests a comparison with expressionism. Was there not in expressionism also an ascent to the cosmic, an emphasis on force? Was there not the will to form and renew the world, to free man and overturn the age? Thus we read for example in Kurt Liebmann's *Das kosmische Werke*: 'Expression-ism is the primal rhythmical-alogical experience of the cosmic-universal. It is the moulding of the world-background, of the essence, of the absolute. It is annunciation, revelation, vision. Let no one confuse vision with hysteria, neuroticism, modernity, mysticism, romanticism. Expressionism is the extreme clarity of the measureless.'[85]

In view of this interpretation of expressionism we might relate the neo-Africans much more readily to expressionism than to surrealism. Yet a closer comparison reveals more points of differ-ence than agreement.

Expressionism has in common with surrealism the fact that it accomplished less than it wished to accomplish. Its creations are modest compared with its loud manifestoes. There is much storm and stress, much enthusiasm, much eagerness to experi-ment, useful destruction and hopeful searching for new paths. All this is already untrue of neo-African lyric poetry. It does not experiment, but, as we have shown, applies traditional methods. It does not seek paths, for it knows them. It does not storm and stress, but demands.

In the introduction to an anthology, Gottfried Benn has ex-pounded in retrospect the nature of expressionism.[86] The fol-lowing passages from his exposition exhibit both the likenesses and the differences between expressionism and neo-African lyric poetry. Benn writes: 'It was 1910–20, it was a world doomed to destruction, ripe for the storm that did in fact come, but before-hand there were this handful of expressionists, believers in a new reality and an old absolute.' The neo-Africans are also believers —but in a new reality? And in an old absolute? African culture knows no absolute and no new reality in the European sense. The Africans believe in the malleability of reality with the help of old, we may almost say eternal, rules. They too are struggling against a world doomed to destruction—that of colonialism, which does indeed resemble very closely the world against which the expressionists rebelled. But the revolutionary goal of African writers is more concrete.

Benn writes: 'We may say that expressionistic realization is a constituent of all art.' This is especially true for African culture.

147

Since Nommo, the procreative word, represents the form-giving principle as such, every taking on of form *is* expression. Benn: 'A theme is not presented methodically, but inner agitation, magical and compulsive relationships of a purely transcendental character provide the connection.' Here we find essential differences from neo-African lyric poetry. The latter has no 'theme' whatsoever, but 'motives' and contents; it does not discuss or expound anything, but speaks by 'imagining': it creates images. Its 'compulsive relationships' are 'magical' but not transcendent. And their agitation is not an inner agitation in Benn's sense. In their case the inner agitation is not the cause of the statement, but one of its instruments. Benn writes of the 'breaking of cosmic boundaries and the visionary ecstasy which are ascribed to expressionism'. Visionary ecstasy the African poet also has, but it is disciplined: it is not a breaking of bounds but a binding of the ego, and the cosmic does not take boundaries away from him, but gives him laws.[87] Benn writes: 'Our (that is, the expressionists') background was Nietzsche: his drive to tear apart one's inner nature with words, to express oneself, to formulate, to dazzle, to sparkle at any risk and without regard for the results—the dissolution of content for the sake of expression.' In African poetry, on the other hand, the expression is always in the service of the content; it is never a question of expressing *oneself*, but of expressing *something*, and, indeed, with a view to the results, for African poetry exists as *function*. Nor is the African poet ever concerned with his inner nature, with *his* individuality.

Here lies an essential difference between African and modern European poetry in general. Benn writes: 'The expressionistic poet is expressing nothing different from poets of times and schools: *his* relation to nature, his love, his sorrow, his thoughts about God.' This is indeed true to a great extent for western poetry from Sappho to Benn. But for African poetry it is not true at all. The African poet does not express *his* relation to nature, but places 'Nature' (Kintu) at his service, rouses it into life, steers and manipulates it. In the love poem he does not express *his* love, but love as such, a force in which he shares. The love poem is more than conversation, courtship, play: it is Nommo, word seed in the most concrete sense. 'When one speaks to a

woman, one makes her fertile,' writes Ogotommêli. 'Or at least
one introduces into her a celestial seed, one puts her in condition
to become humanly fertilized.'[88] In the same way the poet expresses sorrow as such, and expresses not his own, but *the*
'thoughts' about God. 'For in the last analysis every artistic
manifestation is collective, created for all and shared by all,'
writes Senghor. 'Because they are functional and collective,
Negro-African literature and art are committed. They commit
the person, and not merely the individual.'[89]

The European poet is an individual and expresses what *he*
feels, thinks, has experienced, and wants. The African poet is a
person, and that means sorcerer, prophet, teacher. He expresses
what *must be*. His 'I' is not therefore 'collective' in the European
sense; it is not non-individual. He speaks *to* the community and
for them. He has a social task which raises him above the community: the most important poets, Césaire, Senghor, Rabémananjara, Guillén, Ortiz and many others are politicians who exercise an official function. Their functional character does not
prevent them from saying 'I', but this 'I' is always a 'we', and
every I-statement includes a binding imperative.

From this it follows that African poetry, old and new, poetry
and prose, is determined by responsibility. Poetry does not
describe, but arranges series of images which alter reality in the
direction of the future, which create, produce, invoke, and bring
about the future. The present interpreted by the poetry is
subordinated to the future. African poets take no delight in
drawing the present for its own sake or for the pleasure of the
drawing. The present is material for transformation; it is Kintu.
It is dissolved into particular images, which the poet arranges
anew according to their power as examples, sometimes to terrify,
sometimes to attract. He counts up what he holds to be true and
what false, and groups it, not according to a system inherent in
the things, but according to the force inherent in the images
themselves. This does not exclude a rational context; on the
contrary, since all the images are related to a purpose, each one
has its meaningful relation to it. But reason is—as in all poetry—
the slave of expression. The poem is meant to convince not
through logic but through fascination.

The past has a double function. On one side it is Kintu, the stuff of forces, which is awakened in images and ordered and transformed with reference to the future. On the other hand it is a pattern for the future, for it contains the wisdom of the ancestors, the knowledge of the order which is held to shape the present. It is magara, the spiritual force of the bazimu, of the departed, or concretely speaking: it is traditional poetry which, because of its paradigmatic quality, must be truly preserved. The work of the contemporary poet who is fulfilling his function as a teacher with responsibility for the community, will also, after his death, become a magara force and set an example for the living men of the future. Thus in traditional Africa works of poets and words of practical wisdom were passed on verbally from generation to generation. Except where destruction of the culture by slave hunts, colonization and missionary work violently ripped the chain apart, whole epics were preserved: in Ruanda alone, for example, 176 great dynastic poems have been preserved since the eleventh century.[90]

The same holds, fundamentally, for prose as for poetry. Even modern African and Afro-American novels tell nothing for the pure joy of story-telling. Only in contrast to lyric poetry, they do have a 'theme'. But the individual is never in the foreground; everything is example. No figure is portrayed for the sake of his experiences or his interesting situation, but for the sake of the instruction which the author hopes to achieve through his story. And yet the African author never teaches 'didactically', never with that school-masterish sort of demonstration that sometimes makes European productions with a pedagogical intent seem laboured or dry—for the African author knows that he convinces only through the fascination of the images, through word magic. Even Tutuola's love of story-telling, which the uninitiate may consider *l'art pour l'art*, is anything but that: it teaches the power of the Nommo, the mechanism of sorcery, the laws and the order of forces.

It will be said: much of this is true also of certain periods of European poetry and literature, for the mystery plays of the Middle Ages, or for the modern 'literature of commitment' (*littérature engagée*). Certainly. One finds something in common among all literatures of the world, otherwise they could never meet. But when we are dividing literatures into groups, we must emphasize their differences. And one of the essential differences between Western and African poetry is the different function of the image. In Western poetry the image precedes the word. Images are 'ideas' in the Platonic sense, they are given in advance, even for the surrealists, who wanted to press on to new and deeper images through the use of trance and automatic writing. And they set images from different levels experimentally alongside one another in the hope that the magic of a new image would spring up from the absurd combination, that absurdity would have the power to transform the already available imagery. *In African poetry, on the other hand, the word is there before the image.* It is the word, Nommo, that creates the image. Before that there is Kintu, a 'thing', which is no image, but just the thing itself. But in the moment when the thing is invoked, appealed to, *conjured up* through Nommo, the word—in that moment Nommo, the procreative force, transforms the thing into an image: 'I have nothing but my word,' writes Césaire. 'It is enough to *name* the thing, and the *sense* appears in the *sign*,' writes Senghor.[91] An image like Césaire's 'coal laughter of the daggers',[92] consists of three concrete objects, of which two are Kintu (coal, dagger) and one Kuntu (laughing). Coal, dagger and laughing are not ideas or symbols or images; they are nothing but 'frozen forces' available to the muntu and waiting for him to actuate them, to make them an image, to give them symbolic value, sense and meaning —in short, to cast a spell on them. Since they have no meaning of their own, Nommo can give them whatever symbolic value it likes. The poet speaks and transforms thing-forces into forces of meaning, symbols, images. Depending on the intention of the poet, the same 'things' acquire different symbolic value: 'coal laughter of the daggers', 'coal age of our horror',[93] 'lizard laughter',[94] 'sun daggers'[95]—each time 'coal', 'laughter' and 'dagger' have, as symbols, a different value. Sometimes the stress is enough to transform one and the same kintu into a threatening, an exulting, a shudder-raising or a comforting symbol. A kintu is not a coin of fixed value like the European concept; on the contrary, only Nommo by its magic makes of kintu a value, a modal force or kuntu.

So Césaire uses European words in an African way. For example, in Yoruba the mere word itself does not yet convey a concept or idea. The muntu who utters a word must first designate it by his utterance. It is he who gives it its immediate meaning, while giving a new interpretation to every word he speaks, and so finally giving the specific meaning to the vocable or the phoneme. 'Not only are the Yoruba highly conscious of the meaning of names,' writes Beier, 'but they also like to interpret each word they use. They believe that every word is really a sentence that has been contracted through a series of elisions into a single word.'[96] Thus 'in Yoruba many words are open to different interpretations,' Beier continues, 'and can therefore be used by different speakers in such a way as to evoke a different set of associations.' For the European a word like 'God' conveys a stable concept. Dr. Idowu, in a lecture given at the University College, Ibadan, in 1957, gave five interpretations of the Yoruba word for 'God' (Olodumare):

1. *Olodu-Omo-Ere.* The supreme one, offspring of the boa.
2. *Olodu Ma Re.* The supreme one, who remains constant.
3. *Olodu Mo Are.* The supreme one, wearing the crown.
4. *Olodu Kari.* The perfect one.
5. *Olodumare.* The one to whom I must return.[97]

The words 'wife' or 'mother' also convey stable concepts to Europeans. 'Most Yoruba people, however, using the word "iyawo" (wife) think of a story that is told in the Ifa oracle[98] and which explains that it means "suffering in the town of Iwo". The story says that Orunmila, the deity of the oracle, encountered much suffering in the town of Iwo and that later he was given a wife in recompense. Hence the word "iyawo". On the other hand Mr. T. S. Sowande of Abeokuta has ventured another interpretation: "iya" (mother) is explained as "one who draws an image" and "iyawomi" (my wife) as "one who draws my picture". Again "iya mi" (my mother) has been interpreted by Mr. Abolubode of Oshogbo as: "from where I branch" (the mother and her children likened to a river and its tributaries). Thus in the Yoruba language words cannot become cliches because they are constantly being reinterpreted and charged with new meaning.'[99] The phoneme is therefore only the raw material, the 'flesh' of the meaning. And it is the muntu who designates the vocable as a word, and gives it 'meaning-force', or Nommo-force, then this makes it into a symbol, a picture. The word precedes the image.

This is true of all the poetry of African culture, old and new, on the near or the far side of the Atlantic, and whether the poet is writing in an African or in a European language. It is precisely because the neo-African poet does not treat European terms as concepts and ignores the accepted meanings inherent in European usage that African poetry in European languages appears so amazingly new.

In African poetry the images are not torn from their context and arbitrarily put into another context in order to transform them, as the surrealists tried to do. For the African poet there is, in fact, no relation at all between 'things' as such. Man invokes them, conjures them into a context: 'Out of the sky, the birds, the parrots, the bells, silk cloths and drums, out of a touch of drunkenness and wild endearments, out of copper clanging and mother of pearl, out of Sundays, dancings, children's words and love words, out of love for the little fists of children I will build a world, my world with round shoulders . . .'[100] writes Césaire. How different is the expressionistic programme-poetry, for instance of a Johannes R. Becher: 'I learn. I prepare. I rehearse. How I work—ha! passionately! Against my still unmoulded face—I stretch folds. The new world (—such a one: erasing the old one, the mystical one, the world of suffering) I draw on it, as correctly as possible. A sunny, a highly articulated, a polished landscape floats before me, an island of happy people . . .'[101] Here there is planning, practising, probing how ideas can be realized; but no future is conjured up or magically invoked.

African poetry belongs neither to surrealism, nor to expressionism, nor to any European school of literature. Nor is it in the European sense 'modern lyric poetry', such as would arise from one situation and be made obsolete by another situation, as Sartre believes, for it belongs to no European calendar of time. Only the confrontation with it is a European situation. It does indeed have in itself its differences of style, its epochs, its own historical course. To expound this in detail will be the task of a history of African literature.[102]

In short, the forced classification of neo-African authors into European literary groups, introduced by Breton, has done more harm than good to the understanding of their poetry. Their work becomes more intelligible if we give up the use of European labels. But this presupposes that we recognize its independence. The practice of dividing literatures according to languages had its meaning as long as the languages corresponded to divisions in a single—Christian-European—sphere of culture. English, French, Russian, German literature were sub-divisions of European literature. Their likenesses and differences could be determined. But since another culture, the African, with its common characteristics, has spread over several European languages, it becomes necessary to give up the classification purely by language, since the language alone no longer indicates to what literature an author belongs. It has been considered necessary for much lesser reasons to separate English and American literature—shall we then put Tutuola into English literature? Within African literature Tutuola is intelligible; within English literature he is an oddity. 'Tall, devilish story,'[103] Dylan Thomas called Tutuola's *Palm Wine Drinkard*; 'extraordinary writer,' wrote Pritchett in *The New Statesman* and continued: 'In a violent, bizarre, but quite simple talking manner, Tutuola is describing universal experience in a way that will be deeply interesting to psycho-analysts and anthropologists.'[104] Césaire too one might, without Breton's fake interpretation, have recommended to the psycho-analysts.

Naturally, authors like Césaire *also* belong to French literary history, because, regardless of whether they are interpreted correctly or not, whether they are understood or misunderstood, they do influence French literature, and extend and enrich the French language—just as Shakespeare also belongs to German literature, where he plays an important part different from his role in English literature. But when Claude Roy expresses the opinion that 'the authentic descendants of the Parisians Villon, Voltaire, Diderot, Hugo, etc., are above all those Negroes who in their writing utilize, deepen, and re-discover the French of our great writers',[105] this is close to intellectual colonialism, the appropriation of foreign property.

As soon as an African writes a European language, African philology, interested in linguistics, can no longer take any notice of his works. Thus they are attached to one European literature or another and are interpreted and readjusted until somehow or other they fit into it. Even the spiritual continent of Africa is still split up among the powers; and literary scholars have not yet foreseen the rise of an independent, modern African literature based on its own traditions.

Chapter 6

KUNTU

Immutability of Style

Thou mask face, immaterial and
eyeless, turned away from the
changing, thou art perfect, thou
head of bronze.
LÉOPOLD SÉDAR SENGHOR

I. IMAGE AND FORM

According to African philosophy, the metal, the stone, the clay, out of which the smith, the stone-cutter, the potter moulds a piece of sculpture is a kintu, a 'thing', and nothing more. Only the piece of wood .hat the wood-carver uses for his sculpture is something more than other 'things': it comes from the tree, from the 'road of the invisible ones', as they say in Haiti, from the vertical that unites the water-Nommo of the depths with the cosmos.[1] As 'respository', as the seat of the loas, the wood of such trees is a privileged kintu; the Nommo of the ancestors has given it a certain consecration, a symbolic value— just as a flag is a privileged piece of cloth: the force of respect, a symbolic force has been invested in it. The respect, however, is never for the wood itself, but for the Muntu-beings who have chosen it as their 'seat'. Since it stands closer to the loas, the orisas, the ancestors, it is favoured as a material—for the materials one works with also have a hierarchy. On the other hand, even though wood does come first in this scale, it is still basically a kintu, a 'thing' like stone, clay and metal. 'Things' are 'available' to the muntu.

With the help of Nommo, the word, Camara Laye's father, the

156

goldsmith, makes an ornament out of a piece of gold. He works magic. His manual skill is an addendum, on important addendum, but what is decisive is the word, the 'magic formula', which brings it about that the 'thing' is turned into something else, what it is destined to be: an image. As we have explained in the previous chapter, the image is created through Nommo—that is, it is *designated*. We shall call this process *the designation of the image*.

The designation of the image determines what the image expresses. The woodcarver carves a figure, and says meanwhile, 'let this piece of wood mean Erinle' (an orisha), and so the figure expresses the orisha Erinle, it becomes an ideogram of the orisha. The woodcarver carves a second figure and says: 'Let this piece of wood mean the King of Ondo', and so the figure expresses the King of Ondo. Both carvings may be as like as two peas, but one means Erinle and the other the King of Ondo, in virtue of the designation of the image, which is determined not by the appearances of the figure but by Nommo. In virtue of this act of designation African sculpture was able to dispense with all individual expression and all psychology. Whether an orisha, a king, an ancestor, a peasant or one's neighbour was being represented, one figure could look like another and yet, thanks to its designation, be for the woodcarver in one case the image of an orisha, in another the image of king, ancestor, peasant, neighbour and so on.

Let us assume that the woodcarver has in fact completed a row of figures all similar to one another and set them aside, and some one has disarranged them; and now suppose the woodcarver stands before these figures. The woodcarver has now become a spectator who will use the completed figures, someone who needs an orisha, a king, an ancestor and so on. The act of designation has been forgotten. Thus the figures are once more kintu, 'things', which have no force of their own and await their designation through Nommo. So our woodcarver says: 'You are Erinle, you are king, you are ancestor, you are peasant,' and so on. He does not need at this point to do any more carving, for the figures are all already present; only the Nommo of designation is needed to make the figure mean something. Thus the onlooker must renew the designation; he must say what the image is to mean, what he wants to see in the image. And the designation obtains only so long as the master of the image likes. He can dethrone the image by saying: 'You mean nothing to me any more,' and then the image again becomes a kintu, a piece of wood, which is good for nothing but kindling. For Muntu is master of every kintu, and so of images also. Hence the carelessness with which Africans treat works of art that 'no longer mean anything'.

Carl Einstein and others are mistaken, therefore, when they say that a statue representing a God *is* in the eyes of the African the divinity itself.[2] An African statue is neither an idol nor a 'fetish' (i.e. an artifact) that *is* God. The African does not carve himself Gods that control *him*, but images which *he* controls. 'A carving', writes Beier, 'is never worshipped in itself. A carving in an orisha shrine is no more an idol than is a crucifix in a Christian church. Both are accepted symbols of the spiritual being that is worshipped.'[3] In other words, images are images and not Gods.

This is evident even from the accounts of authors who explicitly emphasize the existence of fetishes. Himmelheber writes: 'If an individual has any worries and problems, he turns to the village sorcerer for advice. The latter may prescribe medication, or recommend the performance of certain actions, and he may also suggest going to an artist and having a fetish made. A fetish is then ordered, usually without the artist's receiving any particular instructions. To make the fetish work, it is usually necessary to offer a sacrifice.'[4] From this exposition it is clear that the woodcarver receives only a general order, and the designation of the image is undertaken by the customer or by the 'village sorcerer'. Only the designation makes of the figure—a totally ineffective and indeterminate thing—a statue representing something definite, the votive image of a higher being. Himmelheber continues: 'To make the fetish work, it is usually necessary to offer a sacrifice, on more serious occasions of a cock, although in minor cases sprinkling with flour or even with white chalk is enough.' The sacrifice differs with the occasion: that is, the image is 'dedicated' to the Muntu appropriate to the matter in hand, whether a muzimu or a muzima. If it is a question of a slight illness, the figure may represent the 'village sorcerer' himself, whose Nommo-force speaks to the patient out of the image and so is always close to him. The image is thus the medicine, which is effective in virtue of the medicine man's Nommo. In more serious cases, however, the image will represent some higher muzimu being. It is this very differentiation in the sacrifice which demonstrates that the sacrifice is made not to the figure but to what the figure represents. Himmelheber continues: 'Thus the fetish has been ordered for a particular occasion, but if it works especially well it is used in future for all needs and wishes. It seems to me that the statements about *one* exclusive function of *one* particular fetish or the fetishes of a whole family often rest on the fact that one has asked too little and then has given exclusive or general validity to one or a few answers.'[6] Thus the so-called fetish appears as the votive image of a particular muzimu whose advice has proved good in one case and whom one therefore consults on other occasions: 'for the cure of sickness, for the pacification of an angry husband, for a good harvest, or quite generally to make things go well, on the occasion of a marriage or a journey,' as Himmelheber writes.[7] The demands made on the fetish presuppose a thinking partner, a muntu, and this no artifact can become. The interpretation of the figure itself as Muntu would flatly contradict the fundamental principles of African philosophy. Nor is there, presumably, any figure which serves a single purpose only, for in that case it would be nothing more than the carrier of a concretely defined Nommo, nothing but a 'medicine'. But since any kintu-substance that has been 'conjured' can be such a carrier, it is not only superfluous to make the substance wood into a muntu-image for this purpose, it would be in fact a misuse of the image unless such 'fetishes' were in fact kintu-images, that is, amulets, and thus once more symbols. All so-called 'fetishes' prove, on closer analysis, to be votive images; an image is never in itself worshipped as divinity; the concept 'fetish' is, as Frobenius rightly remarks, 'a European trade mark'.[8]

On the other hand, by virtue of its designation, a woodcarving is more than an ordinary piece of wood, an ordinary kintu; through its designation it has become an image and has acquired a meaning through the force of the Nommo. In addition, however, the individual may admire the image as such because it is beautiful or because it pleases him. But this has nothing to do with religious veneration and is independent of it. If a picture pleases a person, he gives strength to the picture through the joy and pleasure that he expresses. Prayer strengthens the god and only the god, but joy in the image strengthens the image itself and increases its Nommo-value, its power of expression.

Here we have the other component which enters into the creative process along with the act of designation, and which we shall call the *kuntu* or *modality* of the image.

The designation is, as we have shown, independent of the shape or form of the image. The image receives its meaning through its designation; through kuntu it receives its form. For the understanding of African sculpture it is first of all necessary to separate these two components.

If the woodcarver in cutting his statue determines by the force of his Nommo what the figure is to be, then he carves it in such a way as to make his designation recognizable. The carving 'antelope' must look different from the carving 'king' or the carving 'woman'. The antelope will have horns and the woman breasts. To distinguish the king from the farmer, the sculptor will give the king a crown and the farmer a hoe. We call these kuntu components the *determination* of the image, because they express whatever category or sub-category the image will evoke. The most important category is Muntu, and most images belong to it. They are therefore given human form. This is a determinant of the first degree. But there must also be some indication whether, within the category Muntu, this image is to represent male or female, muzima, a living person, or muzimu, a person without life. These are determinants of the second degree. By means of attributes like crown or hoe the figure is further and more exactly determined, but never more exactly than is necessary. The determination does not individualize the figure but determines its place in the ontological system, in the hierarchy of the world of the living and the dead. The sculpture is individualized, on the other hand, not through its determination, but by virtue of its designation. If a figure is to signify a certain chief, then it will be determined by the woodcarver to the extent of meaning 'chief' or even 'chief of city A' or 'chief of city B', but there is in principle a remainder which can be individualized only through designation. Otherwise the image would become reality and would fail in its purpose, namely to 'reveal' behind the visible world 'a universe of hierarchically ordered life forces'.[9] Even the so-called 'portrait heads' of Benin are not in fact portraits, as they were assumed to be by European scholars who had seen none of the models but sought and believed they saw behind the image the individual instead of the universal. The resemblance of the 'portraits' to one another already suggests that what we have here are variations of a type. The ten female heads of what Luschan calls the 'best period', allegedly 'proper portraits of young, elegant, well-born women',[10] (Plate 5), are not even individualized as 'princesses' or 'noblewomen'. On the basis of the statements of the Nigerian historian Jacob V. Egharevba, Sydow is forced to correct himself and Luschan. 'The woman with the pearl headdress was described to me by Egharevba as the mother of a king. In the light of his information these are certainly not young unmarried princesses.'[11]

The determinants of sculpture differ from nation to nation and from cult to cult. A Yoruba chief is determined by a pointed crown; a bochio, or protective spirit of Dahomey by the position of the hands.[12] But the process of determination holds everywhere.

Determination stresses the general before the particular and begins therefore with the most general, with the ontological category. Thus in the first place human beings are distinguished from animals. Hence Muntu as a class is emphasized. Its mark is the head, the seat of intelligence, of will, the sign of the self, as a Yoruba bridal song puts it:

> *Only my head will follow to my husband's house,*
> *only my head will follow.*
> *You may wear a costly crown,*
> *but only your head can follow.*
> *You may hold a beaded sceptre,*
> *but only your head can follow.*[13]

The head is enlarged in relation to the body and the latter may be neglected, so much so that in the so-called 'head-foot figures' it can be altogether omitted (Plate 4a). Muntu includes muzima and muzimu, living and dead, and the 'determinant of the first rank' expresses this also, for it is not the temporal but the 'eternal' face of the Muntu that is pictured, since it alone has equal validity for bazimu and bazima. The various African peoples have coined various basic forms for the 'Muntu-face', but they all express the Muntu face. Within *one* people the Muntu face is constant, for it is derived from their common ancestor, that muzimu who formed the physiognomy of his people. Thus the artist is not free to think out a Muntu face for himself according to his own conception: the Muntu to be represented must belong to his own people; only foreigners, Europeans, for example, can have other Muntu faces. For the observer, the knowledge of various Muntu faces is usually sufficient to enable him to classify human figures correctly according to the tribe they represent.

The Muntu face does not express 'life', let alone 'liveliness' in the European sense, but 'existence'. For according to African philosophy the bazimu, in common with the bazima, do not have life (buzima) but only existence.[14] In the image, which cannot directly represent something incorporeal, since it is a body, this emphasis on existence in the sense of living beyond death is expressed by the way in which the Muntu face listens, as it were, to existence after death. Thus the Muntu face has either something skull-like about it, or, for example among the Yoruba (Plate 1), the expression of a person ecstatically united with the Muzimu.

'The features are prominent and bulging, particularly the eyes. The round swelling forms seem to be pushed out by some rising pressure from within. The expression is one of concentration and receptiveness at the same time. It is the same expression that appea: ; on the face of the worshipper when he is ready to receive the god in his soul, or just after the mystical union with the god has been accomplished. Every initiate into a Yoruba cult must go through this religious experience, which for want of a better word we call possession.[15] The result of this union between man and the divine is always a complete harmony of the soul, an utter relaxation of the mind and—balance of the personality.'[16] Thus the Muntu face is not only representative of the union of the living with the departed and the—deified—ancestors, but at the same time an example of the religious attitude, of intensive concentration. Like the word-image, the carved image too expresses what it creates. The carved image too commands.

The artist who is commissioned, for example, to carve a 'portrait' of a recently deceased chief from his dead face,[17] is faced with the task of translating the real face of the dead man into a Muntu face, that is, he de-individualizes it. It is then only in name—that is, through designation—a portrait and through determinants of the second degree again made recognizable as a 'chief'. Thus the activity of the artist is not portraiture (according to Brockhaus: to paint, to represent exactly, according to nature), but the very opposite. The 'portrait' too, applied to Africa, is a mistaken European interpretation.

The determinant of the first degree, the Muntu face for man, or the animal shape for beasts, is binding for the artist. With the determinants of the second degree he has more freedom. He may mark the determination 'chief' by the coiffure, by the crown, or by the dress (Plate 4b), or he may set the figure on a horse—which must be small, for a horse, however beautiful, must never outshine a Muntu face (Plate 3)—or he may even use European insignia and medals, in order, for example, to determine an ancestor who lived hundreds of years ago as a person with great power in the world. If biographical material, legend and known attributes of the person in question are available, he will make use of these as far as possible.

In general the determination is the meaning of the sculpture given form. The determination is that aspect of the designation which is precipitated in concrete form. The designation answers the question: 'What does this image mean?', and the determination answers the question: 'How is the designation to be recognized?' But the question: how does this figure look? is only half answered by the determination—that is, insofar as the form is determined by the meaning. The determination is only one of the components of Kuntu.

II. Rhythm

The other component of Kuntu is rhythm, which plays the
same role in sculpture as in poetry. We must go into this more
closely, for the style of all African culture, its mode of existence—
Kuntu—is determined by meaning *and rhythm*. In every concrete
expression of this culture meaning and rhythm are inseparably
interwoven; it is only in theory, and for the purpose of exposition, that the two components can be separated.

'Rhythm', writes Senghor, 'is the architecture of being, the
inner dynamic that gives it form, the pure expression of the life
force. Rhythm is the vibratory shock, the force which, through our
sense, grips us at the root of our being. It is expressed through
corporeal and sensual means; through lines, surfaces, colours,
and volumes in architecture, sculpture or painting; through
accents in poetry and music, through movements in the dance.
But, doing this, rhythm turns all these concrete things towards
the light of the spirit. In the degree to which rhythm is sensuously
embodied, it illuminates the spirit.'[18] Rhythm is, as we can see,
simply the modality, the kuntu of the Nommo. Since 'man' controls things through the imperative of the word, rhythm is indispensable to the word: rhythm activates the word; it is its
procreative component. 'Only rhythm gives it (the word) its
effective fullness,' writes Senghor; 'it is the word of God, that
is, the rhythmic word, that created the world.'[19]

The first of the African arts is therefore poetry, not sculpture.
The art of words is the pure Art of Nommo. In the poem the
metre is rhythmical. When stressed syllables recur at regular
intervals, we have a line of verse and then a poem. Yet even more
essential than verbal rhythm is the rhythm of the drums; for, as
we shall show in the next chapter, the language of the drums is
also speech, it is Nommo, and indeed, privileged Nommo: it is
the word of the ancestors.[20] They speak through the drums and
establish the basic rhythms. Between word rhythm and the
rhythms of the drums there is a kind of rhythmic counterpoint.
Senghor speaks of the principle of 'polyrhythm'.[21]

What Senghor calls polyrhythm Dauer has investigated more

precisely in his recent work *Jazz*, in which he has made the first exact analysis of African rhythm. In this analysis the rhythm itself is shown to be a rhythmical system, which in its turn seems to me to mirror African philosophy. The description of these relationships would need an exposition of its own. Here we can only indicate the general foundation, the practical application of which has already been presented in the chapter on Voodoo.

African percussion rhythm is either polymetric or polyrhythmic. In *polymetry* several different sorts of basic metre are heard simultaneously; in polyrythmics a single basic metre is accented and syncopated in different ways.[22] In polymetry, for example, one drum beats a four-four time, another at the same time a three-four time, and a third a two-four time. Moreover, the entries must not be simultaneous; if one were writing out the full score of such an orchestra, one could not correlate the bars vertically. Yet the duration of the metres is constant, that is, the same sequence of bars is repeated regularly. In *polyrhythmics*, on the other hand, the bars stand, as in European music, vertically under one another, but several rhythmic versions of the one metre are combined together.[23]

Common to both basic forms is the principle of *crossed rhythms*; that is, the main accents of the basic forms employed do not agree, but are overlaid in criss-cross fashion over one another,[24] so that, in polymetry, for example, the particular basic metres begin not simultaneously but at different times. 'In this way', writes Dauer, 'the African produces those fascinating accent sequences, which are to be explained as the result of extremely simple basic forms interlaced cross-rhythmically. These accent sequences are the true music which the African is trying to create by his combinations of rhythm.'[25] In Voodoo the ecstatic patterns of accents[26] are as it were the Nommo words of the loas, through which the dancer is designated the Choual, the embodiment of a particular loa. The drums 'speak' the Nommo, the 'magic word', which *designates* a particular person to be the 'image' of a particular loa.

Since all these rhythmical forms are peculiar to African culture and are absent in western music, their occurrence furnishes us with a reliable criterion for ascertaining how far African culture reaches in the field of music. In the West Indies and in Latin America, as Dauer points out, both polymetry and polyrhythmics still survive in Afro-American music, but in North American polyrythmics alone survives as a traditional African element and continues to be definitive all the way to the swing style of jazz.

Poetry also, embedded in polymetry or polyrhythmics, appears 'as a piece of architecture, a mathematical formula founded on unity in diversity'.[27] For like the drums, but using language, it forms secondary rhythms based on alliteration, word play, and reiteration, that is, on the repetition of sounds or phonemes, which strengthen the effect of the whole.[28] A poem as it appears before our eyes in print is therefore incomplete, if it is not given rhythm at least through a percussion instrument.

'Prose narrative also shares in the grace of rhythm. In Black Africa there is no fundamental difference between prose and poetry. The poem is only a piece of prose with stronger and more regular rhythm. The same phrase can become poetry through the accentuation of its rhythm, expressing in this way the tension of being, the being of being. It seems that "in the very old days" every recital was strongly rhythmic and so was a poem. As it appears to us, even in the form of fable, which is the most de-secularized form, it is always rhythmic, even though more feebly. To begin with, dramatic interest is not sustained by, or rather does not consist in, avoiding repetition, as in European narrative; on the contrary, the dramatic interest is born of repetition: repetition of a fact, of a gesture, of words that form a *leitmotiv*. But there is almost always introduction of a new element, variation of the repetition, unity in the diversity. It is this new element which underlines the dramatic advance. That is to say, prose narrative does not despise the use of figures of speech based on the repetition of phonemes or the use of descriptive words.'[29]

It is not necessary here to give examples of rhythm in neo-African poetry, for all the verses quoted in this book in other contexts may serve as examples. Afro-Cuban lyric poetry, in which, thanks to the Spanish language, basic and secondary rhythms stand out most clearly, was treated in the Chapter on *Rumba*.[30] As an example of prose rhythm, we may take a passage from Amos Tutuola's *Palm Wine Drinkard*:

'There was a big market in this town from where the daughter was captured, and the market-day was fixed for every 5th day and the whole people of that town and from all the villages around the town and also spirits and curious creatures from various bushes and forests were coming to this market every 5th day to sell or buy articles. By 4 o'clock in the evening, the market would close for that day and then everybody would be returning to his or her destination or to where he or she came from. But the daughter of the head of that town was a petty trader and she was due to be married before she was taken away from the market. Before that time, her father was telling her to marry a man but she did not listen to her father; when her father saw that she did not care to marry anybody, he gave her to a man for himself, but this lady refused totally to marry that man who was introduced to her by her father. So that her father left her to herself.

'This lady was very beautiful as an angel but no man could convince her for marriage. So one day she went to the market on a market-day as she was doing before, or to sell her articles as usual; on that market-day, she saw a curious creature in the market, but she did not know where the man came from and never knew him before.

'He was a beautiful "complete" gentleman, he dressed with the finest and most costly clothes, all the parts of his body were completed, he was a tall man but stout. As this gentleman came to the market on that day, if he had been an article or animal for sale, he would be sold at least for £2000 (two thousand pounds). As this complete gentleman came to the market on that day, and at the same time that this lady saw him in the market, she did nothing more than to ask him where he was living, but this fine gentleman did not answer her or approach her at all. But when she noticed that the fine or complete gentleman did not listen to her, she left her articles and began to watch the movements of the complete gentleman about in the market and left her articles unsold.

'By and by the market closed for that day then the people in the market were returning to their destinations, etc., and the complete gentleman was returning to his own too, but as this lady was following him about in the market all the while, she saw him when he was returning to his destination as others did, then she

Kuntu

was following (complete gentleman) to an unknown place . . .'[31]
The rhythmical kind of narrative in which the repetition intensifies the dramatic quality of the action, makes Tutuola's story oral literature. We listen to it as we would to story-tellers in the market-place, and its forcefulness underlines the significance of the events. For rhythm is no more an end in itself than is the image of poetry or carving; it hammers image after image, statement after statement into our ears for 'only rhythm transforms copper into gold, isolated words into living speech'[32]—that is, into words with a meaning. Rhythm make prose too imperative.

Intensification through repetition as a traditional African element can be traced all the way to North America, where we still find this urgent rhythm as the driving power of the narrative in the Afro-American novelists Ralph Ellison, Chester Himes and above all James Baldwin. In many West Indian authors also the African narrative style is clearly marked. It is especially pure in the Barbados writer George Lamming. When he writes in his novel *The Emigrants* about his countrymen who had come with a ship to the coast of England, his style becomes entirely African:

'For in the dormitory it was as though they were in a cage with the doors flung open, but they couldn't release themselves. Nothing mattered outside the cage, because there was no-thing. So they remained within the cage unaware of what was beyond, without a trace of desire for what was beyond. It was unnatural and impossible to escape into something that didn't matter. Absolutely impossible, for within the cage where they were born and would die, the only tolerable climate of experience was reality which was simply an irreversible instinct to make things matter. Only where things mattered could they breathe, and suffer. There seemed some agreement with the silent dead that this should be so, for the habit of making things matter had become an instinct, human and, it would seem, eternal. Life was what mattered, and reality was part of the instinct that gave life some meaning. The instinct would make no claim on what went beyond, for beyond there was no-thing. No-thing that mattered. The door remained open and the cage festered with its reality which mattered for innumerable reasons and in innumerable ways.'[33]

A rhythm that matters, that means something and emphasizes

168

meaning, permeates every African work of art; it is the other component of the 'how', of the kuntu, as much in poetry and prose as in sculpture and painting. The parts are always rhythmically grouped and related to one another. Senghor uses a Boula carving of a woman as an example of this: 'Two themes of tenderness here sing an antiphony. Ripe fruits of breasts. The chin and the knees, the buttocks and the calves are here equally fruits or breasts. The neck, the arms and the thighs are pillars of black honey.'[34] In a Bambara mask representing an antelope we have 'the strophe of horns and ears, the antistrophe of tail and neck.'[35] (Plate 6). It is the same in painting. Flat colours, no 'perspective', no shadows. The rhythm results 'from the repetition, often at regular intervals, of a line, a colour, an outline, a geometrical figure, above all of colour contrasts. In general the painter places brightly coloured figures against a dark background which creates space or intervals and gives the painting its depth. The drawing and colouring of the figures follow not so much appearances as the deeper rhythm of the objects.'[36]

Whether painting or carving, the African work of art receives its meaning during its designation. This meaning is expressed through signs, determinants which are rhythmically arranged and the expressive power of which is intensified by rhythm.

III. MASKS

The mask also signifies what it represents; here too the process of designation is a double one: the artist performs the first designation, and the dancer the second. The two kinds of designation can be distinguished in much the same way as the tenses of verbs are distinguished: the artist undertakes the habitual, and the dancer the practical designation.

The mask—even an animal mask—always signifies a muntu. But as distinct from woodcarving the mask has no 'muntu face' in the sense in which we have described it above as the common denominator of living (muzima) and departed muntu (muzimu). It belongs to the function of the mask that it can be only the one *or* the other, for the dancer cannot at one and the same time lend voice and motion to a living and to a dead man. Only sculpture can realize the unity Muntu, because it neither moves nor speaks. But the masked dancer is not performing the designation of a habitual being, a symbol; he is designating a concrete being, that is, muzima *or* muzimu.

Thus we have two types of masks. The muzima masks represent a living person and therefore serve profane uses, mostly entertainment and amusement. The muzimu masks (Plate 2) are employed for the purposes of ritual.

In order to make the muzimu forces perceptible, these masks, in contrast to the carvings, must emphasize those features which distinguish muzimu from muzima: it must be clear that they do not signify living persons. For the same reason the Ñáñigos in Cuba, in their mask dances, execute the most grotesque and extraordinary leaps.[37] And neither is the muzimu mask a fixation of the human countenance: 'The African mask is not the fixation of a human expression,' writes Malraux; 'it is an apparition. The sculptor is not geometrizing a phantom of which he knows nothing, but raising it through his geometry; the effectiveness of his mask is measured not so much by the degree to which it resembles a man as by the degree to which it does *not* resemble him.'[38]

Since a muzimu has no body, neither has it any face (see Plate 15). The muzimu mask is not, therefore, the *real* face of an 'apparition'; it is an image that goes beyond reality, the negation of the muzima face, and the artist has therefore—in theory—the greatest possible freedom in the creation of the mask, so long as he is able to produce a more than real face, a non-face. The mask becomes the non-face of *a particular* ancestor only through designation. As everywhere, however, traditions have developed, so that it is possible to recognize a particular ancestor in a particular non-face, a particular muzimu mask.

There are all sorts of possibilities for making a mask signify muzimu rather than muzima: white, the colour of death, non-human, that is, non-muzima-like form—what Sydow calls the 'phantastic' form—or animal form. The animal mask, accordingly, signifies, *not* a dead animal—we have already pointed out that nothing is left of animals after death,[39] but the non-face of an ancestor. 'Masks, oh masks, I greet you in silence, and not last you, my panther-headed ancestor,' says a poem of Senghor.[40] The animal-image too means what it produces: 'the elephant', for example, 'is strength, the spider prudence; horns are the moon, and the moon fertility.'[41] Animal form expresses what is above reality (Plate 6).

For a muzimu mask it is idle to ask what expression it has. Only in a muzima mask, which represents a living person, can the question whether the person represented is laughing or crying possibly have meaning. In the case of the muzimu mask, which is not a face but a non-face, the question is meaningless. Whether it evokes joy or terror depends not on its appearance but on its designation—on the first designation, that of the artist, if for example it is to represent a particularly terrifying muzimu; and on the second designation, that of the dancer, according to the rôle which he happens to express. For just as the poem is incomplete if it is not recited, so the mask is incomplete so long as no one wears it, so long as it is not used. If, for instance, a certain Egungun mask of the Yoruba represents a certain dead man, then his relatives, for whom the Egungun dancer is lending the mask his voice, will approach the departed, through the mask, with respect and love; they will be afraid if he reveals his supernatural powers, and they will laugh if he amuses them and plays the fool. Only in the unity of mask and dancer, only in action is the muzimu mask the carrier of supernatural forces, the carrier of the muzimu forces which the dancer conjures up in a disguised voice. In this process the dancer never asserts that he *is* a 'spirit', as has been often alleged. 'Every pagan is fully aware that there is a human being under the mask. Most people will clearly recognize the human shape under the mask. After all the "owner" of the mask who is *not* a cult member knows quite well that he has had the mask made himself and that he asked the alagba to find him a dancer. But it is believed that the spirit of the deceased may be invoked to enter into the masquerader during the dance.'[42] By virtue of this designation the mask and the dancer are sacrosanct and can, if desecrated, bring about the death of the miscreant. A mask as such, on the other hand, as it hangs in a museum, is Kintu, a 'thing', a piece of wood, or a shape of bone and skin, of leather or bronze, of pearls, or whatever it may be.

The African work of art, whether poetry, music, carving or mask, is 'complete' only when it is Nommo, productive word, effective word, or function. If it loses its functional efficacy it becomes valueless. 'Because he is committed,' Senghor writes, 'the worker-poet does not care about creating a work for eternity. The work of art is perishable. Even if one preserves its style and spirit, one hastens to replace the old work—by bringing it up to date—before it is dated or destroyed.'[43] This attitude to art has led some Europeans to assert that Africans undervalue art, or do not know what art is; that since there is only functional art and no 'pure' art, no *l'art pour l'art*, there is no art at all. African art, they say, is at best an art industry or handicraft.

As far as the judgement of art is concerned, there are generally two different points of view: that of the creative artist and that of the observer. The artist is primarily interested in the creative process, and the connoisseur in the object, the artistic product. Now in Europe in the last few centuries art has come to a large extent under the dictatorship of the spectator, of the collector, even of the dealer, a situation with which the artists themselves are highly dissatisfied. If the artist did not need the proceeds of his work in order to keep body and soul together, the product of his art would matter even less to him. The artist endeavours to increase his power of expression, his creative power, from one creation to another. For him the completed work, that of his predecessors also, is always only a stage, a transition; in retrospect it becomes a preparatory exercise. For the connoisseur, on the other hand, the work of art is a work in itself, by reference to which he compares, measures, and develops aesthetic laws.

For this reason outstanding European artists—Kirchner, Brancusi, Picasso, Braque—when they made the acquaintance of African visual art, at once understood its creative magic. On the other hand, the cataloguing, classification of styles, and criticism of African carving was undertaken to a large extent by professional connoisseurs, that is, by the curators of museums, who extended their preference for one or another European school to African works of art accidentally resembling their favourite style, and judged it accordingly. Thus in the 'standard works' on

African carving one finds over and over again the most subjective judgements of taste. Glück, for example, praises the 'baroquising element of form' in the masks of the Cameroons, the style of which 'has understood so consciously how to master the grotesque and exaggerated',[44] while Kjersmeier ascribes to the same masks 'little artistic value',[45] but predicates of the works of the Boula a 'refined sensibility and technical delicacy', which 'lifts them far above the works of most African races'.[46] Luschan praises the 'great grace' of certain Benin heads,[47] while Einstein places them in a 'degenerate coastal tradition', which has recovered in the Cameroons 'in a late primitive rebirth'.[48]

Kjersmeier does indeed classify African art geographically and thus finds himself on the sure ground of ethnography. Sydow, on the other hand, distinguishes 'pillar carving', 'figure carving', and 'fantastic carving', a classification in which the degree to which the wood has been worked determines the artistic achievement. According to this interpretation the abstract 'pillar style' remains most 'banal' and achieves only in 'exceptional cases' 'ceremonial representation' and 'figures of a coarse monumentality' expressing not so much the 'will' as the 'instinct' for 'sublimity', while the 'naturalism of figure carvings', which are sometimes imbued with a 'joy of life of a loose and frivolous sort' occasionally attains 'beauty'. Thus the goal of African as of European art is thought to be the naturalistic portrait with its 'lively expression', which the African does indeed achieve only at a 'lower level'.[49] According to Sydow, therefore, African art is distinguished from that naturalism which for him is *the* European art form, only by its inferior quality, and, presumably because of want of application, remains for the most part at the 'pillar style' stage. Only Einstein—who is also a curator—has an artistic relation to African art; yet he postulates it as 'fetish', whether erected as 'type of the power being worshipped' or as 'the God who preserves his separate and mystical reality'.[50]

With the help of certain tendencies in European aesthetics, Sydow's judgements can indeed be given a philosophical foundation; but the theory of naturalism finds no support whatsoever in African philosophy. African philosophy stands consistently on the side of the artist; for it the finished work as it stands in the museum has nothing more to do with art; it is a 'thing', it is wood, vocable, lead, ivory, glass, colour—nothing more. It is not the artistic product that is important in African philosophy, but the fashion in which the creative, form-giving process takes effect.

An African aesthetic rests, therefore, on the aesthetics of Kuntu, and that means, on the harmony of meaning and rhythm, of sense and form. This is already apparent from the fact that in almost all African languages the word for 'beautiful' also means 'good'. 'When I say, "that is good", this term carries at the same time the meaning "beautiful",' writes Kagame.[51] Beauty is identified with quality, above all with effective force.[52] If therefore the rhythm, the division of accents, fails to correspond to the meaning, then Kuntu, and therewith art, has failed, there is no effect, Kuntu is bad and therefore ugly.

For the European, the difficulty of the African use of aesthetic standards consists in our inability to separate Kuntu from Kintu. We always see the 'work' as an object *having* meaning and rhythm. But the African sees Kuntu in action: the poem as recited, the carving in its function as stimulus in the worship of an orisha, the mask in the movement of the dance, that is, when it *is* Kuntu. In action Kuntu is complete, and here Kuntu is art and displays its efficacious value, its Nommo value, the standard of African aesthetics. Kuntu—and therewith art—is in Africa a force, and the force is accordingly the essential not of the art-*object* (Kintu), but of the exercise of art (Kuntu!). Art in Africa is never a thing but always an attitude or activity.

It has been asserted that the Africans have no feeling for beauty, because they do not know beauty as 'uninterested, free gratification'. But 'interested' gratification does not exclude gratification. Functional beauty is also beauty. In the light of African philosophy, in fact, disinterested beauty is no beauty at all, for it would be ineffective and meaningless, and a thing without meaning and effect cannot be beautiful, but only empty: 'ubusa', nothing. And in Africa one does not create nothings.

This statement is not contradicted even by Himmelheber's report, according to which there is in Africa 'art for art's sake'. He tells us that among the southern Atutu a number of things were brought to him, which very much surprised him: little figures of animals, carved out of wood, leopards, birds, a chameleon, a snail—all highly ornamented. When he inquired he was told that all this had nothing to do with religion, and had in fact no particular purpose, '*ça, c'est rien*'.

Stranger still was a group of things executed in the same richly ornamented fashion: signal horns, which were extremely exact indications of proper horns, but were so huge that one could not blow on them. The purposelessness was especially emphasized, for at the wide end, which should have been opened, the unnatural filling of the hollow was ornamented with a mask. Their was an ointment jar which could not be opened because it was just as solid and made of a single piece.

'My astonishment can well be imagined,' writes Himmelheber. 'What were these things? They could not be toys, for one thing because I had at once been told so, and besides though one can play with wooden animals one cannot play with a horn on which one cannot blow. After it had been stubbornly explained to me again and again that "*ça c'est rien*", came the explanation, whose significance the reader might ponder. "*Les jours de fêtes on met les choses devant soi et puis on est content*"—on feast days one puts these things in front of one and then one is satisfied.'[53]

Is that then *l'art pour l'art*? It looks as if we have here a misinterpretation induced by putting the wrong questions. Himmelheber asked the *purpose*, not the function, and got the answer, 'That is nothing.' In other words, these things have no 'useful' purpose, one cannot blow with them. Himmelheber is dissatisfied with the answer, and presses further. Apparently the person questioned now believes that Himmelheber has asked him not for the purpose, but the function, and answers, 'one puts these things in front of one and then one is satisfied'. So the things do indeed have a function, that is, to produce satisfaction—Kagame would say magara. Beauty is, as we know from Tutuola,[54] a force, a Kuntu—not the beauty of something, but beauty itself. The designation of these things is accordingly that they shall take on their function as forces of beauty, in order to give satisfaction to man. The works are therefore created for a meaningful function. The misunderstanding arose because the European easily overlooks the fact that in African culture function is directed to meaning, not to purpose.

Even with so secular an object as a hoe it is, in Africa, not the purpose but the meaning that is decisive; for the hoe cannot *intend* anything; Nommo, the word, makes the maize germinate and grow.[55] Man's activity with the hoe is only an addition. For the smith who makes the hoe also, the manner of his activity is more important than the purpose and the thing, Kuntu more important than Kintu. In his novel *The Radiance of the King*, Camara Laye makes a smith say: 'But what is a hoe? I have made thousands on my forge, and this one will surely be the most beautiful, all the others have been trials so that I might finally succeed in making this one; so that this hoe will be the aim of all I have learned, it will be as it were my life itself and the effort of my life. But what do you want the king to do with it? . . . He will accept it; at least I hope he will accept it, and perhaps he will even deign to admire it, but he will only accept it or admire it to please me. In fact, what pleasure will he have in it? He will always find hoes infinitely more beautiful and sharper than any I could make. . . . Yet I am making it. . . . Perhaps I can do nothing else: perhaps I am like a tree which can only bear one kind of fruit. Certainly I am like that tree . . . And perhaps, despite my shortcomings, perhaps because I am like that tree and lack means, the king in spite of himself will consider my good will. But the hoe in itself. . . .'[56]

In Laye's novel this smith is engaged all his life in making the sharpest and loveliest hoe, which he wants to give to the king. When one is finished, he begins a new, lovelier, sharper one. For the king who will come some day, hoe after hoe. The hoes already made: dethroned works of art—let the farmer have them! But the one on which he is working, the last one so far, is for the king. It is intended not to serve a purpose, but to delight.

IV. THE NEW ART

Traditional African plastic art is dying out. When the missionaries appeared, they raised a storm against images, and

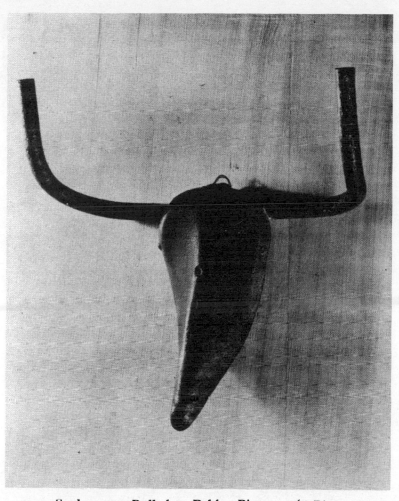

13. Sculpture: *Bull* by Pablo Picasso. (© Photo: Chevojon)

14. *Diviner for Obatala*. Silk screen by Susanne
Wenger (cover of *Yoruba Poetry* by B. Gibadamosi and U. Beier)

advancing Islam was no more friendly to the carvings. European influences of all kinds robbed African sculpture of its prestige, and the former patrons of the woodcarvers, the cults, secret societies and chiefs, became impoverished. The new stratum of African bourgeoisie, cocoa planters and merchants who had grown rich, would like to embody 'progress', and so introduce emphatically new forms of life, and they are afraid that if they admire traditional carvings they will be considered 'pagans' or 'savages'. 'I have asked many Africans', writes Beier, 'why they do not like my collection of African carving. Usually they had their answers ready: the carvings were "ugly", "crude" and "not true to life", I was told.'[57] The woodcarvers have become cabinet-makers or carve mass-produced articles for the souvenir trade.

Recently, various attempts have been made to preserve the African carver's art or to attract new artists to it and to stimulate an African art on a new basis among them.

A carver who still carves masks for the Gelede secret society of his village but can no longer live on this, Laniba Koumouhi of Dagbé, was commissioned by the colonial government of Dahomey to make a door for the government building in Porto Novo. The artist has spread figures in the traditional style, symbols, masks, carvings, implements, over the door. They have become Kintu, requisites serving a purely decorative purpose. While the carved columns of the chief's palaces expressed his power, wealth, force or history and every detail had a meaning, in the government building the symbols have been frozen into museum pieces. No designation, no determination, no rhythm—hence no African art. The value of this carved door lies beyond the sphere of art: it produces prestige once more for the despised art of carving and so may help to preserve it.

The Roman Catholic church has been trying for some years to draw African artists into its service. One of the most successful of these attempts was that undertaken by Father K. Carrol in Oye-Ekiti, in Nigeria. He gathered about him young carvers already schooled in the traditional art, and urged them to portray Christian themes. 'They were permitted to continue their activities for their pagan customers in the village. But at the same time

Father Carrol told them the story of Christ. Then he commissioned them to portray this or that saint or the Virgin Mary or Christ himself. No European models were shown them.'[58] The resultant carvings show their new designation, but were uncertain in determination and rhythm. The determinants are in part traditional—the crown for one of the three kings, the Muntu face for Mary—but in part also acquired additional paraphernalia such as the haloes and cross. One notices the concern of the artist to bring the determinants of different origins into one rhythm, and in this way external harmony and stylization are achieved, but at the expense of the expressive force of the determinants themselves. The rhythm does not strengthen the determination, but weakens it. Yet in contrast to the door, these works are not sterile, they are a beginning which still lacks courage—the courage to *transform* the new 'things' (Bintu) such as halo and cross. (Plate 8.)

The circle of Father Carrol also included those carvers who are decorating the chairs of the 'speaker' and the president of the lower house in the new parliament building of Western Nigeria. They portray dignitaries with rich headdresses and garments, with swords and guns and all the determinants of traditional power. But in this case the designation is wanting: the figures carry their faces like empty masks, their garments like actors' costumes. The meaning has perished in the decoration. Here too the value lies beyond art, in the prestige that accrues to the art of carving as such. Yet one should give African artists more and more of such 'profane', and not only religious, commissions, for African art has always consisted in significant function, and is therefore eminently suited to undertake the work of a parliament building, if only the artists do not 'decorate' the building, but make a place *mean* 'parliament', if they are allowed to set up *their* symbol for *their* representation, *their* freedom: to *transform* things into images.

Alongside these efforts to give traditional art new themes and new tasks, stand the attempts to call directly to life a new African art. At Makere College in Kampala, Uganda, at Elizabethville (Congo) and in Poto-Poto near Brazzaville in the French Congo, African pupils are placed under the guidance of European art teachers and artists. In Kampala young painters and draughts-men made a series of pictures from the life of the people which were printed in England and distributed throughout the class-rooms of Uganda. In the 'Academy of Fine Arts' at Elizabethville and in Poto-Poto European artists, Pierre Romain-Defossé, Laurent Moonens and Pierre Lods, have formed 'studio com-munities' with African artists. The value of these experiments lies in the fact that young Africans become acquainted with new materials and techniques. The disadvantage is that the whole conception of art proceeds from European ideas. 'In Poto-Poto too,' writes Italiaander, 'the motto is: let the inspiration be Africa alone. Neither colours nor themes are prescribed.'⁵⁹ But the very word 'inspiration' is a term which has nothing to do with African art. The poets of Négritude have no 'inspiration', they have something to say. To produce African art, one may safely specify the themes and colours for the artists: insofar as themes and colours mean something to them, they will transform them into images, and Kuntu will be art. Italiaander unwittingly gives a pretty example of this. He writes: 'It is scarcely possible to give them commissions. One day in Paris I went with one of them to the Folies-Bergère. My young African friend was in Europe for the first time and was much taken with the perform-ance of the charming ballerinas. The morning after, I asked him to paint what he had seen. Result: a group of Negroes dancing with a background of primeval forest. Thus he was not in a position to make a transposition.'⁶⁰ In reality, however, the African had both 'transposed' and executed the commission: he had represented the occurrence by grasping its meaning and transposing or transforming it into an image through *his own* determinants. This image then *produces* dance; it does not copy it. Italiaander demanded a copy, but the African made a symbol.

To the Africans the demands of well-meaning European patrons are downright unintelligible—and rightly so. Italiaander took copper and zinc plates along to Africa, in order to create there a new art form: the art of etching. When he had introduced the new technique in Poto-Poto, he announced 'categorically': 'if they were now to learn a new technique, then they must themselves outgrow the world of their traditional ideas.'⁶¹

Italiaander himself explains how he means this: 'If for example they took up the themes "Dance to the tom-tom" or "Life in the market place", their work was for the most part not realistic. . . . When it came to revealing themselves, my young etchers shrank from every sort of realism or naturalism. Even prizes which I set for them, and which certainly attracted them, could scarcely move them to give up rendering their long cherished themes in the traditional style. In this their uncertainty before the world of progress was paradigmatically expressed.' Thus Italiaander demands 'categorically' that they should retain the themes but alter the manner of presenting them. That is like demanding of Césaire that he give up the drum-beat of his words and string rhymed garlands of sonnets together instead.

Yet just as the Neo-African poets write *African* poetry in French, Spanish, or English, even—and especially—when the themes are not at all African, but quite contemporary and quite general—in the same way African painters, etchers, sculptors, and draughtsmen create works of art in the African manner: as they have been doing all along both in Africa and America without 'categorical' patrons.

In Haiti a North American artist, Dewitt Peters, had a good idea. He thought that if one simply put brushes, paints and canvas at the disposal of people who would enjoy using them, 'something curious' would surely result. There arose a neo-African art whose achievements are amazing. Hector Hyppolite, a Voodoo priest, painted the world of Voodoo deities; Castera Bazile, formerly a domestic, created Christian pictures: St. George and the dragon, the adoration of the Virgin, surrounded by a world of marvels: saints sit—like loas[62]—on trees, dead men rise from their graves and walk to church. Préfète Dufaut decorated a protestant church with vèvè symbolism. An observer who is unfamiliar with the Afro-Haitian cults and the African fashion of making images out of 'things', of conjuring up and invoking images, does indeed misinterpret the paintings, but nevertheless makes it clear that Kuntu is at work here.

'The very strange works of young Enguerrand Gourgue (Plate 12) are frightening and malevolent pictures of sorcery, of the terrible mysteries of Black Magic, as filled with symbols as

Bosch or Dali, and more horrifying than the latter. Usually the rites take place in windowless rooms, and presumably at night. Human beings are sacrificed, blood spurts from their hearts to be drunk by serpents. Little demons with sinister preoccupied faces are busy with peculiar ritual. Like the others, Exume seems to take it all for granted. Rigaud Benoit may paint leaves and shrubs in the same spirit as Miss Rhoda Jackson, the Jamaican decorative painter of Mandeville, carefully presenting each one and making the most of its decorative possibilities as if he were polishing and cataloguing them, but ghosts, women whose legs have turned into snakes, and African gods wearing crucifixes are un-Mandevillian. A painter who takes the mystery into the bedroom is Louverture Poisson. His best pictures seem concerned with some very personal incident only a glimpse of which we are given . . .'[63] Nearer to the European style of painting are the pictures of Wilson Bigaud, Fernand Pierre, Sisson Blanchard, Luckner Lazare, Roland Dorcély, Antonio Joseph and others.

In Africa itself various cult groups found new materials and therewith new possibilities of expression. If one travels through the land of Ibibio in South East Nigeria, it looks like a huge park full of concrete sculptures: 'The male figures are often wearing European dress, mostly of a noticeably old-fashioned style reminiscent of a missionary of the 19th century. The women, on the whole, appear to be dressed in the African fashion and most of them wear the traditional Ibibio hair-style. Some figures are shown reading a book and some are shown preaching. Some are seated in state, surrounded by their family; some are on horseback.'[64] These concrete statues are relatively new; in 1923 none of them existed. According to ancient custom the Ibibio erected for their dead open houses, in which, on the back wall of the interior, were painted the deeds of the departed. When the Nwomo house had been erected and the ceremony was over, the building was allowed to collapse. The Ibibio who had become Christians, however, did not want to be backward in honouring the dead, and they began to set up grave sculptures of concrete, for which they found a stimulus in the style of European memorial sculpture, but transformed with gay colours according to their own custom. Soon the non-Christians found the new memorial art more representative, and so there arose from the competition between Christians and non-Christians, who copied forms and symbols from one another and tried to excel one another, a landscape full of statues (Plate 9).

Where European patrons do not play the teacher the transition to another material sets the artists, for the most part simple masons, new tasks, and preserves the African style and method at its purest. In many new dwelling houses in Yorubaland animal figures of cement have appeared.[65] In Iboland, in the richly painted Mbari houses, bright clay figures have been erected, and the artists have not been afraid to work European objects such as neckties, umbrellas and even sewing machines into their compositions both in painting and sculpture.[66] These Mbari houses, which are erected even at the behest of Christianized communities in honour of the earth goddess Ala, disintegrate quickly. In a couple of years the colours are faded and the clay figures crumbling. Ritual and art occur in the living activity, in the honouring, shape-giving designation, and end with the completion of the work. The goddess, who proclaims her will through the oracle, takes care that ritual and art, the force of worship and the force of artistic creation, do not cease to act.

Independent artists are still rare in Africa. Only a few have not surrendered to European influences. The majority believe that with European materials and techniques they must also accept European forms and methods. European art—with the help of African art—has scarcely set itself free from naturalism, while African artists, as apprentices to Europeanism, are struggling to copy landscapes, fix situations, model realistic portraits. Some found a relation to their native tradition—the carvers Idah and Felix Idubor in Benin (Plate 10)—but only a few found their way back to the artistic attitude of the African. In Ghana, Ampofo and in Nigeria, Ben Enwonwu have found their way, after long detours, to some neo-African expression. Necessary as patrons are to African artists, these patrons are also a danger: Ben Enwonwu was commissioned to model the Queen of England, who sat for him for many hours. That Enwonwu achieved the desired naturalistic copy bears witness to his skill as a craftsman, but not to his art, which is revealed in his magical neo-African figures and paintings (Plate 11).

Today, therefore, various European artists are closer to the African attitude to art than are many artists in Africa. What we have in mind here is not so much those European works of art in which elements of African form have been adopted: Picasso's women of Avignon, the figures of Kirchner, Brancusi or Modigliani. To borrow and assimilate models is not the African attitude to art. But 'when Picasso transforms a bicycle saddle and handlebars into a bullock's head with horns, he is transferring a thing with one blow from the utilitarian to the aesthetic sphere.'[67] (Plate 13). Here is Nommo at work: a spell is cast upon a kintu. The bull's head lacks only the designation which makes it the symbol of a particular expression and therefore a function; with that it would be the purest African art, like Picasso's illustrations for Césaire's 'Corps perdu', like the batiques of Susanne Wenger, who transforms African myths into African symbol images (Plate 14). Paul Klee was close on the track of the nature of African artistic creation: 'What is striven for is to make the accidental essential; art is related to creation in the manner of a simile. It is always an example, as the earthly is a cosmic example.'[68] Indeed, the equivocal pictures of Wols force the spectator to undertake that second designation which brings out again the cosmic structure.

The renewal of African visual art is still far behind that of literature. Nevertheless the break-through has already begun: the first great artist of neo-African painting, the initiator of a visual 'négritude' is the Afro-Cuban Wifredo Lam, of whom Aimé Césaire writes: 'The painting of Wifredo Lam sails with a freight of mutiny: men filled with leaves, sprouting sex-organs turned backwards, hieratic and tropical Gods. In a society where money and machines have immeasurably increased the distance of men from things, Wifredo Lam conjures up on his canvas the rite for which they are all there: the rite of the physical union of man and world (Plate 16).

'Committing intelligence and technical skill to a unique fable-making adventure, he celebrates the transmutation of the world into myth and enchantment. He has broken with the mighty post-card lovers. Broken with those who fear that a raid on their conscience might rob them of the treasure of lazy comfort and dull rest that their bit of cunning had enabled them to acquire. Wifredo Lam did not hesitate to make himself a rebel.

'Painting is one of the few weapons that we have against the deafness of history. Wifredo Lam confirms this. And this is one of the meanings of his overwhelmingly rich painting: it stops the march of the Conquistador; it means that from now on something is happening in the West Indies, that men who were besieged by doubts, contradictory temptations and uncertain invitations, and were irresolute, have, despite nervous groping, despite inconsistencies and obstacles, found themselves. In the name of these people, in the name of those who have risen up again from the greatest shipwreck of world history, Wifredo Lam *speaks*.'[69]

Chapter 7

HANTU

History of Literature

And when 'Drum' started to beat himself all the
people who had been dead for hundreds of years,
rose up and came to witness 'Drum' when beating . . .
AMOS TUTUOLA

I. WRITING

We had our own civilization in Africa before we were captured and carried off to this land,' says Richard Wright. 'We smelted iron, danced, made music and folk poems; we sculptured, worked in glass, spun cotton and wool, wove baskets and cloth. We invented a medium of exchange, mined silver and gold, made pottery and cutlery, we fashioned tools and utensils of brass, bronze, ivory, quartz and granite; we had our own literature, our own systems of law, religion, medicine, science, and education.'[1]

Two essential cultural achievements were missing in the old Africa, however: architecture and writing. Since science has long ago abandoned all other criteria by which civilization and barbarism were supposed to be distinguished, the division of peoples into those who know how to write and those who do not is more popular than ever. Those who have writing are thought to be capable of retaining past experience and so of hastening from progress to further progress, while those without writing are said to be at the mercy of historical accident.

On the other hand, the French ethnographer Lévi-Strauss insists that nothing that we know of writing and its role in human development justifies such a view. One of the most creative phases of human development, he points out, falls in the Neolithic age, to which we owe the cultivation of the fields, the domestication of animals and other arts. In order to achieve such results, small communities of men must have observed and experimented for thousands of years, and have passed on the fruits of their reflection, even though there was no writing. And on the other hand, he points out, from the invention of writing till the rise of modern science the western world lived through 5000 years in the course of which its knowledge was static rather than increasing, for there was no great difference between the way of life of a Greek or Roman townsman and the way of life of a European townsman of the eighteenth century. Writing and cultural progress, he argues, cannot therefore be directly correlated.

But on the other hand, he points out, the rise of handwriting always stands in an immediate relation with the establishment of cities and empires, the organization of men into a political system and the formation of classes and castes. 'Writing', writes Lévi-Strauss, 'seems to favour the exploitation rather than the enlightenment of men.'[2] Its main function, he believes, is to make possible the enslavement of men. Thanks to writing, the Egyptians could summon thousands and put them to work on monumental buildings—and here is the connection between writing and architecture. According to this view, the use of handwriting for the purpose of intellectual and aesthetic satisfaction is a by-product, if not in fact only one of the means of strengthening, justifying, or concealing the fact of enslavement.[3]

This relation between writing and power appears in an especially striking way in the recent history of Africa. When the Portuguese came to Guinea, African and European culture were roughly on the same level. What the Europeans had in advance of the Africans were writing, architecture, navigation and gunpowder—and through these the power to subjugate Africa.

Why, we must ask, did the Africans south of the Sahara never until the modern age of Europe, use writing?*

* It would be wrong to ask why they did not 'invent' writing, for firstly, our writing probably was invented by Africans in Egypt and then developed further by the Phoenicians; and secondly, various scripts were constantly invented south of the Sahara also, some of which even came into limited use: the writing of the Vai, which, like the Egyptian, was a picture writing[4] , the Nsibidi, a syllabic script of an Efic secret society, and others as well.

Writing has the important function of preserving what has once been thought. Chiselled in stone, inscribed on rolls of parchment or papyrus, it fulfilled this function in ancient Egypt with pre-eminent success. There were stones there in plenty and the climate was so dry that the rolls of papyrus lasted for thousands of years. South of the Sahara, however, stones are rare, inaccessible, and hard to move. One might indeed have inscribed papyrus or tooled leather—but would this have served the purpose? Not even woodcarvings last more than a short time, for every organic substance falls a prey to the damp climate or the jaws of termites. What would be the sense in entrusting human thoughts to a piece of parchment or a piece of wood, when experience showed that these things would not even survive the scribe? In the material sense also the word is mightier and more permanent in Africa than any kintu.

On the other hand, the preservation of knowledge is only a secondary function of writing. It is more important as a means of communication. 'Writing: signs, produced by drawing, painting, scraping, scratching, or imprinting, which are employed by men in order to make a communication,' writes *Der Grosse Brockhaus*. Writing is Western culture's most important instrument for conveying information, and for thousands of years it had no other. The Africans, however, did not need an alphabet to convey information; instead they developed the drum language, which is superior to writing for that purpose. It is quicker than any mounted messenger and it can convey its message to a greater number of people at one time than telegraph or telephone. Only recently has the wireless come to excel in this respect the language of the drums.

If we take the concept of 'writing' in a somewhat broader meaning than is contained in the word derived from the verb 'to write', and, as it comes more naturally to Europeans to do, understand the concept not by its method but by its purpose, as 'signs produced and employed by men for the purpose of making a communication', then the language of the drums is a kind of 'writing'. Looked at more closely, therefore, African culture is not a culture without writing. Both western and African culture possessed writing, one an alphabetical script, the other a drum script. The alphabet can be used to preserve information longer, and the drum script can spread it more quickly.

Many African languages are of musical character and can be adequately transcribed by an alphabet only in the most circuitous fashion. When, in recent years, the Latin alphabet was introduced for African languages, it was necessary to utilize accents in order to make it possible to write the language in letters at all. Thus for example the Yoruba language has three different pitches: high, middle and low. A word like ǫkǫ (the cedilla is necessary to distinguish the open from the closed O) has a different meaning for each different pitch. Alphabetical script therefore distinguishes the high pitch by the accent Ó, the low by the accent Ò, the middle tone remains unmarked and the intermediate pitches disappear. Thus ǫkǫ means married man; ǫkǫ́, hoe; ǫ̀kǫ̀, spear; ǫkǫ, canoe. What expense, what trouble, how many auxiliary marks are necessary in order even to write a name such as Láyíko Ǫrǫ̀kúlábę̀bę̀jà. We can see from the orthography how inadequate an alphabetic script is for rendering this language. The drum script, on the other hand, is well suited to the task. The dundun, the commonest type of Yoruba talking drum, with its two membranes, of which one is beaten (referred to by Europeans, because of its appearance, as the hour-glass drum) is especially well suited to represent the Yoruba language, because it can reproduce not only all the tones but also all the modulations. For the drummer holds with his left hand the leather string that joins the membranes, and the more he stretches it the more he raises the note of the drum. Pitch is in fact more important in Yoruba than vowels and consonants. 'Just as a Semitic language is intelligible if written with the consonants only, so many African languages are intelligible if represented by their tones alone. The talking drum does not use a kind of morse system, as imagined by most non-Africans.'[5] The drum language is the immediate and natural reproduction of speech, it is a 'script' intelligible to every trained person, only it is directed not to the eye but to the ear. The young European learns in school to connect optical phonetic signs with their meaning, and in the same way the young African had formerly to learn the art of understanding the acoustical phonetic signs of the drums.

And did the drum script really handle so badly that other task of preserving information? In the earliest period of European poetry information which was considered worth preserving was put into verse and handed on by word of mouth. Rhyme, alliteration and rhythm were aids to memory; verses are more easily retained than prose. But how much more exactly does the drum script preserve the text, since, out of the structure of the musical language, it not only keeps the rhythm and melody but, in melodic and rhythmical fashion, the whole sound of the words. The drum script of the specific rhythmic pattern still summons the orishas in the santería, and calls up the loas in Voodoo. Among the Ñáñigos the encrícamo, the drummer, gives the decisive commands; and thanks to the drum script fragments of African speech have been preserved in Cuba up to the present day.[6] In Africa the official drummer was not simply a conveyor of information: he presented on ceremonial occasions news of the ancestors, most sacred Nommo, the Epics of the past. Among the Akun in Ghana he was called 'the Creator's Drummer' or 'the Divine Drummer'.[7] About his knowledge and his social standing African ethnographers like Dr. Danquah tell us: 'Drummers should become acquainted with the heroic deeds of our glorious dead and they should be versed in the traditions of the country to strengthen their knowledge of the lyrical, heroic and eulogistic verses used in drumming. . . . A drummer in the act of drumming is considered a sacred person and is immune from assaults and annoyances—nor must he be interrupted.'[8] Nketia describes the hierarchy of drummers, beginning with those who perform only for popular entertainment, up to the official drummer, who needed a training of decades. The official drummer 'is closest to the spirit of the Ancestor chiefs whom he addresses. He is in a very enviable position . . . He could be mildly unpleasant to the chief on the drums and go scot free.[7] The official drummers were the historians of Africa.

The influence of the missionaries, who tried to suppress the 'heathen' drumming, was directed especially against the highly sanctified profession of official drummer. While European historians were up in arms about the 'unhistorical' character of Africa, and were taking counsel from auxiliary disciplines, archaeology, philology, anthropology and so on, their compatriots were busy silencing the African historians and thus destroying the most reliable historical sources. Not all is lost, to be sure; recently in a great many places historical epics have been tape-recorded and transcribed. Yet countless irreplaceable works have altogether vanished.

Today the drum script is as good as extinguished. 'The tom-toms beat no longer!' writes the Liberian poet Carey Thomas. 'The jungle's never failing wireless no longer beats upon the hills.'[9] European schooling has conquered in Africa. Today, therefore, 'it is very difficult to get orikis (songs of praise) trans-lated. . . . Few educated Yorubas can still understand the talking drum. Even if one gets the drummer to give one the words the younger Yoruba will mostly find the ancient language beyond them. They have learned Shakespeare at school, but many of them were forbidden to speak Yoruba in their colleges. Since January 1955 all children aged six have been sent to school com-pulsorily; and the talking drum is not on the new curriculum.'[10]

The Africans' zeal for learning, which so delights the educators, is not the zeal of an illiterate people, to whom writing comes as a revelation. It is the zeal for learning of a civilized people whose own script has been destroyed and who therefore need a new medium for communicating and preserving information. Thus under the compulsion of events the Africans have replaced their own acoustic symbols with foreign optical ones. In the Cameroons even small children know what the new script really means for Africa; according to Matip, they call the blackboard 'that black wall where one speaks with the dead'.[11]

II. CULTURE IN TIME AND SPACE

Hantu is the category of place and time. If one wants to characterize African culture, one must not separate place and time. This sounds obvious, and is true for every culture. Yet European scholars, in treating what we call African culture, have always separated place and time. Westermann wrote a *History of Africa* and Frobenius a *Cultural History of Africa*. But the

'Cultural History of Africa' is not a history of African culture. A history or cultural history of Africa remains tied to the place, to the continent Africa, to which, however, in consequence of the course of history, or of the temporal component of Hantu, African culture is not limited. That extra-African part of African culture which survived and developed on the American continent is usually treated in its purely temporal aspect, as 'History of Slavery' or 'History of the Emancipation of the Negroes'. The spatial component, namely Africa as starting point, as a conscious cultural heritage, as the true home of the exiles, is ignored, and where relationships are needed, where ways of living, thinking or acting are to be interpreted and explained, the term 'Negro' is used instead of 'African', so that the historical relations are lodged in the individual, and cultural traditions are falsely translated into racial traits. In this way the African has become the 'Negro'—understood as a designation not of skin colour but of a person who feels, thinks, reacts, dances, paints and writes poetry in such and such a way.

The word 'Negro' is applicable only where—as so often in North America—'Negro' and 'non-Negro' are distinguished only by the colour of their skins, not by their culture. Strictly speaking, no adjective can be formed from the word 'Negro', for such a term ('Negroid') would carry with it the assertion that human culture is a biological datum like the culture of bees.

In the preceding chapters, above all in those on Voodoo and Rumba, we have cited sufficient examples to make it clear that Afro-American culture belongs to African culture and that we may consider the two together. This does not mean that there are no differences between Ruanda and Haiti. There are differences also in Western culture between Lisbon and Moscow; and between San Francisco, Hammerfest, Vladivostok and Sydney there are the greatest possible variations.

If we ignore pre-history, the history of African culture can be divided into the following periods:

1. *Antiquity*. Nubians penetrate into the Nile valley and there found Egyptian culture, which, favoured by the oasis character of the country, endeavours to seal itself off on all sides.[12] Into the Nile valley, which is harder to defend on the north and north-

west than on its other boundaries, foreign invaders—Lycians, Libyans, Assyrians, Persians, Greeks, Romans, Hyksos—occasionally make their way.[13] The early conquerors are assimilated and accept African culture, but at the end of its age-long history the country succumbs to the Romans. Its culture fructifies the cultures of the Near East, of the Mediterranean peoples.

2. *Middle Ages.* As in Europe, the rest of the continent had failed to keep step with the people on the shore. As in Europe also, Medieval culture had to be constructed anew out of the heritage of antiquity. Europe had an easier task in this; it was favoured by the climate and retained its ancient areas of culture, Greece and Italy, within its cultural circle, while for Africa Egypt was lost. The drying up of the Sahara cut Africa off from foreign influences, while Europe was open to the Near East, so that near Eastern and ancient (Greek) influences flowed in on it, above all through Moorish Spain. Struggling with an inhospitable and hostile Nature, who did not permit the use of an alphabetical script, African culture reached in the middle ages a level which was materially only a little inferior to Europe, and ethically probably superior, for African standards of law and faith were not only striven for, as in Europe, but actually lived by every individual.

3. *Modern times.* Europe discovers Africa. The discoverers are received with friendliness and repay this friendliness badly. They transport people from Africa to America. In order to spare their own subjects, the rulers on the African coasts make alliances with the slave traders and organize attacks on the interior. One people is inflamed against another, unceasing civil wars tear the continent apart and the prisoners are brought to the ships. The morale is lowered everywhere, general chaos and tyranny spread. Nevertheless, in those areas which are not affected by the slave hunts or which take part in the exploitation and so become prosperous —for example, Benin—African culture produces great achievements. On the whole, however, the era of the slave trade is a time of decline. The continent suffers as much as its enslaved and kidnapped members. Richard Wright says: 'For every hundred of us who survived the terrible journey across the Atlantic . . . 400 of us perished. During three hundred years—the seventeenth,

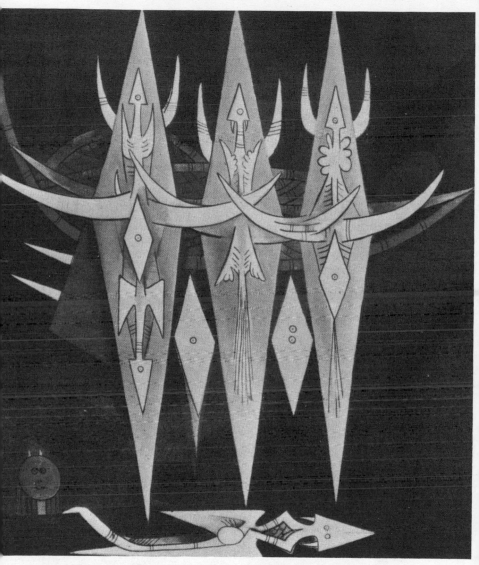

15. *Umbral*. Oil-painting by Wifredo Lam, Cuba, 1950. (Photo: Marc Vaux)

16. *The Jungle*. Gouache by Wifredo Lam. (Museum of Modern Art, New York)

eighteenth, and nineteenth centuries—more than 100,000,000 of us were torn from our African homes.'[14]

Slave trade and a slave economy made an important contribution to that wealth which enabled the Western World to build its modern civilization. 'The European Renaissance was built on the ruins of Negro-African civilization,' writes Senghor, 'American power grew fat on Negro sweat and blood.'[15] 'London, Paris, New York, Amsterdam,' writes Césaire, 'all these cities surround us like stars, like victorious moons. But consider under their repose and their dignity and their equilibrium and their movement and their noise how much was needed of my nervousness, of my panic, of my cries of eternal torment and beads of sweat from my sweating face to make that.'[16]

In 1791 the slaves of Haiti rebelled and in twelve years of war fought through to freedom. Between 1807 and 1830 the slave trade died out. In 1833 slavery was abolished in the British colonies, in 1848 in the French colonies as well, in 1865 in the United States, in 1888 in Brazil. Yet the exploitation of Africa and the Africans continued by other means. Colonialism, discrimination and segregation serve the same purpose and they persist up to the present day. The view is indeed spreading gradually that Africa and the Africans have a right to independence and self-reliance. And in all these periods the best forces of the West have, at first ineffectively, but with increasing success, opposed the exploitation and its methods.

The Africans who were shipped off to America, whose families were torn apart, who were individually auctioned, treated as chattels and thrown together into working groups, lost in this process the languages of their ancestors and adopted in large part the languages of the slave owners. The slave owners did not reflect on this change, for they did not think of African languages as languages, but as noise or stammering, means of communication among animals, like the barking of dogs and the twittering of birds. Recently, on the other hand, it has repeatedly been asserted that the Afro-Americans abandoned African culture along with their African languages, and travelled into the new world without cultural baggage, so to speak. Since they express themselves in European languages, they are said to belong not to African but to European culture. In European culture the language, the mother tongue, is the epitome of the national heritage; through it a European nation understands its own cultural unity. A European emigrant who gives up his mother tongue and teaches his children another language sets himself adrift from his native culture and enters another culture. And the struggle of Europeans overseas for schools teaching the language of their homeland, is the expression of their devotion to a particular cultural heritage.

In African culture, language does not have this weight, for Nommo, the word, precedes the image. The vocable as such is not loaded with ideas, it is not the carrier of sensations, it is not idea or image in the European sense. It is only the phonetic script for an object and has therefore no cultural value in itself.[17] Only the muntu gives it cultural significance, when he makes of it a word-seed or image. If he changes his vocabulary and creates images from the new vocables in the same way as in the former language, he has nevertheless preserved the essence of his language, the creative transmutation of the material of speech. It is not the vocabulary, but the way of using speech that is his real language. Kuntu, the way or manner, is an independent force. It is in Kuntu that the character of African culture is expressed.

In the Afro-American world some hybrid languages have arisen: Creole, Surinaams, Papiamento and others, which are generally designated as dialects. Creole counts as spoiled French, Surinaams is also called Negro-English. The vocabulary consists predominantly of European words, but the syntax and word formation follow the rules of African grammar. It is wrong therefore to call these languages 'spoilt' English or 'spoilt' French. If one considers the essence of a language to be its vocabulary, Creole and Papiamento must be called the youngest of the Romance languages, Surinaams must be called the youngest of the Germanic languages. But if one considers the grammatical structure of a language more important than its vocabulary, then the three languages mentioned do not belong to the Indo-European group. In the light of African culture, which places function ahead of object, for which Kuntu is more important in concrete life than Kintu, Creole, Surinaams and Papiamento must be described as neo-African languages.

Thus we see clearly that it is unimportant in this context, what language an author happens to employ. Whether he was born to a European or an African language one may not accuse him of 'betraying his mother tongue' if he speaks a European language. Nor can one simply include his works in modern African literature because the author of these works does not have a white skin. Whether the work of an author, whatever his colour, belongs to Western or to African culture, depends on whether we find in it those criteria of African culture which we have set forth in the preceding chapters. The fact that so far very few white authors belong to African culture is due to the fact that there were scarcely any who were aware of these criteria. This may change in future.

Where African and European culture overlap—and that is the case today both on the African and the American continent—two groups must be distinguished in modern African literature and poetry. The one, despite European influences, preserves African traditions in more or less pure form, and more or less consciously, but would like to get free of them. We shall call this group the conservative-African or residual African. The other group consciously revives its African heritage, and we call it therefore renaissance-African or neo-African. Residual African and neo-African elements may overlap and intensify one another even in a single work. This is true not only for literature, but also for religion, dance and art.

III. RESIDUAL-AFRICAN LITERATURE

The history of African literature corresponds to African history. Ancient Egyptian literature will have to be investigated in order to discover to what extent the criteria of African culture are preformed in it. Various authors, the Senegalese Sheikh Anta Diop, the Nigerian Olumide Lucas and others, basing their view on linguistic comparisons, derive traditional African culture directly from the ancient Egyptian.[18] The extent to which this is justified would have to be investigated through comprehensive comparative analyses of style. The literature of the African Middle

Ages, insofar as it escaped destruction, would have to be collected, translated into visual script and classified according to type. It would also be necessary to investigate the extent to which the Arabic literature produced in the Sudan and in East Africa by African authors from the seventh to the nineteenth century belongs to African or to Islamic culture.

In Africa, as in America, modern African literature begins with the acquisition of the Latin script. Since both African and European languages use this script, it would be necessary to investigate all these works according to the criteria we have established and to classify them accordingly under African or European-American literature. In this connection it is possible that the works of many authors who are to be counted unequivocally with African culture also play, by virtue of their influence, an important role in European literature.

All these investigations would exceed the scope of this book and must therefore be reserved for a history of African literature. But I do want to give here a survey of modern African literature and poetry, to point out the principal trends and groups, and mention the most important names.

In America as in Africa, modern African literature begins shortly before the turn of the century. In South Africa the Xhosa writer Samuel Edward Krune Mqhayi writes his songs of praise and a story; in Haiti in 1884 Oswald Durand writes his first poem 'Choucoune' in Créole; in 1893 Paul Laurence Dunbar of Ohio publishes his first volume of verses, *Oak and Ivy*, containing verses in the dialect of the North American Afro-Americans. The writings of North American Negroes before Dunbar were exercises without literary value. In Haiti Durand had a great number of predecessors who wrote verses of some merit, but despite their patriotism these belong entirely, in style and language to nineteenth-century French literature, which they have taken as their model.

The first great modern African author is Thomas Mofolo of Basutoland. He is the first African author who takes account of the new age. His parents were Christians and he grew up in mission schools. In 1904, after he had earned his teacher's diploma and had learned cabinet-making, he became a proofreader at Morija, where the Paris Evangelical mission published religious works. It was as a proofreader in Morija that he wrote his three books, the first of which appeared in 1906 in the mission's periodical *Leselinyana*. Written in Sesuto, it is the story of *The Traveller to the East*, which later appeared in English under a false title. It begins: 'In the blackest dark, which was very black, in the time, when the tribes devoured one another like wild beasts, there lived a man named Fekesi.'[19] Fekesi, a chief's son from Basutoland, is seeking for truth. He leaves his home, journeys on adventurous roads to the East, where he hopes to find the truth which visions have promised him. On the sea coast he collapses and is nursed back to health by three Europeans in their ship, taken back to Europe and brought back again on their next journey. During the voyage he has many conversations with the strange white men. They ask him where he is going and he answers, 'The place I go to is . . . where God lives.'[20] They answer, 'Among all the lands there is no such land. Moreover God does not live on the earth. He lives on high in the heavens, above the clouds, the stars and the sun. We pray to God when we are on earth; and he hears us. We abide by His laws and His commandments. . . . That is the reason why we took such care of you when we found you. . . .'[21] 'Fekesi was full of joy when they explained all these things; he felt that most of the things they told him were the very things he was looking for. He asked them questions about their government and their customs; but most of all he asked about things touching the word of God.'[22] Fekesi's attitude to the Europeans is the attitude of the young Mofolo himself: 'He was taught to read and write. His heart rejoiced exceedingly; when he found that the things he was seeking exist; and even others which he did not know. He accepted all they told him, he believed them.'[23]

Thomas Mofolo accepted everything they taught him; he believed them. He glorified Christianity in *The Traveller to the East*, and he condemned paganism in his novel *Chaka*, the first historical novel of modern African literature. Chaka is the first great king of the Zulu, the black Napoleon. Mofolo makes Chaka ally himself with sorcery, and this drives the king through one bloody deed after another to mass annihilation. 'When Chaka had

given his full consent the witch doctor began his work . . . He
. . . inoculated him on the chest, and rubbed in the medicines
with his eyes shut . . . The doctor said this was a fine medicine
to bring good fortune . . . The second thing the witch doctor did
was to pierce Chaka's forehead just where the hair began, and to
lift up the skin. Then he inserted a medicine made of a little
powder mixed with part of a crocodile's brains. While he did this
hurriedly his eyes were staring; he said that this was the medicine
of chieftainship. . . . The witch doctor said he had not the remaining medicine with him; it was one that caused bloodshed and
murder. "It is very evil, but of great power. Choose." "I desire
it," said Chaka. And now the decision had been made; of his own
free will Chaka had chosen death in place of life.'[24]

Although Mofolo equates sorcery with death and condemns it,
the missionaries saw in this novel a reversion to paganism and let
the manuscript lie unpublished for twenty years. Disappointed
by their narrowmindedness, Mofolo left them and stopped
writing. But he did not lose his faith in the good cause of the
Europeans. He displayed an industry that was positively American on behalf of the new age, travelled about, solicited labour for
the diamond mines, opened a steam mill, acted as postman and
trader and bought himself a farm in East Griqualand. When he
came to feel the injustice of the white world for which he had
lived, his spirit was broken. A Christian in his inmost being, he
resigned himself. He uttered no word of revolt.[25]

Mofolo's biography is as it were the biography of all modern
African literature, which begins with Christian belief and then
turns away disillusioned—though not in resignation. With
Mofolo's black and white drawing, in which the blacks are black
as pitch and the whites are white as snow, we have the beginning
of a whole literature of tutelage, supported by missionaries and
colonial officials, which still has its authors today, especially in
South Africa. If they do not chose to escape political pressure by
taking refuge in historical themes, animal stories and tales of
hunting, they produce novels like *Jôhannie giet die Beeld*, by
Arthur Nuthall Fula, a South African Bantu who writes in
Afrikaans. It is a novel in which even the evil practices of the
South African policy of Apartheid are justified. Nothing is said

of the police terror, the lawlessness, the low wages. But Fula
turns all the more sharply against the few amusements left to
Africans in the wretched slums of the Union. ' "Now, Maringo,
let's dance." "No, old man, I'm done with that—that is the voice
of the devil that lures men here onto the slippery slide." '[26] After
further instructive experiences Maringo says: 'I am now really
afraid of dancing and the cinema. The dazzling lights and plea-
sures only hide temptations, suffering and tears.'[27] Dancing,
movie-going and the enjoyment of drink are the three devils
against which the hero of the novel wins his victories. Now and
then he does touch on a genuine problem. 'You say we must
return to the land. But where is the land to which we must
return?'[28] Fula and his hero leave us without an answer. Instead
they pray.

Even authors like this, however, who are trying to soothe and
pacify their compatriots in the service of the ruling power, do for
the most part attach themselves to the African tradition of story-
telling and so write in a sure and vivid style. But none of them has
attained the stature of Mofolo. Their failure to criticize the
Europeans is a conscious silence, a voluntary justification, where-
as Mofolo, shut off in the bosom of the mission from every Western reality, could see, and so unconditionally respect, only the
bright side of his European masters. His passion is genuine, his
purity without stain, his integrity absolute. When he left the ideal
world of the mission and came closer to reality, he wrote no more.

Yet it is not the integrity and honesty of his faith that places
Thomas Mofolo in the ranks of world literature, but his style.
Even though he accepted unreservedly the conceptions and
valuations of the European world, he had no extra-African
literary model except the Bible, and so he reached back to the
African art of story-telling, Mofolo carried further the epic tradition of his own people and provided it with new material.

Mofolo's period, the first quarter of the twentieth century,
Peter Sulzer calls 'the golden age of Bantu writing'.[29] In this
period Zakea D. Mangoaela, a friend of Mofolo's, wrote his
hymns, *Lithokotsa marena a Basotho*, as well as animal stories in
the Sesuto language, and among their compatriots Azariele M.
Sekese wrote humorous-satirical animal stories, David Cranmer

Theko Bereng a long epic poem about the great Basuto chief Moshoeshoe and Everitt Lechase Segoete two partly sarcastic stories in which the life of the past is contrasted with the moral degeneration of the present. In London, during the first world war, the Bechuana writer Salomon T. Plaatje, one of the first to write in English, composed an extensive report on the life and treatment of the Africans in South Africa, which contains some stirring scenes. The story of his historical novel *Mhudi*, also in English, is well told, but weak in comparison with other works, for Plaatje tries to individualize his characters in the European fashion and thus the African pathos of the dialogue becomes empty.

'A period of rich literary harvest,' writes Sulzer of the Bantu literature of South Africa, 'was followed at the end of the twenties by a period of extreme sterility. Calm prevailed after the first clap of thunder.'[30] It was no accident that the calm began when in 1924 the party of Boer nationalists under General Hertzog took over the government of the Union for the first time.

Meantime in North America that period had begun which has been called the 'Negro Renaissance'. It was the time after the first world war when 'black became fashionable'. After the great old masters Paul Laurence Dunbar and James Weldon Johnson, who, at the turn of the century had created folk poetry with artistic merit out of Afro-American folklore, the second generation came to be heard in the twenties, with Langston Hughes, Countee Cullen, and the Jamaican Claude McKay. Dunbar and Johnson had proceeded from the Spirituals in full sounding verses through which swung the ecstasy of hope. Johnson's 'Negro National Anthem begins:

> *Lift every voice and sing,*
> *Till earth and heaven ring,*
> *Ring with the harmonies of Liberty;*
> *Let our rejoicing rise*
> *High as the listening skies,*
> *Let it resound low as the rolling sea.*[31]

Here is the pathos of the revivalist preacher, the imperative style, the intensification through repetition; here is Nommo, which transmutes the old Biblical images into new, living, actual

images. Here is the same responsibility of the word as in the old
spiritual,

> *Go down, Moses,*
> *'Way down in Egypt's land,*
> *Tell ole Pharaoh*
> *To let my people go!*[32]

Johnson himself is a Moses, who speaks for his people as Secretary of the NAACP. We shall call this style the 'spiritual style'.

The second generation has lost this deep voice. It is related
not to the spirituals but to the blues. Its form is small and subtler
and more European. Claude McKay likes to write sonnets with
paradoxical tunes and charming bits of impertinence, which
tickle the public without offending them. But one knows just
how far to go. The white public, which applauds Negro poets at
evening parties as one would dancing poodles or horses that do
sums, likes to hear impertinences that are not *too* impertinent.

Thus Countee Cullen writes of a woman who

> *Even thinks that up in heaven*
> *Her class lies late and snores,*
> *While poor black cherubs rise at seven*
> *To do celestial chores.*[33]

Is this 'sorcery' or are these adaptations, imitations and subtleties
to show that 'I am the dark brother . . . I, too, am America . . .'[34]
I too am human; rhymes, jokes—please, may I make them too?

The 'Blues style' or 'Harlem style' lies at the extreme boundary of African culture and for a large part no longer belongs to it.
Yet there is more of residual African culture here than one would
think at first glance. There is the responsibility, the 'I' of the
speaker and the image of the river in Hughes' poem 'The Negro
talks of rivers':

> *I've known rivers:*
> *I've known rivers ancient as the world and older than the flow*
> *of human blood in human veins.*
> *My soul has grown deep like rivers.*
> *I bathed in the Euphrates when dawns were young.*
> *I built my hut near the Congo and it lulled me to sleep.*[35]

And there is the antiphonal African style in Hughes' 'Midnight in the Negro bar':

> *Shut and wiggle*
> *Shameless gal*
> *Wouldn't no good fellow*
> *Be your pal.*
> > *Hear that music . . .*
> > *Jungle night . . .*
> > *Hear dat music . . .*
> > *And the moon was white . . .*
> *Sing your blue songs*
> *Pretty baby*
> *You want lovin'*
> *And you don't mean maybe.*[36]

The paradigmatic quality is lost here; the personal experience is in the foreground, even though the social function has not been dropped. The poet often takes more delight in description, in characterization. Description is more than an instrument. Yet again and again in the verses of Langston Hughes we get flashes of purely African imagery.

> *A Bright bowl of brass is beautiful to the Lord.*
> *Bright polished brass like the cymbals*
> *of King David's dancers . . .*
> *A clean spittoon on the altar of the Lord . . .*[37]

There is no blasphemy in this: the spittoon (Kintu) is transformed by the word (Nommo) into a sacred object.

From the Spiritual, the blues style or Harlem style took over the Biblical analogies, from the Blues the 'melancholy' mood and tragi-comic tone. On the whole it is sad and plaintive and begs for pity. Especially touching are the little genre pictures from the life of messenger boys, the spittoon cleaners in 'Brass Spittoons',[38] the 'Trumpet Player',[39] the 'Minstrel Man',[40] of Langston Hughes, the scullery maid of Waring Cuney in 'No Image',[41] the 'Banjo Player'[42] of Fenton Johnson, the 'two brown boys in a Catholic church'[43] of Frank Horne. The Harlem style was the weeping of the enslaved in a time of laughter, a defiance of the human creature, without any assurance of victory, without hope, but with a longing to be set free.

> *You, too, will suffer under Pontius Pilate*
> *and feel the rugged cut of rough-hewn cross*
> *upon your surging shoulder—*
> *They will spit in your face*
> *and laugh . . .*
> *They will nail you up twixt thieves*
> *and gamble for your garments.*
> *And in this you will exceed God*
> *For on this earth*
> *You shall know Hell . . .*[44]

The verse of the Harlem style is no 'Negro Renaissance'. It is the plaint left from the great tumult, the legacy of the time of confusion that vanished forever in the great crash of 1929.

In the thirties Afro-American poetry in North America became more American in style during the crash, 'the crash that sent Negroes, white folks, and all rolling down the hill towards the work progress and administration',[45] Langston Hughes tells us in his autobiography *The Big Sea*. The tone becomes sharper, not only the plaint but the accusation makes itself heard. The pathos of the preachers becomes the pathos of the agitators. The verses gain in direct force and realism, but lose in imagery and transforming power.

> *They weigh the cotton*
> *they store the corn*
> *we only good enough*
> *to work the rows;*
> *they run the comissary*
> *they keep the books*
> *we gotta be grateful*
> *for being cheated . . .*

writes Sterling A. Brown.[46]

The toughly accusing, arresting realism of those poets, of whom Frank Marshall Davis, Sterling A. Brown, Robert Hayden and Melvin B. Tolson are the most significant, and whose works we may group together under the designation of 'agitation style', leads directly to the prose realism of Richard Wright.

Wright's first book, *Uncle Tom's Children*, a collection of four stories, or rather, short novels, which appeared in 1938, puts him in the first rank of North American narrative writers. His next novel, *Native Son*, the story of the fate of the Africans, *Twelve Million Black Voices*, and his autobiography, *Black Boy*, won for him world-wide renown. Each of his books does indeed set an example, yet neither his style nor his thought is African. Western literature possesses in him a great writer, but to African literature he does not belong.

To sum up: the literature of tutelage on the one hand and the North American spiritual, blues, and agitation styles on the other all exhibit a tendency to move away from African cultural traditions. In every one of these groups, the names of which do not imply any value judgement, the residual African elements decrease the further we go in time. Mofolo and Hughes and Wright are authors of world-wide standing and all three are 'black'. Mofolo's works belong entirely to African, and Wright's entirely to Western culture. In Mofolo we have *only* and in Wright *no* residual African elements. In the 'spiritual style' the African component predominates, and in the 'agitation style' the Western. In the 'blues style' of Langston Hughes' poetry the two elements are evenly balanced.

IV. Neo-African Literature

Shortly after the first world war a French civil servant in the colonial service in Ubangi-Shari wrote a novel, *Batouala*, which took up the cause of the oppressed Africans. The author was an Afro-American from Martinique who had studied in Bordeaux. In 1921, when the novel won for him the Prix Goncourt, he was forced to leave the colonial service. Since then René Maran has been living in Paris, where he has written many other works. *Batouala* is the first book in which a non-African consciously writes in the African way. For many pages his style remains wholly European, above all when he is engaged in political argument, but then again he succeeds, for example in the description of the chase, in casting spells with words in the African way. He is a forerunner of 'Négritude'.

Afro-Cuban lyric poetry originated in Cuba in 1928 with the 'Rumba' of José Zacarías Tallet, with Ramón Juiraós' 'Bailadora de Rumba' and Nicolás Guillén's first volume of poetry, *Motivos del són,* all consciously dependent on local folklore. At the beginning were descriptions of folk dances in the rhythm of the rumba, but soon African images flare up:

> *Your forest sign,*
> *with your red corals,*
> *your bracelets of curved gold,*
> *and this dark crocodile*
> *swimming in the Zambesi of your eyes*

we read in a poem by Guillén.[47] 'Submarine men reborn in trees,' writes Baquero.[48] Guillén, Ballagas and Arozarena are the masters of this type of lyric poetry. It is the refutation of the 'African soul', of the 'rebirth of Africa out of the soul': 'Ballagas is white, Arozarena is black. The fascinating rhythm swings out over all Latin America. Luis Palés Matos in Puerto Rico, Adalberto Ortiz in Ecuador, Solano Trinidade in Brazil, León Damas, Martin Carter and Jan Carew in Guiana, Virginia Brindis de Salas in Uruguay, and many others have taken up and elaborated their method.

Césaire's poem 'Cahiers d'un retour au pays natal', which introduced 'Négritude', appeared in Paris in 1939 and was unnoticed. Although it was overlooked in Europe, it must have exercised an immense influence in Africa and the West Indies, for when it was re-published in 1947 with a preface by André Breton, and caused a sensation, the poets of 'Négritude' with their poems composed in the African spirit were already there: Damas in Guiana, Tirolien and Niger in Guadeloupe, Laleau and Roumain and Camille and Brière in Haiti, the Africans Senghor, Birago Diop and David Diop, and the three writers from Madagascar, Rabéarivelo, Rabémananjara and Ranaivo. Had they all simultaneously rediscovered Africa? Had Césaire pushed open a dam? One thing is certain: the African method of verse-writing was for them all beginning, liberation and avowal all at once.

'Négritude' was a beginning: authors were embarking upon a journey, they were making a beginning which was to have, and could have, no end. For 'Négritude' was liberation: these authors were freeing themselves from the European paradigm. If nearly everything that had been written in the colonies had till then been subjected to European standards, if Europe with its literature had furnished the model for thought and style, these European values and examples were now cast aside. 'Négritude' was avowal: avowal of Africa. It became permissible to think and write in the African way; Africa was rediscovered, re-awakened; from now on African culture was to, and did, furnish the standards. Enthusiastically, these writers embraced African traditions—and lo and behold, they restored a libelled and despised culture—and themselves—to dignity. They became free.

Once this road was taken, there was no going back and no choice. Henceforward anyone who followed European models would be a lackey, a bootlicker, deserving only contempt:

> *And here are those who do not console themselves for being made*
>   *not in the image of God but of the devil,*
> *those who consider that being a Negro is like being a second-class*
>   *official: waiting for better and with the possibility of rising*
>   *higher,*
> *those who capitulate to themselves,*
> *those who live in a little cellar of themselves,*
> *those who flaunt their proud pseudomorphosis,*
> *those who say to Europe: See, I know like you how to make*
>   *courtesies,*
> *how to present my respects, in short, I am no different from you;*
>   *pay no attention to my black skin, it is the sun that has*
>   *burned me.*
> *And there is the informer Negro, the askari Negro, and all these*
>   *zebras shake themselves in their own way to make their*
>   *stripes fall off in a dew of fresh milk.*
> *And in the midst of all that I say Hurrah! my grandfather is dying,*
> *I say hurrah!*
> *The old negritude is gradually becoming a corpse.*[49]

Thus 'Négritude' could not be the phenomenon of a particular time. Once for all it took the stain from Africa; it demonstrated that poetry and literature were not only possible in the African manner and out of an African attitude of mind, but that only such poetry was legitimate and only such poetry really found a hearing —even in Europe. 'Négritude', therefore, is at bottom not a 'style', but an attitude: the practical application of the extremely obvious knowledge that every artist achieves his best work when he attaches himself to his own tradition. 'Négritude' is nothing more nor less than the conscious beginning of neo-African literature.

If, then, similar features of style occur, as in Césaire and the poets of 'Négritude' whom Senghor gathered in his famous anthology, and since then in nearly all writers in Africa, the West Indies and Latin America, we cannot say that these writers are influenced by 'Négritude', nor that they are disciples of Césaire. One or the other may indeed have been stimulated by Césaire, Senghor, and the rest, but this is by no means necessary. 'Négritude' has broken the spell that had lain over all things African, and now no African or Afro-American writer need be ashamed any longer to create works directly out of the African tradition. 'Négritude' has restored the legitimacy of belonging to African culture.

Therefore we call the recent writers who have since appeared not writers of 'Négritude' but simply neo-African writers as such. The process of 're-Africanization' reaches far: Africans like Tutuola (Nigeria), Dei-Anang (Ghana), Okara (Nigeria), Mbiti (Kenya) or Mopeli-Paulus (Basutoland) may never have read a line of the poets of 'Négritude'; they write directly out of the African tradition. Depestre (Haiti), Calixte, Carbin and Glissant (Martinique), Bolamba (Congo), Tchicaya U Tam'si (Central Congo), Dadié (Ivory coast), may be influenced or stimulated by 'Négritude' or they may, like Vesey and Mason (United States), McFarlane (Jamaica), Telemaque (Trinidad), Carew, Carter and Seymour (British Guiana), have found their own way back to their African cultural heritage.

Not all the works of these poets are of the same intensity, of the same importance and certainty in their re-adoption of African tradition. If, however, we arrange them according to dates of publication, we find that the African elements are increasing, and increasing to a greater degree, the greater the writer's talent.

The same is true of the novelists, for whom 'Négritude', which was at first expressed purely in lyric poetry, could not have been a direct stimulus, especially of the non-Africans, the great story tellers of the West Indies, like the Haitians Pierre and Philippe Marcelin, Cinéas, Trouillot, Roumain, Saint-Amand and Alexis, the Jamaicans Reid, Mais and Hearne; Glissant, Tardon and Zobel of Martinique, the Barbadian Lamming, the Trinidadian Selvon, the Ecuadorian Ortiz. Lamming, Selvon and Reid elevated the West Indian dialect to a literary language and thus achieved more than local colour—immediacy, imperative style, magical, ideogrammatic images and African rhythms become more and more prominent. In Selvon's novel the rhetorical narrative style is intensified, and Victor Reid's novel *New Day* is narrated altogether in Jamaican dialect; his second novel, *The Leopard*, which takes place in Kenya and makes an epic of an episode in the Mau-Mau movement, convinces the reader, not because Reid furnishes documentary details of East African customs, but because he understands African philosophy in all its depth and makes it come to life. African rhythmics with its primary and secondary rhythms determine the architecture of this book, which excels the works of Mofolo in intensity, although Reid is free of Mofolo's Christian affiliation. He writes: 'The doctrine of brotherly love which the white man preached from his god was like the wings of the ostrich. No ostrich has ever flown by his wings.'[50] Even the most un-African of the West-Indian novelists, Hearne, whose first novel, *Voices under the Window*, tells an individual story in entirely European form, in his third novel, *The Faces of Love*, sets a society of the future in which there is no longer any race question quite simply in the present, and uses indirectly that imperative present which is one of the characteristics of African culture. If this particular trait is not sufficient to justify his inclusion in neo-African literature, at least it does illustrate the general tendency to Africanization in Caribbean literature.

V. MODERN LITERATURE IN AFRICA

In Africa itself it is difficult, in the case of many authors, to make a neat division between 'residual African' and 'neo-African' elements. Since education is controlled by the missions and a Christian upbringing and the knowledge of a European language give the graduate a higher social standing, a young person with a gift for writing is subjected from the first to strong European influences. If he writes in his mother tongue, there is a prospect of publication only if his work is of use to the missions or can be used for instruction in the schools. These authors are Christians and make the missionaries' point of view their own. Thus the 'literature of tutelage' has its greatest authors, as we have already shown, at the beginning of this century. Yet this genus does find its continuation still in South Africa after the 'calm', since the Africans there cannot express themselves freely. 'The Bantu writer feels it above all as a handicap and an unbearable limitation of his freedom that he must as far as possible avoid taking a stand on political questions if he is to find a publisher. "Manuscripts should be suitable for use in schools and should therefore deal neither with political nor with church conflicts" is a condition laid down by a publishing house for coloured writers opened in Johannesburg in 1953. A novel by the Zulu historian R. R. R. Dhlomo, which is concerned with the African-Indian unrest in Durban in 1949, remains unpublished.'[51] Many writers therefore retreat into history, whether to eulogies, or—like Mofolo—to the novel. Dube, Fuze, Molema, Jordan, Segoete and others write historical tales; Jolobe, Vilakazi and Tayedzerhwa write poems. Now and then there is a flash of criticism between the lines, as in the novel *Headman's Enterprise*, written in Cewa by Samuel Yosia Ntara. We read there, for example: ' "You have done well," said the European. "Now the reason for my coming is tax. We are going to look after this land and we want to find men who will go and take employment at Blantyre. They will work for a period and will then get a chit to certify that they are free of debt to the Government." "Have you then," asked Msyamboza, "found any men?" "I have indeed: men have come to me to be enrolled to go for work at Blantyre." '⁵² In another part of the book the central figure, Chief Msyamboza, has to part with his wives in order to become a Christian. He does it with the words: ' " I have fired this gun today as a sign that from now onwards I shall follow Jesus! You, my wives, all of you! I put you away for Jesus' sake and I do not wish to leave out even one of you all since it is my life and your lives that are concerned. I know that you will have anxiety and sorrow but I cannot give up honouring Christ who is the Master of Life. I have no cause of any sort against you. What I do I do according to the desire of Jesus that I may receive freedom and release in my heart through his love! Farewell!" '⁵³

Thanks to the historical material and the Bantu languages in which these authors write, much of the genuine African tradition remains.

The South African writers who use the English language are subjected to the same compulsion. The most important are the brothers Herbert and R. R. R. Dhlomo, Silas Modiri Molema and D. D. T. Jabava. Katie Mandisodza (really Katie Hendriks) has written a gay autobiographical novel. Arthur Nuthall Fula writes in Afrikaans. The 'literature of tutelage' is not limited to South Africa, but it is a sign of immaturity outside the Union as well. The author is practising the foreign language, follows foreign models and expresses his thanks to his teachers.

> *Thank you*
> *sons and daughters of Britannia*
> *you gave me hospitals,*
> *you gave me schools,*
> *easy communication too,*
> *your western civilization.*⁵⁴

That is how the Nigerian Dennis Chukude Osadebay begins his poem 'Young Africa thanks'.⁵⁴ But most writers soon pass this stage—only in Africa are pupils expected to learn not for living but for their teachers—the young talents take issue with their time, and then criticism begins, the discussion of religious and political questions. We shall call this group the 'literature of emancipation'.

This literature is written in European languages. The writers at first may follow European models and find their strength in debate. But from one work to the next most of them take on more and more of African tradition, especially in recent years since the poetry of 'Négritude' has lifted the ban and made the tradition respectable once more. This finally leads to the complete acceptance of African tradition, first among the lyric poets, and then also in the great story-tellers, until finally the European elements are simply assimilated as necessary materials into neo-African poetry and prose. There is a smooth transition from the 'literature of emancipation' to neo-African literature.

Of the South Africans only three belong to this group, Mopeli-Paulus, a Basuto chief who works with English collaborators, and the two emigrants Peter Abrahams and Ezekiel Mphahlele. Abrahams could only start writing when he had been hired as a stoker and reached England after a two-year voyage. Even his first novel, *Mine Boy*, shows his complete craftsmanship, the economy and responsibility in the use of language. 'The traditional African narrative', writes Senghor, 'is woven out of everyday events. In this it is a question neither of anecdotes nor of things 'taken from life'. All the events become images, and so acquire paradigmatic value and point beyond the moment. None of the actors is in the European sense an individual confronting society. Every figure represents in the first instance a type, it is paradigmatic, like an African mask.'[55]

That is just how Peter Abrahams tells a story. *Mine Boy* portrays a young man who comes from the country and goes to the mines at Johannesburg; *Wild Conquest*, a historical novel, treats the struggle of the Matabele against the Boers, and in *The Path of Thunder* a young Negro and a Boer girl pay for their love with their lives.

Mopeli-Paulus takes issue with the South African race question as well as with the abuses of tradition in his homeland. In *Blanket Boy's Moon* a miner, and in *Turn to the Dark* a teacher become involved in a ritual murder. Mopeli-Paulus also writes poetry.

In his autobiography, *Down Second Avenue*, Ezekiel Mphahlele treats his own life as a symbol of the situation in South Africa. Just because he tells the story without passion, almost without reproach, every experience becomes a paradigm, every personal oppression a general experience. 'It is the lingering pain of a past insult that rankles and hurts me more than the insult itself,'[56] he writes, when he has escaped from the coercion of the Union, about a freedom which is still new to him. 'I, breathing the new air of freedom, and now the barrel of gall has no bottom any more. I shall soon know what to do with this freedom.'[57]

We should expect to find a greater number of significant writers in South Africa if there were more freedom there. And conversely, the number and type of writers in other parts of Africa can be inferred from the conditions in each area. In the Spanish areas there is not a single author, since, as the Spanish Colonial Ministry wrote me, 'the characteristics of the society in our African territories are not favourable to the individual expression of poetic feeling.' In the Portuguese areas there are a number of poets writing in Portuguese; in Angola, Ósar Ribas, Agostinho Neto, Mario Pinto de Andrade, Virato da Cruz and Antonio Jacinto; in São Tomé, Francisco José Tenreiro and Alda do Espírito Santo; in Moçambique, Noémia de Sousa. Andrade's anthology of Africans writing in Portuguese includes twenty authors, also from Portuguese Guinea and the Cap Verde Islands. In East Africa Shaaban Robert and Sahele Kibwana (Tanganyika) write in Swahili, and the young story-teller Mbiti (Kenya) in Kibamba and English. In Ruanda Kagame wrote a long Biblical epic in Kinyaruanda. In the Congo we need mention only the poet Bolamba and the young novelist Lumani-Tshibamba, who received a prize for his novel *Ngando*.

Writers are numerous only in West Africa. Cameroon has three important novelists. In *Une Vie de Boy* and *Le Vieux Nègre et la Médaille* Ferdinand Oyono, a pre-eminent word sorcerer, pictures with biting irony and pitiless precision the weakness of prominent Europeans as well as of Africans. Both novels are African satires in French prose, alternating almost from one sentence to another between jest and earnest; this is neo-African realism. Benjamin Matib describes the disturbances caused in a village of the Cameroons by the outbreak of war in 1939. Mongo Beti, who wrote his deservedly successful first novel *Ville Cruelle* under the name Eza Boto, portrays in his novel *Le Pauvre Christ de Bomba* a missionary, seen through the eyes of his faithful servant, who comes to see that the mission he has built up over many years is only bringing disorder and evil to the country. When the priest asks himself why the people are no more receptive to Christianity than they were twenty years ago, his African cook answers: 'The first of us who came flocking to religion, to your religion, came there as if to a revelation—that's it, as a revelation of your secret, the secret of your power, the power of your aeroplanes, your railways and so on . . . the secret of your mystery in fact. . . . Instead of that, you started to talk to them about God, the soul, eternal life, and so forth. Do you think that they didn't know about that already long before your arrival? . . .'[58] It is not such arguments, however, that move the priest to close his mission, but his conscience and his Christian responsibility. He recognizes that the mission has no chance as long as it 'sits in the same boat' as colonialism.

In his novel *Doguicimi*, the Dahomey writer Paul Hazoumé draws, with ethnographic accuracy, an impressive picture of the old kingdom of Dahomey, Bernard B. Dadié, of the Ivory Coast, writes stories as well as poems, and also a biographical novel, *Climbié*. In his second novel, *O Pays, mon Beau Peuple*, Sembène Ousmane (Senegambia) tells how an African returns home with his European wife. The first novels of Jean Malonga (Central Congo) and A. Sadji (Senegal) give reason for some hope. The most significant narrative writer of French Africa is Camara Laye of High Guinea. His autobiography, *Enfant Noir (Dark Child)*, which describes his childhood between initiation and school, in his father's goldsmith's workshop and at the rice harvest, has already won him the Charles Veillon prize. His second novel, *Le Regard du Roi (The Radiance of the King)* is, to date, the high point of neo-African literature in French prose. In an action which is symbolic from beginning to end, a European exiled by his own people is 'delivered over' to Africa and as it were initiated into African thought. First doctrines are expounded to him. Alongside a beggar he watches the procession of the African King, whose arms and legs are heavy with gold. ' "He is young and he is fragile," said the beggar; "but at the same time he is very old and very strong. . . . If he were less laden with gold, no doubt nothing would keep him among us." "Why would he leave you?" said Clarence. "Why would he not leave us?" said the beggar. "Do you imagine he is made for creatures like us? But the weight of that gold chains him." "The gold . . ." said Clarence bitterly. "Gold can also be something besides gold," said the beggar. "Is gold among white men nothing but gold?" . . . "We throw ourselves avidly upon the tiniest speck of gold." "Yes, at the beginning, when you came, we thought gold was your food. But gold can also be one of the signs of love, if love attains its purity. It is that sort of gold which holds the king a prisoner, and that is why his arms are so heavily laden.'" [59] The European Clarence entreats the beggar to get him employment with the king, any employment at all. The beggar goes and returns. 'Clarence tried to read the face of the beggar, but he could read nothing; he had been too short a time in the country and was not used to deciphering black faces. "Well?" he said. "I am sorry," said the beggar. "There is no post you could fill." "But I would have taken any post at all!" "I know, but he hasn't any." "The very smallest would have satisfied me," said Clarence. "Alone," he thought, "I find myself each time a little more alone!" And he realized that despite himself he had been nursing a last hope; he had stayed there on the Esplanade out of despair, and yet, despite all his rebuffs he had not altogether given up hoping, and it was this reflection of hope—a reflection only, for one could not properly call that obscure remnant that had survived a hope—it was this wretched remnant, this miserable phantom, that he was now pursuing. "I could . . ." he said. But what could he have done? What did he know? "A simple post as drummer, for example . . ." "That is by no means a simple post," said the beggar. "The drummers are of noble rank, and with us this position is hereditary; certainly you could have beaten the drum, but that is not what counts; your beatings would not make any sense. There too, one must know. You are a white man!" "I know that," said Clarence. "It is useless to tell me it over and over; I have known it longer than you. You distress me, in fact . . ." "Yes, but the whites think they know everything," said the beggar, "and what do they know?" '[60]

And after a long conversation the beggar says: ' "Perhaps I

made a mistake when I presented your request. . . . Perhaps I should not have said that you were ready to take any employment; for one might perhaps distrust a man who was ready to take up any post at all since that would indicate that at the same time he was not really fit for any of them." '61 The usual pedagogic relationship of Europe and Africa is here reversed: here the European is the pupil, who must learn justice and pass examinations. Image succeeds image, often to the vexation of Clarence, the European. None of his scales of value hold any longer, they fall away from him, he senses his own nothingness, where, in this strange world of African wisdom, he fails again and again. When at last he understands that he is nothing, when in extreme humility he appears naked before the king, the king covers him with his robe. The king too is a symbol. He is happiness, merit, favour, grace, king and redeemer, all in one. Camara Laye reckons the sum of all religion, all humanity in this novel—and behold: at the bottom they are all equal.

The poets of French Africa were enumerated above in the discussion of 'Négritude'. In Ghana we should mention Dei-Anang and Efua Theodora Sutherland (Morgue), in Nigeria Gabriel Okara, Wole Soyinka, and Mabel Imoukhuede, and the novelists Chinua Achebe and Cyprian Ekwensi. Ekwensi's first novel, *People of the City*, is not yet free of journalism. Achebe's first novel, *Things Fall Apart*, presents the collapse of a traditional village community as a tragic defeat. In the Yoruba language there are the poets Adeboye Babalola; Sola Adekambi and Oladele Ajao and the story-teller Daniel Olorunfemi Fagunwa, whose works, such as *Ogboju Ode Ninu Igbo Irunmale* (*The brave hunter in the zombi wood*) are written from the same source as the stories of Tutuola.

Tutuola has created the purest expression so far of neo-African prose. What others had sought to achieve through moulding language, fell into the lap of his naiveté. Compared with Reid or Salvon his style sounds like a first effort; yet compared with Laye, Tutuola remains purely African even in diction. And he does not try to take issue with the western world; he simply borrows the necessary materials which he assimilates into his own purely African world. Tutuola writes English without taking over the way of thinking characteristic of European languages. He fits European objects, modern customs, even economic forms, seamlessly into his mythological world. Taxes are paid there—for the rental of fear; death is purchased for £70 18s. 6d.; a terrible voice sounds out of a big room 'as if a lot of people were talking into a big tank'; then a 'half-bodied child' speaks lightly 'like a telephone'. In the hall of the merciful mother, a kind of fool's paradise, all the lights are in technicolour and change every five minutes. The sober materials of the technological age are transformed in these strange contexts and are turned from objects of technology into subjects of magic. They too are only bintu, 'things', which are transformed by Nommo. Thus they acquire existential powers which they do not possess in themselves. A tension arises between the thing and its function, and since Tutuola sees everything from the point of view of function, this distorts the original thing in ironical fashion. In other words, in the hierarchy of the ontological system of forces which Tutuola presents to us, the achievements of western technology appear on the level of magic toys, which have only humble functions like frightening and surprising and which are easily overcome by forces of a higher order—such as beauty.[62]

Surveying the fifty years of modern African literature, we may say that it began with the rejection of the African tradition and the emphasis on Christianity, but turned further and further away from Christianity, and has now returned to the African way of thinking.

Chapter 8

BLUES

The Conflict of Cultures

To keep from cryin' I opens my
mouth an' laughs.

LANGSTON HUGHES

I. RESIDUAL AFRICAN ELEMENTS IN NORTH AMERICA

The peculiar development of African culture in North America began with the loss of the drums. The Protestant, and often Puritan, slave owners interfered much more radically with the personal life of their slaves than did their Catholic colleagues in the West Indies or in South America. The slaves were allowed no human dignity and their cultural past was ignored; or else it was considered a humane task to educate them into being 'better' human beings, and this process was initiated by teaching them to be ashamed of their African heritage. And to forbid the drums was to show a keen scent for the essential: for without the drums it was impossible to call the orishas, the ancestors were silent, and the proselytizers seemed to have a free hand. The Baptists and Methodists, whose practical maxims and revivals were sympathetic to African religiosity quickly found masses of adherents.

Their nearness to God, their intimately personal relation to Him, and their ecstatic possession by the Holy Ghost won the highest praise for the converts in many Christian circles. People talked of the renewal of Christianity, of a 'fervour of faith akin to early Christianity',[1] and the like. And certainly, the intensity of this religious feeling cannot be doubted, but the question whether it is really Christian might well provoke some theo-

logical dispute. According to Christian doctrine man designates
by the word God that unworldly-supraworldly (transcendent)
reality, by which he knows that the experienced world including
his own being is governed and sustained.[2] But of what sort is the
transcendence of the Christian God in the Negro churches of the
United States, when the Pulitzer Prize winner Gwendolyn
Brooks in one of her poems makes the preacher murmur at the
end of his sermon:

> *Picture Jehovah striding through the hall*
> *Of His importance, creatures running out*
> *From servant-corners to acclaim, to shout*
> *Appreciation of His merit's glare.*
> *But who walks with Him?—dares to take His arm,*
> *To slap Him on the shoulder, tweak His ear,*
> *Buy Him a Coca-Cola or a beer,*
> *Pooh-pooh his politics, call Him a fool?*

Gwendolyn Brooks' preacher positively feels sorry for the
Good Lord, because—to use our Haitian expression—he has to
remain 'Bon Dieu' and is not allowed to become a loa like his
son Jesus or the Holy Ghost. The revivalist ceremonies in the
Negro churches, which no one describes better than the Afro-
American poet James Baldwin in his novel *Go Tell it on the
Mountain*, contain so many residual African elements, that the
comparison with the Arada rite of Voodoo is inevitable. However,
we are concerned here with the differences. In the first place the
drums are missing. The percussion instruments are replaced by
hand-clapping and foot-stamping. But no polymetry can be produced in this way and there are no specific formulas permitting
the invocation of a number of loas. The singing is therefore
directed to the *one* Christian divinity, to whom the sermon was
also addressed, and the faithful, usually many of them at a time,
are 'ridden' by a single divinity. The procedure which in the
African orisha cult evokes ecstatic immobility, and in Haitian
Voodoo different types of ecstatic movement, produces, in the
Negro churches, 'mass ecstasy'.[4]

A faith, like African art, is an attitude. It is the relation between
men on the one hand and one or more divine or deified beings on

the other. In Christianity this relation is unequivocally determined by God alone: God created man, commanded him, forbade him; God enlightens, punishes and redeems him. The bond of man with God (*religio*) is expressed in man's obedience. In African religion this relation is reversed: *religio*, active worship, 'creates' God, as the expression 'She Orisha'[5] puts it: that is, the living person (muzima) in his active worship installs the divine being as such. Analogously to the designation of an image[6] we may speak of the *designation of divinity*. Necessarily, therefore, this divinity must be other than transcendent, for it is concretely present during the act of worship—or better, it is produced by the congregation during the act of worship. This occurs in the African cults, in Haitian Voodoo, in the Cuban santería, in the Jamaican pocomania, in the Brazilian macumba,[7] in the Winti cults of Guiana and in the Negro churches of the United States. But while the cults of the West Indies and South America have remained polytheistic, through the equation of the loas and orishas with saints (the equation is a pure act of designation), the Negro churches perform the designation of a single divinity.

With the designation of a Christian God Christian standards penetrate the cult, above all the sharp separation of good and evil; but the nature of worship, the *service* of God, remains to a great extent African. For God is not only served but invoked, called up and embodied by the faithful. As in art, so also in religion, the Kuntu is unchanging and remains the hallmark of African culture. Even the Christian images are treated in prayer in the African manner. Thus an old woman in Baldwin's novel *Go Tell it on the Mountain* prays: 'Lord, sprinkle the door-post of this house with the blood of the Lamb to keep all the wicked men away.'[8]

Musically, the change is expressed by the fact that with the loss of the drums, the polymetry which carries polytheism is lost, and all that remains is polyrhythm, which is constructed on the basis of a single metre. The hymns of Christian European origin used by the missions are Africanized, producing *jubilees*, 'original songs of praise, in which, as they are sung stanza after stanza, a more and more marked Africanization takes place, sometimes leading in the end to sporadic outbreaks of possession'.[9] Kuntu, the manner of singing, remains African, and where European melody and harmonics begin to penetrate, in the ballads, spirituals and blues, this becomes apparent through the fact that the African *way* of singing alters the melody in many ways unknown in Europe. First of all there is that melodic technique which Dauer calls 'heterophony of variants', impromptu variations by means of 'singing separately', for which in classical jazz 'the misleading title "improvization" has become widespread'.[10] Then there are changes of tone, of intonation, of pitch and timbre, variations, paraphrases and slurring of the text and many other African devices which Dauer expounds in detail.

Nor did the Afro-Americans have to wait to learn melody and harmony from European Americans. The very first slaves brought to America and passed on to their descendants their own tonality, harmony and a rich treasure of musical means of expression. 'If in this connection anything had surprised them in "white" music,' Dauer believes, 'it would have been at the most the fact of an amazingly large tonal and harmonic kinship.'[11] Yet the familiarization of the Afro-Americans with European church music (which was by no means always voluntary) produced 'a perceptible approach to the European melodic form and a new type of Afro-American harmony'[12] in the true spirituals, which differ considerably from the concert hall spirituals as they are presented by concertizing Negro choirs and soloists. For between 1860 and 1870 University choirs like the Fisk Jubilee Singers or the Hampton Student Singers began to collect spirituals in great numbers, to 'purify' them of 'ugly and unlovely' Africanisms and then to copy and record them in choral fashion. Through this 'purification' all the basic elements were destroyed.[13] The definiteness prevents designation, Nommo cannot take shape or be given shape; in the concert hall Kuntu freezes into a dead form. The true folk spirituals, on the other hand, are residual African folk art, and the part played in their origin by Christian influences is still considerably exaggerated.

The secular parallel to the jubilee and the spiritual is that music which is usually so completely misunderstood: the blues. 'A white song—black: that is, reduced to a simplified formula, blues.'[14] This is a widespread view. People also think that the *blue notes* and the modulation of tone exhaust the African part of the blues.[15] What is correct in all this is the fact that the blues did originate from the contact of African and European music. How the different contributions are divided, in what way these two very different styles affected one another, Dauer has described and determined. It is not the formula of the blues that is the true hallmark of blues but the sequence of voices, which is founded on the African antiphony. 'This consists in appeal and answer and explains the division of phrases in blues singing, as well as the function of the individual phrases. In the simplest case the phrase sequence runs A B and corresponds to the functions of an appeal and an answer. In the 12-beat blues, which have become classic, the sequence runs A A B, which corresponds to two appeals and one answer.'[16] Only in the blues the separate events of appeal by the first singer and answer by the chorus are 'consolidated into a single event, since they are all executed by a single voice'.[17] One song *in* the community becomes one song *before* the community, for the community is now only a listener. Instead of a chorus answering the singer, there are instruments accompanying the singing. In Africa the drums lead the singer's performance; one might say that the song accompanies the drums. In the blues this relation is reversed. First there is unaccompanied singing, then in the course of the development the instruments are added, but they are only accompaniment and the singing remains the most important part of the performance.

The texts of the blues follow the African narrative style almost entirely. They stem from the Afro-American ballads, which in turn continued the tradition of the African fable. 'In the fable', writes Senghor, 'the animal is seldom a totem; it is this or that one whom every one in the village knows well: the stupid or tyrannical or wise and good chief, the young man who makes reparation for injustice. Tales and fables are woven out of everyday occurrences. Yet it is not a question of anecdotes or of "material from life". The facts are images and have paradigmatic value.'[18] The boll weevil ballad, which comes from Texas, may serve as an example.[19] The weevil is the arch enemy of the cotton planter.

Fahmah say to de weevil
'whut makes yore head so red',
weevil say to de fahmah
'it's a wonder ah ain't dead,
lookin' foh a home, lookin' for a home!'

Nigger say to de weevil,
'ah'll throw yo in de hot san'!'
Weevil say to de nigger
'ah'll stand it like a man,
ah'll have a home, ah'll have a home!'

Say de Capt'n to de Mistis
'what do yo think ob dat?
Dis Boll Weevil done make a nes'
inside my Sunday hat;
he will have a home, he'll have a home!'

The weevil, which bores into the bolls of cotton with its proboscis, is the plantation worker in his eternal search for a home. In the farmer's Sunday hat, his best piece of property, the weevil will have a home. Here again is the imperative future, which, in the form 'has made a nest', is set back into the perfect tense but means that the weevil *is to* make a nest there.[20] It is the same technique that Césaire uses. The ballad is a song that invokes liberation; in the most harmless fable it conceals the call to rebel.

The old ballad was later turned into a blues song, for the two types fade imperceptibly into one another. In the Boll Weevil Blues the weevil then becomes the living symbol of liberation.[21] The blues cannot therefore be reduced to the formula: 'a white song—black'; for both textual and musical structure stem from African traditions.

Nor are the blues 'sad', although the legend of 'melancholy' blues has been influential for a century and for a couple of decades there have in fact been melancholy blues. In accordance with the common view we do indeed find in the *Negro Caravan* of 1941 the statement: 'In contrast to the spirituals, which were originally intended for group singing, the blues are sung by a single person. They express his feelings and ideas about his experience, but they do this so fundamentally, in an idiom so recognizable to his audience, that this emotion is shared as theirs.'[22] But this is the exact contrary of the real situation.

For the blues singer does not in fact express *his* personal experiences and transfer them to his audience; on the contrary, it is the experiences of the community that he is expressing, making himself its spokesman.[23] Even when there is talk of loneliness, of the beloved who has run away, of the neglected wife, of nostalgia for the South, it is not the personal experience that is emphasized, but the typical experience of all those rejected by society in the Negro districts of the North. And even though indirectly, the note of rebellion is always heard too:

> *I'd rather drink muddy water, sleep in a hollow log,*
> *dan to stay in dis town, treated like a dirty dog.*[24]

The melancholy is a camouflage, the 'plaint' hides a *com*plaint.

If we read the text of the blues songs without prejudice and notice the double meaning, which all authors emphasize, we find them mocking, sarcastic, tragi-comic, tragic, dramatic and accusing, often crudely homorous—there is only one thing that they are only exceptionally, and then usually when they have been turned into a cabaret number, and that is—melancholy. Yet we read in the *Negro Caravan*: 'The mood is generally a sorrowful one; the word "blues" is part of the American vocabulary now as a synonym for melancholy, for unhappy moodiness.'[25] This widespread misinterpretation has various causes. The *blue notes* characteristic of the blues, which go back to the middle pitch of the West African tonal languages,[26] and have a modality between sharp and flat, sound sad to European ears. Besides, we are accustomed in Europe to interpret poetry and music psychologically as expressions of an individual soul. For African art, on the other hand, this means a confusion of means and meaning. Of the Afro-American *Work Songs*, which go back to the traditional form of communal work, and which are called *dokpwe* in Dahomey, *egbe* in Yoruba, *coumbite* in Haiti, *troca dia* in Brazil, and *gayap* in Trinidad, even Dauer writes: 'The basic law of the work song is to increase energy through music. Its effect consists in turning work into a kind of game or dance which in turn invokes an excitement that cannot be produced by pack mule work. This excitement increases energy and when reduced to a form that excludes all unnecessary movements itself becomes a driving force. The constant sequence of game and dance distracts the mind from the burdens of labour, the evenly rhythmic singing and playing becomes a (pretended) reality, work goes on automatically, and becomes subconscious.'[27] This interpretation of Dauer's correctly perceives the effects but not the causes. Song and dance do not have the purpose of lightening the work, but in song and dance Nommo is doing the real work, and conjuring up the latent forces of nature, while the work itself is only an addition.[28] The meaning of the work lies in the song and dance; they are not a purposive means for the end of lightening the work, even though their influence has that effect. The song is not an aid to the work, but the work an aid to the song.

The same is true of the blues. The blues are sung, not because one finds oneself in a particular mood, but because one wants to put oneself into a certain mood. The song is the Nommo which does not reflect but creates the mood. And this mood is melancholy only from the romantic point of view current since the time of the abolitionists. The picture of the poor slave full of yearning, singing his sad song, corresponded to the mood awakened by Harriet Beecher Stowe with *Uncle Tom's Cabin*. Much as we may admire the sentiments of the abolitionists, we must not overlook the fact that they saw the slaves as alienated, helpless beings who were longing for freedom but ought not to rebel: enslaved by white men, they should also be set free by them. So they were drawn as patiently suffering lambs, helpless, pitiable and sad. Help and support was to be given the slaves, but from agitators one kept one's distance and tried to pacify them. This attitude was apparent as late as the beginning of this century in the generous help that was given to the pacifist Booker T. Washington, while every possible obstacle was put in the way of W. E. B. DuBois, who made rigorous demands.

The abolitionists opposed their picture of the sad slave with his melancholy songs to the picture of the willing, confident, happy slave which the slave owners habitually drew. For the latter, the song of the disenfranchised sounded by no means melancholy;

they considered it the expression of a carefree and happy mood. But both pictures are distorted. Frederick Douglass, the runaway slave, writes in his autobiography the telling sentences: 'The remark is not infrequently made, that slaves are the most contented and happy labourers in the world. They dance and sing, and make all manner of joyful noises—so they do; but it is a great mistake to suppose them happy because they sing. The songs of the slave represent the sorrows, rather than the joys, of his heart. Slaves sing to *make* themselves happy rather than to express their happiness through singing.'[29] The blues do not arise from a mood, but produce one. Like every art form in African culture song too is an attitude which effects something. The spiritual produces God, the secularized blues produce a mood. Even there residual-African Nommo is still effective.

II. STATES OF CONFLICT

The blues lie at the boundary of African culture, where residual African elements pass over into American. They are always in danger of crossing the boundary but are held back by their musical traditions and mode of singing. Where, however, the song becomes a poem which is no longer sung, but written and printed, Africa is hardly even a memory. The poetry of the 'blues style' lives on both sides of the boundary. Often the 'I' no longer means a 'we', and the exemplary expression on behalf of a community becomes the expression of individual feeling.[30]

Nevertheless the poetry stands closer to the African tradition than the prose. The Afro-American novelists have almost entirely adapted themselves to North American style. These writers often differ only in the colour of their skins from their European-American colleagues, and so the colour of their skin and the prejudice, contempt and oppression which accrue to them because of it form the theme of their books. The characters of their novels are split personalities who are struggling with their true selves and who furnish material for the widespread view that a split personality results from the conflict of two cultures.

It is not in the United States, however, where with a few exceptions only vestiges of African culture are still alive, and where even these are becoming more and more adapted to western forms—it is not there that two cultures come into conflict, but in Africa. In Africa men with European education do indeed stand between the civilizations.

> *I'm tired*
> *I'm tired of hanging in the middle way*
> *—but where can I go?*[31]

writes the Nigerian poetess Mabel Imoukhuede. And the Ghanaian Dei-Anang says:

> *Here we stand—*
> *poised between two civilisations*
> *Backward? To days of drums*
> *And festal dances in the shade*
> *Of sun-kist palms.*
> *Or forward?*
> *Forward!*
> *Toward?*
> *The slums, where man is dumped upon man? . . .*
> *The factory*
> *To grind hard hours*
> *In an inhuman mill*
> *In one long ceaseless spell?*[32]

This either-or is usually put before the African by the European with the demand that he make up his mind; and since there can be no turning back, he expects the answer that will make the African his pupil. This question corresponds to the schema which we mentioned at the beginning of our argument.[33] But the question is falsely put. Césaire said of it at the first world congress of Negro writers in Paris: 'They demand of us: "Choose . . . choose between loyalty, and with it backwardness, or progress and rupture." Our reply is that things are not so simple, that there is no alternative. That life (I say life and not abstract thought) does not know and does not accept this alternative. Or rather that if this alternative presents itself, it is life that will take care of its transcendence. We say that it is not only black societies that have to face this problem; that in every society there is always an equilibrium, always precarious, always in need of remaking, and in practice always remade by every generation between the new and the old. And that our black societies, our civilizations, our cultures will not escape from this rule. For our part and for that of our particular societies, we believe that in the African culture to come or in the para-African culture to come, there will be many new elements, modern elements, elements if you like borrowed from Europe. But we believe also that there will survive in that culture many traditional elements. We refuse to surrender to the temptation of the *tabula rasa*. I refuse to believe that the African culture of the future can oppose an end of total and brutal non-acceptance to the ancient culture of Africa. And to illustrate what I have just been saying permit me to use a parable. The anthropologists have described what one of them proposes to call cultural fatigue. The example that they cite deserves to be recalled, for that example rises to the level of a symbol. This is the story: it takes place in the Hawaian Islands. Some years after the discovery of the islands by Cook, the king died and was replaced by a young man, the prince Kamehameha II. Won over to European ideas, the young prince decided to abolish the ancestral religion. It was agreed between the new king and the high priest that a great festival would be organized and in the course of the ceremonies the taboo would be solemnly broken and the ancestral gods annulled. On the appointed day, at a sign from the king, the high priest hurled himself upon the divine images, trod them under foot, and broke them, while a great cry was heard: the taboo is broken. Several years later the Hawaians did indeed welcome the Christian missionaries with open arms. The sequel is known. It is the most complete case that we know of a cultural subversion preparing the way for enslavement. And then I ask if that renunciation by a people of its past, of its culture, is what they expect of us? I say simply: among us there will be no Kamehameha II!'[34]

Accordingly, African literature takes issue with the age, follows the traditional style even in European languages, and as we have shown in the chapters on Nommo and Kuntu in the cases of Tutuola and Laye, assimilates European elements to the

African conception. In Peter Abrahams, Ferdinand Oyono, Mongo Beti and many others there may be passionate discussion of an African revival, of technology, progress and independence and of the place of tradition within the synthesis still to be produced—but the human being always remains sound. There is much talk to the effect that the African has been uprooted through the intrusion of western civilization—but the literature shows little indication of this. The African suffers, fights, rebels, seeks new paths, but he is not neurotic. There is a division of choice, an uncertainty of content, but existence is not split apart. Even where the traditional social order is shattered, where as in the slums of Johannesburg a new black proletariat has grown up, the individuals themselves have for the most part remained sound and well. Peter Abrahams, the great South African writer, in his novel *Mine Boy*, describes how an African woman named Leah fights for her existence against the inhuman oppression of apartheid. One night a stranger stands at her door seeking shelter. Abrahams characterizes the figures in brief dialogue: ' "Sister, do you know a place where a man can rest and maybe have a drink?" His voice was deep and husky. "It is late," the woman replied. "It is very late," the man said. "Make a light for me to see you," the woman said. "I have no matches." "What have you?" "Nothing." "And you want to rest and drink when it is so late?" The man inclined his head, but the woman could not see in the dark. "Have you money?" "No." "Huh. You're a queer one. What are you called? Are you new here?" "Xuma. I come from the North." "Well, Xuma from the North, stay here and I will be back with a light." ' [35] After the light has tested him Xuma from the North is given shelter in the house in which Leah is in charge of several people. ' "Then you can go to sleep," Leah said. Dladla and Ma Plank went out. Only the man who had been silent throughout remained. He looked at Leah and then at Xuma. "What is it?" Leah asked him. "How do we know he's not from the police?" "I know," Leah replied and her whole face creased in a smile.' [36]

Psychological explanations are not necessary. Soul image and apparent image are identical, the meaning is revealed in the sign. Personalities recognize one another, and the boundaries are clearly marked. The conversation comes around to Leah's husband. ' "Yes," she repeated softly. "My man. He's in jail. He's been there for one year, and he must stay there for another two years. He killed a man. A big man with a big mouth who tried to kiss me. He is strong, my man, and he fights for his woman, and he kills for his woman. Not like Dladla who is all mouth and knife and nothing. He's a man, my man. You are a man yourself, Xuma, you are strong. But my man can break you like a stick! I don't lie, you can ask people . . . Here," said Leah, going into the little room, "this is where the teacher lives but she will not come till day after tomorrow so you can sleep here." She struck a match and lit the candle. "And listen to me Xuma from the North, don't you think because I do this I am soft or easy and you can cheat me, because if you do, I will cut you up so that your own mother will not want you . . ." Xuma laughed. "You are a strange woman. I don't understand you. The only thing I can understand is your kindness." "You're all right," she said softly. "But the city is a strange place. Good night." '[37]

The people in Abrahams' novel are fighting against race madness and against oppression but they have no inferiority complex. They move from the country to the city, from village society to industrial society, as one exchanges a loin cloth for an overall. They remain the people they are, retain their values and their style, even if the struggle for existence forces on them new rules of play. They assert themselves in race society but do not accept it. There is no part of them which admits the rightness of their oppressors; if they defend themselves their consciences are clear. They are far from the dividedness of the coloured North Americans. Mofolo admired the white man's notions and rejected the African tradition. Recent African writers do not do this. Peter Abrahams describes the forces which are creating in Africa a modern, but an African society. The whites are for him not gods but fellow human beings, whose technology one accepts and whose arrogance one rejects. The cultural conflict that characterizes Africa today does not produce any split in consciousness. The slogan of the 'dividedness of the African' is wrong. The African writer who writes in a European language is not a divided person. He uses the freedom to choose one, another or any of a thousand hybrid forms, and by his decision brings past and future each time into harmony. Every decision is a weighing up, a compromise, a harmonization of contradictories.

Thus split consciousness and all the problems connected with it arise not in African writers but in the works of those Afro-Americans who know no conflict of cultures and to whom the freedom of choice is therefore denied. For centuries Afro-Americans have had no direct contact with African culture. In tradition, education and mother tongue they are Americans and do not want to be anything else. But the full citizenship of their homeland is denied them. Their colour, which alone is reminiscent of their African descent, becomes a stain which prevents their being entirely what they in fact are, namely Americans. They protest against the unjust prejudices of their lighter skinned fellow citizens, in order to become their equals—that is, in order to share their prejudices. Their situation is tragic. There is no alternative, no possibility of a choice, of a decision. Since only their skins prevent them from being Americans like other Americans, and since they are nevertheless Americans, they would like most of all to get rid of this burdensome skin of theirs. Therefore the hatred they feel against the resistance of their environment easily becomes hatred of their own skins, hatred of themselves. Added to this is the fact that their prejudiced neighbours are unwilling to see them as Americans, but see them as American Negroes, as people who are supposed to behave childishly, deferentially, and above all submissively—a type of behaviour which contradicts the democratic American attitude. Thus a role is forced on the Afro-American: he is supposed to be someone other than himself: a 'nigger' instead of an American —and he himself wants to be someone else, namely a light-skinned rather than a dark-skinned American. The role that he has to play revolts him and the role he wants to play he is not allowed to play, yet plays it all the more. So we find in Afro-American literature countless examples of split personalities. The Afro-American flees from the role forced on him into a thousand other roles, and changes his personality, the identity of his 'I', until the individual becomes invisible.

In his autobiography *Black Boy*,[38] Richard Wright shows how from childhood on an unnatural role is forced on the young Afro-American. In Ellison's novel *Invisible Man* there is a passage in which the narrator buys a pair of green sun-glasses and a big hat and so to his amazement falls into the role of another person, which he plays with effortless perfection.[39] When he is disguised the question of the identity of the person arises, and that means, it is placed in doubt. But the role one plays, so easily interchangeable, is what others see. The person behind the role, Ellison believes, is invisible. Everyone sees into the other person what he wants to see, but never the reality. The *designation of the person* has lost its sense and meaning: still a force, it becomes negative. It is as if 'wizards' were at work: instead of constituting personalities, unauthorized 'designators' have pushed man into the shadow-existence of a role and so dissolved his identity.

The same thing happens in the novel *Go Tell it on the Mountain* by James Baldwin. After a knifing a young man is brought wounded to his parents' house. But the father refuses to see that this son Roy, whom he loves, has brought the danger on himself, directs his reproaches against the brother John and slaps the mother when she defends her boy. Then the wounded Roy sits up and shouts at his father: ' "Don't you slap my mother. That's my mother. You slap her again, you black bastard, and I swear to God I'll kill you." In the moment that these words filled the room, John and his father were staring into each other's eyes. John thought for that moment that his father believed the words had come from him, his eyes were so wild and depthlessly malevolent.'[40]

Again the confusion of identity and also the hatred for one's own self. It is not enough that others strike one, one must strike oneself also. This dividedness cannot be ignored in any of these Afro-American writers. Alston Anderson writes about the two I's in his story 'Schooltime in North Carolina'. The pupil La Verne is lying in bed and thinking of his sweetheart, the coloured girl Del, but the image of the white founder of the school, Susanne Weber, becomes confused with her in his imagination: 'I'd try hard to see Del but I couldn't so I'd open my eyes and stare into the dark. When I closed them again I could see myself as Susan Weber's husband but that wasn't the black me but the white me with wavy black hair and sideburns and a full dress suit.'[41]

Disunited with himself under the pressure of prejudice, the Afro-American is in a hopeless situation. Richard Wright gives one of the clearest pictures of this in his novel *Black Boy*. The young Richard has taken the liberty of asking his white overseers when he could learn something about the work. 'This is a white man's work around here,' is their answer, and from now on they persecute him with their hate. 'The climax came at noon one summer day. Pease called me to his workbench; to get to him I had to go between two narrow benches and stand with my back against a wall. "Richard, I want to ask you something," Pease began pleasantly, not looking up from his work. "Yes, Sir." Reynolds came over and stood blocking the narrow passage between the benches; he folded his arms and stared at me solemnly. I looked from one to the other, sensing trouble. Pease looked up and spoke slowly, so there would be no possibility of my not understanding. "Richard, Reynolds here tells me that you called me Pease," he said. I stiffened. A void opened up in me. I knew that this was the showdown. He meant that I had failed to call him Mr. Pease. I looked at Reynolds; he was gripping a steelbar in his hand. I opened my mouth to speak, to protest, to assure Pease that I never called him simply Pease, and that I never had any intention of doing so, when Reynolds grabbed me by the collar, ramming my head against the wall. "Now, be careful, nigger," snarled Reynolds, baring his teeth. "I heard you call 'im Pease. And if you say you didn't, you're calling me a liar, see?" He waved the steel bar threateningly. If I said: No, sir, Mr. Pease, I never called you Pease, I would by inference have been calling Reynolds a liar; and if I had said: Yes, sir, Mr. Pease, I called you Pease, I would have been pleading guilty to the worst insult that a Negro can offer to a southern white man. I stood trying to think of a neutral course that would resolve this quickly risen nightmare, but my tongue would not move.'[42]

The situation of the Afro-Americans in the United States is hopeless because for the most part they are distinguished from other Americans only by the colour of their skins, and often hardly by this, since 'the "Negro race" is', as Gunnar Myrdal writes in his important investigation sponsored by the Carnegie Foundation, *An American Dilemma*, 'defined in America by the white people. It is defined in terms of parentage. Everybody having a known trace of Negro blood in his veins—no matter how far back it was acquired—is classified as a Negro. Legislation in this respect tends to conform to social usage, although often it is not so exclusive. In some states one Negro grandparent defines a person as a Negro for legal purposes, in other states any Negro ancestor—no matter how far removed—is sufficient.'[43] Most of these 'Negroes' have entirely relinquished their African cultural heritage. There is no conflict of cultures and the 'race question' has to do with African culture only in so far as prejudices about it play a role in the debate. The problem itself belongs to western culture and can be resolved only within it. A book which has the aim of defining and describing African culture can dispense with its analysis. It offers a contribution to this problem only insofar as it shows that culture has nothing to do with 'race'. If African culture were tied to skin colour, the Afro-Americans would not be able to give up African culture and one would be able to see by the shade of each of them whether he belonged to African culture or not. When the Afro-American Richard Wright had visited Ghana, he wrote in the account of his journey, *Black Power*, 'I was black and they were black but it didn't help me.'[44] With as little understanding as any white-skinned American he stood before the Africans and their culture. It is therefore idle to make him, as so often happens, a star witness for African relations simply because of his colour.

Nothing shows more clearly than the North American 'Negro problem' that culture is not tied to chromosomes. Therefore one should not try to trace the character of African culture back either to physical or even psychological traits of the black race. Since history offers countless examples of the fact that on the one hand culture can be carried over and passed on, and that on the other hand it changes with the transformation of thought, the 'how', the Kuntu of a culture cannot be derived from the psychology of its bearers. When Senghor writes that the Negro is a sensual person, a being with open senses, that he is first of all sense, smells, rhythms, forms and colours, that he is sensation before vision as the white European is,[45] this attitude is indeed explicable as a consequence of African culture and the forming force of its style, but not as the physio-psychological cause of African culture, as Senghor suggests; for then the attitude would be a property, which could not be lost. For the analysis of African culture which Senghor presents, it is immaterial whether the attitude of the African is formed by the culture, or whether the culture arose from an attitude. Senghor would not really need to work with a false premise, for it changes nothing in his results. Since the attitude is directly derivable from the philosophy of the culture, there is no reason to reduce it to undemonstrable 'racial' characters. For the answer to the question why African philosophy and culture differ from other cultures, there are enough historical reasons which could be investigated, for one to do without physio-psychological arguments which are on the one hand vague and on the other dangerous.

III. EUROPE, THE PARTNER

'It is a fact: the whites consider themselves superior to the blacks,' states Frantz Fanon. This proposition is indeed a generalization, yet unfortunately in most cases Fanon is right. This arrogant assumption is sometimes given a 'racial', sometimes a cultural basis. The racial arrogance is easy to refute but hard to combat, since the majority of those who suffer from it are scarcely accessible to rational arguments. The cultural arrogance —which we must clearly distinguish from the self-consciousness which every culture needs and develops—is indeed hard to refute, so long as there is no universal standard for cultures and each, as we said at the outset, is superior to every other by its own standard; yet to objective argumentation this form of arrogance is less deaf. Only it is often unaware of itself and is frequently to be found in people who reject every form of arrogance. It is too easily hidden behind good will, unasked-for advice, or patronizing instruction.

In a world in which more than ever before everyone depends on everyone else, true partnership is a necessity of the hour and of reason. But it can come about only if every culture allows to every other its own unique nature and reciprocal influences and borrowings voluntarily follow. The attempt to force on others the acceptance of one's own views, forms of life and judgement, instead of simply offering it to them, lies so deep in the nature of western culture and of all its ideologies, that the hurtful presumption of such an attitude, especially towards Africans, is something of which the European is often unaware. 'I am the Lord and thou shalt! . . .'—so speaks in effect, the military commander, the merchant, the farmer, the tourist, the big-game hunter, the dogma salesman. So they speak, whether they want to exploit Africa or to save her. They go along and teach and baptize in the name of the Father, in the name of civilization, in the name of democracy, in the name of communism.

And the one who is addressed, the African, is asked no questions. Freedom? Equal rights? 'Yes, but only when you have been baptized in the name of Christianity, in the name of civilization, in the name of economics, in the name of democracy, in the name of communism'—according to the particular faith in question. For all these Gods are the children of the one who says: 'I am the Lord . . . and thou shalt!'

Plans are elaborated, programmes made, books written as to what is to happen to Africa, how it should be opened up, in what direction it should be led. But the Africans are for the most part ignored. Nearly everyone who writes, speaks, arranges, recommends—disposes of them, because he thinks: 'I am . . . and thou shalt!'

'A true Copernican revolution must be imposed here,' writes Aimé Césaire, 'so much is rooted in Europe, and in all parties, in all spheres, from the extreme right to the extreme left, the habit of doing for us, the habit of arranging for us, the habit of thinking for us, in short the habit of contesting that right to initiative which is in essence the right to personality.'[47]

In their rejection of this constant guardianship neo-African writers have written many lines which scarcely sound flattering to European ears. Yet we find in neo-African poetry and literature less hatred and more co-operation than the state of things would lead us to expect. Neo-African intelligence, for all the self-consciousness with which it defends its own character, has not produced an opposing arrogance of 'racial' or cultural colour. The polytheistic basis of their culture permits them to be more patient towards foreign gods. And even where hatred is heard, it is in many cases love turned to its opposite. Thus the Barbadian writer George Lamming makes a labourer who hates the English as representative of all Europeans confess: '. . . if they'd just show one sign of friendship, just a little sign of appreciation for people like me an' you who from the time we born, in school an' after school, we wus hearin' about them, if they could understan' that an' be different, then all the hate you talk 'bout would disappear . . .'[48]

On the European side, if we leave aside those who are protecting vested interests, there is more ignorance than ill-will in the case. Europe has not yet played out all her sympathies. Guardianship can still be changed to partnership. But there does not seem to be much time left for this. Lamming makes his labourer say: '. . . because we'd be remembering that for generations an' generations we'd been offerin' them a love they never even try to return. 'Tis why colonial wars will be de bloodiest . . .'[49]

Where the problems of neo-African culture are discussed, in the periodical *Présence-Africaine* in Paris, founded and edited by the Senegalese Alioune Diop, in the world congresses of black writers and artists convoked every second year by that periodical, in the poems, novels and essays of all the poets who are at the same time active politically, and of all the politicians who are at the same time poets and whom we have presented in this volume, the demands are moderate but firm. Over nearly all their publications and speeches stand as it were the verses of Césaire:

> . . . *my heart, preserve me from all hatred,*
> *do not make of me that man of hate for whom I have but hate . . .*
> *you know that it is not through hate of other races*
> *that I make myself a digger . . .*[49]

These are verses in which we hear self-control, but also concern lest the partnership striven for fail through the hardness of folly of the other side, and so force hatred to break out.

IV. CONCLUSION

Every cultural encounter stimulates comparison, demands and effects self-knowledge. The influence of European culture on African made the latter more conscious of itself and after the shock of conquest a self-consciousness developed which made possible the survival and spiritual rebirth of the culture.

How does this survival show itself in a world which can no longer dispense with railroads and machines, roads, mines and factories? One may object that the wheel necessitates roads and rails, railway travel necessitates the organization of travel, and all this necessitates a society based on division of labour and the reorganization of a society which does not correspond to these requirements. With this alteration of the society the culture is also altered; the acceptance of machines, it is asserted, necessarily produces the acceptance of the culture of its inventors.

These consequences hold, however, only for the purely material aspects of culture, not for the whole of it. 'Culture is everything,' Césaire said at the first world congress of black writers and artists in Paris. 'Culture is the way we dress, the way we carry our heads, the way we walk, the way we tie our ties—it is not only the fact of writing books or building houses.'[51]

Now African culture is, as we have shown in this book, in a special degree a culture of the 'How', of the Kuntu, while present day European culture has become a culture that emphasizes the thing, the Kintu, above everything. And the above objections spring from this emphasis. The justifiable complaints within the west, that our age of technology levels cultures, makes them too like one another, makes our world 'more boring', can be interpreted as an appeal to give more meaning to Kuntu once more. To this appeal we find an answer in African culture, which has Kuntu to offer, while European culture helps Africa to acquire the things of which it stands in need. If western culture reflects on itself, it cannot, precisely in view of the machine age, wish for the destruction of African Kuntu. On the contrary, in a world where ends are sought without regard to means or—at the opposite extreme—no end is sought at all, nothing would be more valuable than a revivified style in which sense and meaning are once more fully expressed. The Africans and Afro-Americans who were born into and raised in the western world have known and felt this discomfort, from which western culture suffers. So they have also developed a sense of calling in the conviction that they have a joyous message to bring from African to western culture. 'For who would teach rhythm to the dead world of machines and guns? Who would utter the cry of joy to awaken the dead and the orphans at dawn? Tell me, who would restore the memory of life to the man of disembowelled hopes?'[53]

It is here that African intelligence sees its task, and out of the consciousness of being able to give as well as needing to receive, comes the African's faith in the future, his victorious optimism:

> *For it is not true at all that the work of man is finished,*
> *that we have nothing more to do in the world*
> *that it is enough that we should set ourselves in the steps of the*
> *world*
> *but the work of man is only beginning*
> *and it remains for man to conquer every immobilized prohibition*
> *at the corners of his zeal*
> *and no race possesses the monopoly of beauty, intelligence, force*
> *and there is room for all of us at the rendezvous of victory.*[53]

The enlivenment of existence which is expressed in the creative attitude of Kuntu and which makes possible a new designation of the meaning of the world, may be the contribution of Africa to the world culture of the future. 'A new rhythm will penetrate the world, an unknown colour will settle in the rainbow,'[54] writes Paul Niger.

Since culture is tied to a particular conception, but not to a special psyche or a special race, men and nations can accept and adopt other cultures in whole or in part. Usually a person takes over in early childhood the culture into which he is born, the culture which is set before him in his home and environment. Yet, if he will, he can act like Kamehameha II, throw off his past, let himself be re-educated and adapt himself fully to foreign ways. The Africans could become 'black Europeans' if they wished. But they do not want to do so, as their representatives unanimously insist. Nor do they wish to preserve their inherited culture in all its details. But they do want to preserve its basic conception, of which they have become conscious in their contact with other cultures. According to this conception Kuntu is of higher value than Kintu and so they gladly alter things and their organization yet keep their own style. They are convinced that it is not the thing which determines the style and the person, but that man through his style can and must give things a meaning, that the dignity and force of man lie in his capacity to give meaning to things, even when the things themselves were made for an explicit purpose.

Without this common will of African and Afro-American intelligence African culture would indeed be in danger. But the will to self-assertion is documented in the products of neo-African culture, of which some parts have been presented in this book. There is evident in them also an irrepressible will to freedom, because an independent cultural conception can be shaped and actualized only without guardianship from outside.

NOTES

CHAPTER 1

1. Cf. Jaspers, K., *Vom Ursprung und Ziel der Geschichte*, Frankfurt am Main, 1955.
2. *ibid.*, p. 53.
3. *ibid.*, p. 76.
4. Malinowski, p. 24.
5. *ibid.*, p. 157.
6. *ibid.*, p. 153.
7. *ibid.*, p. 161.
8. Friedell, vol. I, p. 13.
9. Frankenberg, pp. 465, 461.
10. Fanon, F., *Peau Noire Masques Blancs*, Paris, 1952.
11. *ibid.*, pp. 114 f.
12. *ibid.*, pp. 115–19.
13. *ibid.*, pp. 120 f.
14. *ibid.*, pp. 122 f.
15. *ibid.*, pp. 125 f.
16. Senghor 1, pp. 49 f.
17. Fanon, pp. 129 f.
18. *ibid.*, p. 131.
19. *ibid.*, pp. 133 f.
20. *ibid.*, p. 26.
21. Cf. Ch. V, p. 141.
22. Fanon, p. 141.
23. *ibid.*, p. 24.
24. Friedell, vol. I, p. 3.

CHAPTER 2

1. Herskovits 3, pp. 42 ff.
2. The Reports of the Lords of the Committee of Council appointed for consideration of all matters relating to trade and foreign plantations, London, 1789.
3. Quoted from Ramos, p. 92.
4. Moreau 2, pp. 44 ff.
5. Cf. Williams, p. 106.

Notes

6. Dorsainvil in an address to the historical and geographical society of Haiti in 1924, quoted from Williams, p. 99. Cf. Dorsainvil 1, p. 48.
7. Price-Mars 1, p. 32.
8. *ibid.*, pp. 37 f.
9. *ibid.*, p. 119.
10. Williams, p. 106.
11. Leiris 2, pp. 22 ff.
12. Marcelin, M., 1, 2; Maximilien, L.
13. Alexis 3; Deren, Maya; Rigaud, Milo; Rigaud, Odette; Métraux 2.
14. The gourd rattle comes from the Shango cult which will be described in Chapter 3. But in Dahomey an *asson* is not a gourd rattle but a metal symbol which stands on an altar or is carried before the king.
15. Métraux gives a different description, according to which only those of the same rank dance with one another. The accompanying picture shows how two houngans grasp one another by *both* hands (Métraux 2, pp. 70, 75).
16. Dauer 2, p. 21.
17. Rigaud, O., p. 44.
18. Dauer 2, p. 50.
19. *ibid.*, p. 67.
20. Métraux 1, p. 18.
21. Cf. Saint-Amand, *Bon Dieu Rit*, Paris, 1952.
22. Cf. Alexis 3, p. 173.
23. Cf. Deren, pp. 36 f.
24. Métraux 2, pp. 61 f.
25. Cf. Hazoumé 2, p. 151.
26. Métraux 2, p. 64.
27. Césaire 1, p. 79.
28. Leiris 2, p. 26.
29. Métraux 2, p. 64.
30. *ibid.*, p. 88.
31. Deren, p. 37.
32. Cf. Leiris 2.
33. Hanns Heinz Ewers, *Mit meinen Augen*, Berlin, 1909.
34. St. John, Sir Spencer, *Haity or the Black Republic*, London, 1889.
35. Cf. Williams, p. 75.
36. Métraux 3, pp. 146 f.
37. Cf. ch. V, p. 131.
38. Métraux 2, p. 89.
39. Alexis 3, pp. 195 f.
40. Métraux 2, p. 88.
41. Rigaud, Odette, pp. 37 ff.
42. Hazoumé 1, pp. 3 f.
43. Cf. Métraux 3, p. 143.
44. Roumain, pp. 68 f.
45. Cf. Métraux 3, p. 145.
46. Bonsal, pp. 88 f.
47. Métraux 2, p. 59.
48. Saint-Amand, pp. 13 f.

49. Saint-Amand, pp. 275 ff.
50. Saint-Amand, p. 317.
51. Métraux 3, p. 150.
52. Alexis 3, p. 343.
53. *ibid.*, p. 359.
54. *ibid.*, p. 270.
55. *ibid.*, p. 358.
56. P. Joanne Antonio Cavazzi, *Historische Beschreibung der in dem unteren occidentalischen Mohrenland liegenden drei Königreiche Congo, Matamba und Angola*, Munich, 1694, quoted from Ziegfeld, p. 182.
57. Deren, p. 178.
58. Cf. Ch 4.
59. Cf. Ch. 4, pp. 117 f.

CHAPTER 3

1. In Africa today only a couple of Yoruba tribes scattered in Iboland are called *Lucumi* or *Olucumi*.
2. Frobenius 5, p. 69.
3. Beier 7, p. 9.
4. Frobenius 5, pp. 165 ff.
5. Parrinder 2, from Beier 1, p. 10.
6. Beier 1, pp. 9 ff.
7. Ramos, p. 75.
8. Cf. Legba in Ch. 2, pp. 42 ff.
9. Ortiz, F. 2, pp. 202 ff.
10. Cf. Ortiz, F. 1, pp. 370–419; Ortiz, F. 2, pp. 204–310.
11. Ortiz, F. 2, p. 261.
12. *ibid.*, pp. 209 ff.
13. Ramos, p. 74.
14. Cf. Frobenius 5, pp. 274 f.
15. Ortiz, F. 2, p. 247.
16. *ibid.*, pp. 246 f.
17. Frobenius 5, p. 274.
18. Beier 1, p. 7.
19. Frobenius 5, pp. 274–8, and Frobenius 2, pp. 122–37.
20. Beier 1, p. 7.
21. Ramos, p. 74.
22. Ortiz, F. 2, pp. 235 f.
23. In Yorubaland Oshun is not the goddess of rivers but *a* river, nor can one describe her there as an 'Aphrodite' deity.
24. Cf. Ortiz, F. 2, p. 251.
25. *ibid.*, p. 260.
26. *ibid.*, p. 251.
27. Of the extremely complex Obtala cult group of Yorubaland two main conceptions have survived in Cuba: Ogiyan, the young warrior, and Olufon, the wise old man.
28. Ortiz, F. 2, p. 357.
29. *ibid.*, pp. 375 ff.

30. Beier 1, p. 10.
31. Ortiz, F. 2, pp. 358–9.
32. 'Eku' means 'death' in the Yoruba language.
33. Cf. *asson* on pp. 36 and 39.
34. Cf. ch. 2, pp. 35 f.
35. Cf. Ortiz, F. 2, pp. 383 f. Ortiz' terminology Christianizes the process. 'Rebirth' would be better than 'Resurrection'.
36. *ibid.*, pp. 380–92.
37. Ballagas, p. 302.
38. Ortiz, F. 2, p. 364.
39. Beier 1, p. 10.
40. Cf. Ch. 6, p. 171.
41. Ortiz, F. 3, vol. IV, pp. 196 f.
42. Labat, vol. II, pp. 154–6.
43. Moreau 1, vol. I, pp. 44 ff.
44. Ortiz, F. 3, vol. IV, p. 190.
45. *ibid.*, p. 195.
46. *ibid.*, p. 196.
47. Huet-Fodeba, pp. 40–3.
48. Cf. Ch. V, pp. 124 ff.
49. Ortiz, F. 3, vol. IV, p. 196.
50. Ortiz, F. 2, p. 329.
51. Ortiz, F. 3, vol. IV, p. 197.
52. Ortiz, F. 2, p. 330.
53. Ortiz, F. 3, vol. IV, p. 248.
54. Ortiz, F. 2, p. 330.
55. Günther, S., p. 5.
56. Sachs 1, p. 248.
57. *loc. cit.*
58. Zürich, 1953.
59. Vol. LXX, Bilbao-Madrid, p. 1032.
60. Sachs 1, p. 247.
61. Ortiz, F. 1, p. 2.
62. *ibid.*, pp. 61 ff.
63. Amezua, p. 473.
64. Cf. *asson* in Ch. 2, p. 36.
65. Sachs 1, p. 248.
66. Sachs 2, p. 98.
67. Casanova, vol. X, pp. 517 f.
68. Rudolf Lothar in Sachs 1, p. 235.
69. Friedenthal, p. 109.
70. Dauer 1, p. 69.
71. Cf. Ballagas, p. 111.
72. Tallet in Vitier, p. 223.
73. Guirao, R., *Órbita de la poesía afrocubana*, Habana, 1939.
74. Cf. Jahn 3, p. 68.
75. Ortiz, F., 2, p. 342.
76. *ibid.*, p. 280.
77. Ortiz, F. 2, p. 192.

78. Guillén 2, pp. 68 f.
79. Guillén 2, p. 70.
80. Ballagas, p. 139.
81. *ibid.*, p. 138.
82. *ibid.*, p. 137.
83. Arozarena, in Jahn 3, p. 62.
84. Arozarena, Manuscript, German translation in Jahn 3, p. 35.
85. Senghor 6, pp. 61 f.
86. Jahn 3, p. 72.
87. Senghor 5, p. 123.
88. Kostia, p. IX.
89. Senghor 6, p. 60.
90. Cf. Arozarena in Pereda Valdés, p. 160.

CHAPTER 4

1. Ancestor of the Yoruba.
2. Adesanya, pp. 39 f.
3. Lévy-Bruhl 1, p. 77.
4. Lévy-Bruhl 2, p. 60.
5. *ibid.*, p. 73.
6. Griaule, p. 9.
7. Quoted from Haftmann, p. 96.
8. *loc. cit.*
9. Kagame 2, p. 267.
10. *ibid.*, pp. 247–78.
11. Tutuola 1, pp. 45 f.
12. *ibid.*, p. 25.
13. Tempels, p. 28.
14. *ibid.*, p. 39.
15. Cf. Césaire in Senghor 3, p. 59.
16. *loc. cit.*
17. Sartre in Senghor 3, pp. XXXII f.
18. Kagame 2, p. 351.
19. *loc. cit.*
20. Tempels, p. 27.
21. *ibid.*, p. 28.
22. *ibid.*, p. 35.
23. Kagame 2, p. 179.
24. Diop, B. in Senghor 2, pp. 144 f.
25. Kagame 2, p. 369.
26. *ibid.*, p. 371.
27. *ibid.*, p. 372.
28. *ibid.*, p. 377.
29. Adesanya, p. 41.
30. Tempels, p. 31.
31. Senghor 6, p. 54.
32. Senghor 4, p. 28.

33. Diop, B. in Senghor 3, p. 143.
34. Tayedzerhwa Manuscript, German translation in Jahn 1, p. 35.
35. Cf. Tutuola 1, pp. 96 ff.
36. Tutuola 2, p. 152.
37. Senghor 5, p. 88.
38. Senghor 4, p. 28.
39. *ibid.*, p. 16.
40. Senghor 1, p. 16.
41. *ibid.*, p. 65.
42. An old Kingdom in Senegal.
43. Senghor 1, p. 8.
44. Senghor 4, p. 43.
45. Césaire 10, p. 3.
46. Roumain (Manuscript).
47. Sherlock in 'Kyk-over-Al', vol. 3, Nr. 13, Georgetown (Guiana), 1951, p. 215.
48. McFarlane, p. 7.
49. Vesey, p. 28.
50. Hughes 2, p. 87.
51. Beier 7, pp. 8 f.
52. Cf. Tempels, pp. 37 f.
53. Kagame 2, p. 370.
54. Cf. Tempels, pp. 89 f.
55. Senghor 6, p. 54.
56. Adesanya, p. 38.
57. Senghor 5, p. 56.
58. Césaire 6, p. 71.

CHAPTER 5

1. Cf. Ch. 4, p. 115.
2. Cf. Kagame 2, pp. 190, 199.
3. *ibid.*, p. 186.
4. Cf. *ibid.*, p. 187.
5. On the difference between practical and habitual being, doing, having and being able, which penetrates all spheres of being and existence, see Kagame 2, pp. 126 ff., 174 ff., 184 ff., 192 ff., 217–22.
6. Kagame 2, p. 221.
7. *ibid.*, p. 222.
8. Dantzig, pp. 47 f.
9. Griaule, p. 165.
10. *ibid.*, pp. 25 f.
11. *ibid.*, p. 165.
12. Cf. Ch. 4, pp. 107 f.
13. Griaule, p. 166.
14. Senghor 6, p. 58.
15. Dadié 1, p. 15.
16. Laye 1, p. 32.

17. *ibid.*, p. 39.
18. Senghor 6, p. 56.
19. Cf. Ch. 4, pp. 110 ff.
20. Cf. Jores, p. 37.
21. *ibid.*, p. 39.
22. *ibid.*, p. 48.
23. Wenger, p. 2.
24. Leakey, pp. 47 f.
25. Kenyatta, p. 317.
26. Cf. Mbeba (Manuscript), German translation in Jahn 1, p. 41.
27. Kagame 2, p. 148.
28. *ibid.*, pp. 148 f.
29. *ibid.*, p. 150.
30. The Bible.
31. Communicated in a letter by Susanne Wenger.
32. Sartre in Senghor 3, p. IX.
33. *ibid.*, p. XLIV.
34. Césaire 2, p. 156; Sartre in Senghor 3, p. XLIV.
35. Césaire 1, p. 41.
36. Césaire 1, pp. 70 f.
37. Césaire 6, p. 60.
38. *ibid.*, p. 70.
39. *ibid.*, p. 40.
40. Césaire in Senghor 3, p. 62.
41. Césaire 2, pp. 186 f.
42. Césaire 1, p. 71.
43. Tchicaya U Tams'i, p. 48.
44. Cf. Chapter 2, p. 42.
45. Césaire 3, p. 66.
46. Dadié 1, p. 34.
47. Cf. Ch. 4, pp. 102 f.
48. Césaire 10, p. 3.
49. Césaire 2, p. 112.
50. Césaire 3, p. 81.
51. Tchicaya U Tam'si, p. 35.
52. Césaire 3, p. 88.
53. *loc. cit.*
54. Césaire 2, p. 21.
55. Césaire 3, p. 73.
56. Césaire 1, p. 76.
57. Tutuola 2, pp. 157 f.
58. Senghor 5, p. 57.
59. Ortiz, A., p. 13.
60. Guillén 2, p. 53.
61. Arozarena Manuscript, German translation in Jahn 3, p. 16.
62. Vesey, p. 30.
63. Césaire 2, pp. 171 f.
64. Breton, quoted from Wyss, p. 29.
65. Wyss, p. 29.

66. Sartre in Senghor 3, p. XXVII.
67. *ibid.*, p. XVII.
68. *loc. cit.*
69. Sartre in Senghor 3, p. XXVIII.
70. *loc. cit.*
71. Senghor 6, p. 59.
72. Césaire 2.
73. Césaire 7.
74. Juin, p. 44.
75. Césaire 1, pp. 49 f.
76. Cf. Deren, pp. 38 ff.
77. Sartre in Senghor 3, p. XXI.
78. Senghor 5, p. 55.
79. Attuly in Damas, p. 133.
80. Césaire 2, p. 8.
81. Grabbe, 'Herzog Theodor von Gothland', verse 3899 ff.
82. Césaire 1, p. 72.
83. Cf. Jahn 4, p. 433.
84. Senghor 6, p. 59.
85. Leibmann, K., *Das kosmische Werk*, Dessau, 1925 ; quoted from Meyer, p. 90.
86. Benn, pp. 5–20.
87. Cf. the meaning of ecstasy in Ch. 2, pp. 39 ff.
88. Griaule, p. 169.
89. Senghor 6, p. 56.
90. Cf. Kagame 1.
91. Senghor 5, p. 108.
92. Césaire 2, p. 112.
93. Césaire 3, p. 64.
94. Césaire 2, p. 171.
95. Césaire 3, p. 32.
96. Beier in Gbadamosi, p. 7.
97. *loc. cit.*
98. Cf. Ch. 4, p. 110, note.
99. Beier in Gbadamosi, p. 7.
100. Césaire 2, p. 126.
101. Becher in Benn, pp. 140 f.
102. Cf. Ch. 7, pp. 195–216.
103. Dylan Thomas in *The Observer*.
104. Pritchett in *The New Statesman*.
105. Roy in Juin, p. 11.

CHAPTER 6

1. Cf. Ch. 2, pp. 42 f.
2. Einstein 1, pp. XIV f.
3. Beier 1, p. 4.
4. Himmelheber, p. 44.
5. Cf. Ch. 5, pp. 128 ff.

6. Himmelheber, p. 44.
7. *loc. cit.*
8. Frobenius 5, p. 13.
9. Cf. Ch. 5, p. 146.
10. Luschan, p. 355.
11. Sydow, p. 126.
12. Cf. Beier 8, p. 28.
13. Gbadamosi, p. 51.
14. Cf. Ch. 4, pp. 107–8, 112.
15. Cf. Ch. 2, p. 48.
16. Beier 1, p. 14.
17. Cf. Himmelheber, p. 51 and fig. 4.
18. Senghor 6, p. 60.
19. Senghor 6, p. 61; cf. also Ch. 5, p. 127.
20. Cf. Ch. 7, pp. 189 f.
21. Senghor 6, p. 61.
22. Cf. Dauer 1, p. 13.
23. Cf. Dauer 2, p. 248.
24. *ibid.*, p. 249.
25. Dauer 1, p. 16.
26. Cf. Ch. 2, pp. 38 f.
27. Senghor 6, p. 61.
28. Cf. *ibid.*, p. 62.
29. *loc. cit.*
30. Cf. Ch. 3, pp. 90 ff.
31. Tutuola 1, pp. 17 ff.
32. Senghor 5, p. 111.
33. Lamming 1, p. 105.
34. Senghor 6, p. 63.
35. *loc. cit.*
36. *ibid.*, pp. 63 f.
37. Cf. Ch. 3, p. 78.
38. Malraux, p. 563.
39. Cf. Ch. 4, p. 107.
40. Senghor 1, p. 29.
41. Senghor 6, p. 59.
42. Beier 5, p. 383.
43. Senghor 6, p. 57.
44. Glück, p. 7.
45. Kjersmeier, vol. IV, p. 8.
46. Kjersmeier, vol. I, p. 31.
47. Luschan, p. 357.
48. Einstein 2, p. 17.
49. Sydow, pp. 12 f.
50. Einstein 1, pp. XIV, XV.
51. Kagame 2, p. 385.
52. Cf. Senghor 6, p. 57.
53. Himmelheber, p. 49.
54. Cf. Ch. 4, pp. 103 f.

55. Cf. Ch. 5, p. 124.
56. Laye 2, p. 189.
57. Beier 3, p. 162.
58. Beier 6.
59. Italiaander, pp. 25 f.
60. *loc. cit.*
61. *ibid.*, p. 30.
62. Cf. Ch. 2, pp. 41, 61.
63. Harrison, pp. 312 f.
64. Beier 9, pp. 318 ff.
65. Cf. Beier 4, pp. 144 ff.
66. Cf. Moore, pp. 184 ff.
67. Giedion-Welcker, p. 84.
68. Quoted from Knaur, p. 149.
69. Césaire 9, p. 357.

CHAPTER 7

1. Wright 3, p. 13.
2. Levi-Strauss, p. 318.
3. Cf. *ibid.*, pp. 317–19.
4. Cf. Klingenheben, pp. 158 ff.
5. Beier 2, pp. 29 f.
6. Cf. Ch. 3, pp. 73, 78; Ch. 2, p. 39.
7. Nketia, p. 36.
8. Danquah, p. 51.
9. Thomas (Manuscript), German translation in Jahn 1, p. 15.
10. Beier 2, p. 31.
11. Matip, p. 11.
12. Cf. Diop, Sh. A., *Nations nègres et culture*, Paris, 1954.
13. Cf. Breasted, J. H.
14. Wright 3, p. 14.
15. Senghor 6, p. 51.
16. Césaire 2, p. 173.
17. Cf. Ch. 4, p. 152.
18. Diop, Sh. A., *Nations nègres et culture*, Paris, 1955 and Lucas, O., *The Religion of the Yoruba*, Lagos, 1948.
19. Mofolo 1, p. 7.
20. *ibid.*, 1, p. 110.
21. *ibid.*, pp. 110 f.
22. *ibid.*, p. 111.
23. *ibid.*, pp. 112 f.
24. Mofolo 2, pp. 50 f.
25. The detailed biography of Thomas Mofolo was written by Peter Sulzer as epilogue to Mofolo, 'Chaka der Zulu', Zürich, 1953.
26. Fula, p. 99.
27. *ibid.*, pp. 91, 135.
28. *ibid.*, p. 141.

29. Sulzer, p. 90.
30. *ibid.*, p. 91.
31. Johnson in Schulte-Nordhold, p. 5.
32. Johnson in Berendt 1, p. 24.
33. Cullen in Hughes 4, p. 128.
34. Hughes 4, p. 97.
35. Hughes 2, p. 4.
36. Hughes 3, p. 30.
37. Hughes in Johnson, p. 234.
38. Hughes, 'Brass Spittoons' in Johnson, p. 234.
39. Hughes, 'Trumpet Player' in Hughes 2, p. 114.
40. Hughes, 'Minstrel Man' in Brown-Davis-Lee, p. 370.
41. Cuney, 'No Image' in Hughes 4, p. 145.
42. Fenton Johnson, 'The Banjo Player' in Hughes 4, p. 61.
43. Horne, 'On Seeing Two Brown Boys in a Catholic Church,' in Hughes 4, p. 77.
44. *loc. cit.*
45. Hughes 1, p. 223.
46. Brown in Hughes 4, p. 87.
47. Guillen 2, p. 19.
48. Baquero in Vitier, p. 349.
49. Césaire 6, p. 77.
50. Reid 1, p. 63.
51. Sulzer, p. 95.
52. Ntara, pp. 113 f.
53. *ibid.*, p. 178.
54. Osadebay, p. 14.
55. Senghor 6, p. 60.
56. Mphahlele, p. 219.
57. *ibid.*, p. 220.
58. Beti 1, p. 56.
59. Laye 2, pp. 21 f.
60. *ibid.*, pp. 36 f.
61. *ibid.*, p. 55.
62. Cf. Ch. 4, pp. 103 f.

CHAPTER 8

1. Berendt 2, p. 80.
2. Cf. Simmel-Stählin, p. 111.
3. Brooks, p. 13.
4. Cf. Ch. 2, pp. 39 f.
5. Cf. Ch. 3, p. 63 and Ch. 4, p. 115.
6. Cf. Ch. 6, p. 157.
7. Cf. Verger, *Dieux d'Afrique*, Paris, 1954.
8. Baldwin, p. 59.
9. Dauer 2, p. 61.
10. *ibid.*, p. 59.

11. *ibid.*, p. 183.
12. *ibid.*, p. 63.
13. Cf. *ibid.*, p. 64.
14. Berendt 1, p. 11.
15. Cf. *ibid.*, p. 12.
16. Dauer 1, p. 53.
17. Dauer 2, p. 74.
18. Senghor 6, p. 60.
19. Original in Dauer 2, pp. 146 f.
20. Cf. Ch. 5, pp. 136 f.
21. Dauer 2, p. 60.
22. Brown-Davis-Lee, p. 426.
23. Cf. Ch. 5, p. 149.
24. Brown-Davis-Lee, p. 429.
25. *ibid.*, p. 426.
26. Dauer 2, p. 31.
27. *ibid.*, p. 53.
28. Cf. Ch. 5, pp. 124 ff.
29. Douglass quoted from Brown-Davis-Lee, p. 726.
30. Cf. Ch. 7, pp. 201 f.
31. Imoukhuede (Manuscript), German translation in Jahn 1, pp. 20 f.
32. Dei-Anang, pp. 23 f.
33. Cf. Ch. 1, pp. 11 f.
34. Césaire 12, pp. 203 f.
35. Abrahams 1, pp. 11 f.
36. *ibid.*, p. 15.
37. *ibid.*, p. 17.
38. Cf. Wright 4, pp. 59 f. and pp. 160 ff.
39. Ellison, p. 489.
40. Baldwin, p. 43.
41. Anderson, MS, also Anderson, *Lover Man*, p. 95, where the two selves are missing—at publisher's request?
42. Wright 4, pp. 164 ff.
43. Myrdal, p. 113.
44. Wright 5, p. 123.
45. Senghor 6, p. 52.
46. Fanon, p. 26.
47. Césaire 8, pp. 12 f.
48. Lamming 1, p. 186.
49. *loc. cit.*
50. Césaire 1, p. 77.
51. Césaire, A. in 'Présence Africaine' VIII–X, Paris, 1956, p. 225.
52. Senghor 1, p. 30.
53. Césaire 1, pp. 85 f.
54. Niger in Senghor 3, p. 99.

BIBLIOGRAPHY

Abrahams, Peter, *Mine Boy*, London (1946), 1954.
2. *Wild Conquest*, London, 1951.
3. *Tell Freedom*, London, 1954.
4. *The Path of Thunder*, London, 1952.
Achebe, Chinua, *Things Fall Apart*, London, 1958.
Adesanya, Adebayo, 'Yoruba Metaphysical Thinking', in *Odú* 5, Ibadan, 1958.
Alexis, Jacques Stéphen, *Compère Général Soleil*, Paris, 1955.
2. 'Où va le roman?' in *Présence Africaine* XIII, Paris, 1956.
3. *Les arbres musiciens*, Paris, 1957.
Amezua, Agustin G. de, *Notas a Cervantes*, Madrid, 1912.
Anderson, Alston, *Lover Man*, London, 1959.
Baldwin, James, *Go Tell it on the Mountain*, New York (1952), 1954.
Ballagas, Emilio, *Mapa de la poesía negra americana*, Buenos Aires, 1946.
Beier, Horst Ulrich (Ulli), *Sacred Wood Carvings from one Small Yoruba Town*, Lagos, 1957.
2. 'The Talking Drums of the Yoruba', in *African Music* I, 1. Roodepoort (Transvaal), 1954.
3. 'The Attitude of the Educated African to His Traditional Art', in *Phylon*, Atlanta (Georgia), 1954.
4. 'Yoruba Cement Sculpture', in *Nigeria* 46, Lagos, 1955.
5. 'The Egungun Cult', in *Nigeria* 51, Lagos, 1956.
6. 'Christliche Kunst in Nigeria', *Frankfurter Allgemeine Zeitung*, 21; 12, 1957.
7. 'Die Religion der Yoruba in West-Nigeria', in *Kumba Tam*, Darmstadt, 1957.
8. 'The Bochio', in *Black Orpheus* 3, Ibadan (Nigeria), 1958.
9. 'Ibibio Monuments', in *Nigeria* 51, Lagos, 1958.
Benn, Gottfried, *Lyrik des expressionistischen Jahrzehnts*, Wiesbaden, 1955.

Bibliography

Berendt, Joachim Ernst, *Blues*, München, 1957; *also see* Knesebeck, Paridam, *Spirituals*, München, 1955.

Beti, Mongo, *Le pauvre Christ de Bomba*, Paris, 1956.

2. *Mission Terminée*, Paris, 1957.

Bonsal, St., *The American Mediterranean*, New York, 1912.

Boto, Eza, *Ville Cruelle*, Paris, 1954.

Breasted, J. H., *A History of Egypt*.

Brooks, Gwendolyn, *A Street in Bronzeville*, New York and London, 1945.

Brown, Sterling A., Davis, Arthur P., and Lee, Ulysses, *The Negro Caravan*, New York, 1941.

Casanova, Giacomo, *Mémoires*, Leipsic et Paris, 1926.

Césaire, Aimé, *Cahier d'un Retour au Pays Natal*, Paris (1939), 1956.

2. *Les Armes Miraculeuses*, Paris, 1946.

3. *Soleil Cou Coupé*, Paris, 1948.

4. *Corps Perdu*, Paris, 1950.

5. *Discours sur le Colonialisme*, Paris, 1955.

6. *Sonnendolche—Poignards du Soleil*, Heidelberg, 1956.

7. *Et les Chiens se taisaient*, Paris, 1956.

8. *Lettre à Maurice Thorez*, Paris, 1956.

9. 'Wifredo Lam', in *Cahiers d'Art* XX–XXI, Paris, 1945–6.

10. 'A l'Afrique', in *Poésie* 46, Nr. 53, Paris, 1946.

11. 'Victor Schoelcher et l'abolition de l'esclavage', in Victor Schoelcher, *Esclavage et Colonisation*, Paris, 1948.

12. 'Culture et Colonisation', in *Présence Africaine* VIII–X, Paris, 1956.

Dadié, Bernard B., *La Ronde des Jours*, Paris, 1956.

2. *Climbié*, Paris, 1956.

Damas, Léon, *Poètes d'expression française*, Paris, 1947.

Danquah, J. B., *Akan Laws and Customs*, London, 1928.

Dantzig, Gotthardt Arthus von, *Wahrhafftige Historische Beschreibung der gewaltigen Goltreichen Königreichs Guinea / sonst das Goltgestatt von Mina genandt / so in Africa gelegen / sampt derselben gantzen Beschaffenheit . . .* Franckfurt am Mayn, 1603.

Dauer, Alfons M., *Knaurs Jazz-Lexikon*, München, 1957.

2. *Der Jazz, seine Ursprünge und seine Entwicklung*, Kassel, 1958.

Davidson, Basil, *The African Awakening*, London, 1956.

Dei-Anang, M. F., *Wayward Lines from Africa*, London and Redhill, 1946.

Depestre, René, *Minerai Noir*, Paris, 1956.

Deren, Maya, *Divine Horsemen, the Living Gods of Haiti*, London–New York, 1953.

Bibliography

Dietherlen, Germaine, *Essai sur la religion bambara*, Paris, 1950.

Diop, Sheikh Anta, *Nations nègres et Culture*, Paris, 1955.

Dorsainvil, J. C., *Vodou et Névrose*, Port-au-Prince, 1931.

2. *Manuel d'histoire d'Haiti*, Port-au-Prince, 1949.

Einstein, Carl, *Negerplastik*, München, 1920.

2. *Afrikanische Plastik*, Berlin, 1922.

Ekwensi, Cyprian, *People of the City*, London, 1954.

Ellison, Ralph, *Invisible Man*, New York, 1947.

Fagunwa, Daniel Olorunfemi, *Ogboju Ode Ninu Igbo Irunmale*, Edinburgh, 1956.

Fanon, Frantz, *Peau Noire Masques Blancs*, Paris, 1952.

Frankenberg, Gerhard von, *Menschenrassen und Menschentum*, Berlin, 1956.

Friedell, Egon, *Kulturgeschichte der Neuzeit*, München, 1946.

Friedenthal, Albert, *Musik, Tanz und Dichtung bei den Kreolen Amerikas*, Berlin, 1913.

Frobenius, Leo, *Und Afrika sprach . . .*, Berlin, 1912. (*The Voice of Africa*, London, 1913.)

2. *Die atlantische Götterlehre*, Jena, 1926.

3. *Erlebte Erdteile*, Frankfurt am Main, 1929.

4. *Paideuma*, Düsseldorf, 1953.

5. *Kulturgeschichte Afrikas*, Zürich, 1954.

Fula, Arthur Nuthall, *Jôhannie giet die Beeld*, Johannesburg, 1954.

Gbadamosi, Bakare, and Beier, Ulli, *Yoruba Poetry*, Ibadan (Nigeria), 1959.

Giedion-Welcker, Carola, *Plastik des XX. Jahrhunderts*, Stuttgart, 1955.

Glissant, Édouard, *La Lézarde*, Paris, 1958.

Glück, Julius F., *Afrikanische Masken*, Baden-Baden, 1956.

Grabbe, Christian Dietrich, *Works*, Leipzig, 1910.

Griaule, Marcel, *Dieu d'eau*, Paris, 1948.

Guillen, Nicolàs, *Motivos del són*, La Habana, 1930.

2. *Sóngoro Cosongo*, Buenos Aires (1932), 1952.

Guirao, Ramón, *Órbita de la poesía afrocubana*, La Habana, 1939.

Günther, Helmut, 'Der moderne Gesellschaftstanz und das Lebensgefühl unserer Epoche', in *Das Parkett*, Hamburg, December 1957.

Haftmann, Werner, *Paul Klee*, München, 1950.

Harrison, John, 'Some Haitian Painters', in BIM 12, Bridgetown (Barbados), 1950.

Hazoumé, Paul, *Le pacte du Sang au Dahomé*, Paris, 1937.

2. *Doguicimi*, Paris, 1938.

Hearne, John, *Voices under the Window*, London, 1955.

2. *Stranger at the Gate*, London, 1956.

3. *The Faces of Love*, London, 1957.

Hefel, Annemarie, *Afrikanische Bronzen*, Wien, 1948.

Herskovits, Melville, *Surinaam Folklore*, New York, 1936.

2. *Life in a Haitian Valley*, New York, 1937.

3. *The Myth of the Negro Past*, New York, 1941.

Herskovits, Melville, and Herskovits, Frances, *Trinidad Village*, New York, 1947.

Himmelheber, Hans, *Negerkünstler*, Stuttgart, 1935.

Huet, Michel, et Fodeba, Keita, *Les Hommes de la Danse*, Lausanne, 1954.

Hughes, Langston, *The Big Sea*, New York, 1940.

2. *Selected Poems*, New York, 1959.

3. *The Weary Blues*, New York, 1926.

Hughes, Langston, and Bontemps, Arna, *The Poetry of the Negro*, New York, 1951.

Hendriks (Mandisodza), Katie, *The Bend in the Road*, Cape Town.

Italiaander, Rolf, *Neue Kunst in Afrika*, Mannheim, 1957.

Jabavu, D. D. T., *Bantu Literature*, Lovedale (South Africa), 1921.

Jahn, Janheinz, *Schwarzer Orpheus*, München (1954), 1955.

2. *Schwarze Ballade*, Düsseldorf, 1957.

3. *Rumba Macumba*, München, 1957.

4. 'Aimé Césaire und der Surrealismus', in *Texte und Zeichen* 8, Darmstadt, 1956.

5. *Anders gläubige Kunst*, Stierstadt im Taunus, 1958.

Jaspers, Carl, *Vom Ursprung und Ziel der Geschichte*, Frankfurt am Main, 1955.

Jores, Arthur, 'Magie und Zauber in der modernen Medizin', in *Vom ärztlichen Denken*, Stuttgart, 1956.

Juin, Hubert, *Aimé Césaire*, Paris, 1956.

Johnson, James Weldon, *The Book of American Negro Poetry*, New York, 1931.

Kagame, Alexis, *La poésie dynastique au Ruanda*, Bruxelles, 1951.

2. *La philosophie bǎntu-rwandaise de l'Être*, Bruxelles, 1956.

3. *Umuliribya wa nyili ibiremwa*, Astrida (Ruanda), 1952–3 (La Divine Pastorale, Bruxelles, 1952).

Kaufmann, Herbert, *Nigeria*, Bonn, 1958.

Kenyatta, Jomo, *Facing Mount Kenya*, London (1938), 1953.

Kjersmeier, Carl, *Centres de style de la sculpture nègre africaine*, Paris–København, 1935–8.

Klingenheben, A., 'The Vai Script', in *Africa* VI, 2, London, 1933.

Knaurs, *Lexikon moderner Kunst*, München, 1955.

Kostia, Conde, *Arpas Cubanas*, La Habana, 1904.

Labat, Père, *Nouveau Voyage aux Isles d'Amérique*, Paris, 1722, 1956.

Lamming, George, *The Emigrants*, London, 1954.

2. *In the Castle of My Skin*, London, 1953.

3. *Of Age and Innocence*, London, 1958.

Laye, Camara, *Enfant Noir*, Paris, 1953 (*Dark Child*, London, 1955).

2. *Le Regard du Roi*, Paris, 1954 (*The Radiance of the King*, London, 1956).

Leakey, Louis Seymour Bazelt, *Mau-Mau and the Kikuyu*, London, 1952.

Leiris, Michel, *Race et Culture*, Paris, 1951.

2. 'Sacrifice d'un taureau', in *Présence Africaine* XII, Paris, 1951.

Lévi-Strauss, Claude, *Tristes Tropiques*, Paris, 1955.

Lévy-Bruhl, Lucien, *Les fonctions mentales dans les sociétés inférieures*, Paris, 1910.

2. *Carnets*, Paris, 1949.

Liebmann, Kurt, *Das kosmische Werk*, Dessau, 1925.

Lucas, Olumide, *The Religion of the Yoruba*, Lagos, 1948.

Lumani-Tshibamba, Paul, *Ngando*, Bruxelles.

Luschan, Felix von, *Die Altertümer von Benin*, Berlin, 1919.

Mais, Roger, *The Hills Were Joyful Together*, London, 1953.

2. *Brother Man*, London, 1954.

Malinowski, Bronislaw, *The Dynamics of Cultural Change*, New Haven–London, 1945–7.

Malraux, André, *Les Voix du Silence*, Paris, 1951.

Mandisodza, Katie=Hendriks, Katie.

Mangoaela, Zakea D., *Lithoko tsa marena a Basotho*, Morija (Basutoland), 1950.

Maran, René, *Batouala*, Paris, 1921.

2. *Djouma*, Paris, 1927.

Marcelin, Milo, 'Les Grands Dieux du Vodou haïtien', in *Journal de la société des Américanistes*, vol. XXXVI, 1947.

2. *Mythologie vodou (rite arada)*, Port-au-Prince, 1949; Pétionville (Haiti), 1950.

Marcelin, Pierre et Philippe, *Canapé Vert*.

Matip, Benjamin, *Afrique, nous t'ignorons*, Paris, 1956.

Maximilien, Louis, *Le Vodou haïtien (rite radas-canzo)*, Port-au-Prince.

McFarlane, Basil, *Jacob and the Angel*, Georgetown (British Guiana), 1952.

Bibliography

Métraux, Alfred, 'L'Afrique vivante en Haïti', in *Présence Africaine* XII, Paris, 1951.

2. *Haiti, la terre, les hommes, les dieux*, Neuchâtel, 1957.

3. 'Histoire du Vodou', in *Présence Africaine* XVI, Paris, 1957.

Meyer, Alfred Richard, *Die maer von der musa expressionistica*, Düsseldorf, 1948.

Mofolo, Thomas, 'Moeti oa Bochabela', in *Leselinyana*, Morija (Basutoland), 1906 (*The Traveller of the East*, London, 1934).

2. *Chaka*, London, 1931.

3. *Pitseng*, Morija (1910), 1939.

Moore, Gerald, and Beier, Ulli, 'Mbari Houses', in *Nigeria* 49, Lagos, 1956.

Mopeli-Paulus, A. S., *Ho tsamaea ke ho bona*, Morija (Basutoland), 1945.

Mopeli-Paulus, A. S., and Lanham, Peter, *Blanket Boy's Moon*, London, 1953.

Mopeli-Paulus, A. S., and Basner, Miriam, *Turn to the Dark*, London, 1956.

Moreau de Saint-Méry, Médéric Louis Elie, *Description topographique, physique, civile, politique, et historique de la partie Française de l'isle Saint-Domingue*, Philadelphia, 1797–8.

2. *Loix et Constitutions des Colonies Françoises de l'Amérique sous le Vent*, Paris, 1780.

Mphahlele, Ezekiel, *Down Second Avenue*, London, 1959.

Mqhayi, Samuel Edward Krune, *Ityalalama-wele*, Lovedale (South Africa), 1937.

Myrdal, Gunnar, *An American Dilemma*, New York–London, 1944.

Nketia, J. H., 'The Role of the Drummer in Akan Society', in *African Music* I, 1, Roodepoort (Transvaal), 1954.

Ntara, Samuel Yosia, *Headman's Enterprise*, London, 1949.

Ortiz, Adalberto, *Juyungo*, Buenos Aires, 1943.

Ortiz, Fernando, *La Africanía de la Música Folklorica de Cuba*, La Habana, 1950.

2. *Los Bailes y el Teatro de los Negros en el Folklore de Cuba*, La Habana, 1951.

3. *Los Instrumentos de la Música Afrocubana*, La Habana, 1952–5.

Osadebay, Dennis Chukude, *Africa Sings*, Ilfracombe, 1952.

Ousmane, Sembène, *O pays, mon beau peuple*, Paris, 1957.

Oyono, Ferdinand, *Une vie de Boy*, Paris, 1956.

2. *Le vieux nègre et la médaille*, Paris, 1956.

Parrinder, Geoffrey, *West African Religion*, London, 1949.

2. *Religion in an African City*, London, 1953.

Bibliography

Pereda Valdés, *Ildefonso*: *Antología de la poesía negra americana*, Montevideo, 1953.

Plaatje, Solomon, *Native life in South Africa, before and since the European war and the Boer rebellion*, London, 1916.

2. *Mhudi*, Lovedale (South Africa), 1930.

Price-Mars, Jean, *Ainsi parla l'oncle*, Port-au-Prince, 1929.

2. 'Survivances africaines et dynamisme de la culture noire outre-Atlantique', in *Présence Africaine* VIII–X, Paris, 1956.

Ramos, Arthur, *As culturas negras no novo mundo*. São Paulo–Rio de Janeiro, 1946.

Reid, Victor, *The Leopard*, London, 1958.

2. *New Day*, London, 1949.

Rigaud, Milo, *La tradition voudoo et le voudoo haïtien*, Paris, 1953.

Rigaud, Odette, 'Noël Vodou en Haïti', in *Présence Africaine* XII, Paris, 1951.

Roumain, Jacques, *Gouverneur de la Rosée*, Port-au-Prince, Paris, 1944.

Sachs, Curt, *Eine Weltgeschichte des Tanzes*, Berlin, 1933.

2. *World History of the Dance*, New York, 1937.

Saint-Amand, Edris, *Bon Dieu Rit*, Paris, 1952.

Sartre, Jean Paul, 'Orphée Noir', in Senghor, L. S., *Anthologie de la nouvelle poésie nègre et malgache*, Paris, 1948.

Schmalenbach, Werner, *Die Kunst Afrikas*, Basel, 1953.

Schulte-Nordholt, *Het Volk dat in duisternis wandelt*, Arnhem, 1956.

Selvon, Samuel, *A Brighter Sun*, London, 1952.

2. *An Island is a World*, London, 1955.

3. *Lonely Londoners*, London, 1956.

4. *Turn Again, Tiger*, London, 1958.

Senghor, Léopold Sédar, *Chants d'Ombre*, Paris, 1945.

2. *Hostice Noires*, Paris, 1948.

3. *Anthologie de la nouvelle poésie nègre et malgache*, Paris, 1948.

4. *Chants pour Naëtt*, Paris, 1949.

5. *Éthiopiques*, Paris, 1956.

6. 'L'esprit de la civilisation ou les lois de la culture négro-africaine', in *Présence Africaine* VIII–X, Paris, 1956.

Simmel, Oskar, and Stählin, Rudolf, *Christliche Religion*, Frankfurt am Main, 1957.

Sulzer, Peter, *Schwarze Intelligenz*, Zürich, 1955.

Sydow, Eckart von, *Afrikanische Plastik*, Berlin, 1954.

Swanzy, Henry, *Voices of Ghana*, Accra, 1958.

Tchicaya U Tam'si, Félix, *Feu de Brousse*, Paris, 1957.

Tempels, Placied, *Bantoe-Filosofie*, Antwerpen, 1946.

Bibliography

Thoby-Marcelin, Philippe, et Marcelin, Pierre, *Canapé Vert*, New York, 1944.

Traoré, Bakary, *Le théatre négro-africain*, Paris, 1958.

Tutuola, Amos, *The Palm-Wine Drinkard*, New York–London, 1952.

2. *My Life in the Bush of Ghosts*, New York–London, 1954.

3. *Simbi and the Satyr of the Dark Jungle*, London, 1955.

4. *The Brave African Huntress*, New York–London, 1958.

Verger, Pierre, *Dieux d'Afrique*, Paris, 1954.

Vesey, Paul, *Elefenbeinzähne—Ivory Tusks*, Heidelberg, 1956.

Vitier, Cintio, *Cincuenta años de poesía cubana*, La Habana, 1952.

Wenger, Susanne, 'Magische Medizin eines westafrikanischen Stammes' (manuscript).

Westermann, Diedrich, *Geschichte Afrikas*, Köln, 1952.

Williams, Joseph, *Voodoos and Obeahs*, New York, 1932.

Wright, Richard, *Uncle Tom's Children*, New York–London, 1938.

2. *Native Son*, New York–London, 1940.

3. *Twelve Million Black Voices*, New York, 1941.

4. *Black Boy*, Cleveland (Ohio), 1945.

5. *Black Power*, London, 1954.

Wyss, Dieter, *Der Surrealismus*, Heidelberg, 1950.

Ziegfeld, Arnold Hillen, *Im Reiche des Meergottes*, Stuttgart, 1923.

INDEX OF NAMES

Abolubode, 152
Abrahams, Peter, 211, 228–9
Achebe, Chinua, 215
Adekambi, Sola, 215
Adesanya, Adebayo, 96–7, 110, 117
Ajao, Oladele, 215
Alexis, Jacques Stéphen, 48, 54–6, 208
Ampofo, Oku, 182
Anderson, Alston, 231
Andrade, Mario Pinto de, 212
Arozarena, Marcelino, 91, 92, 140, 205
Attuly, Lionel, 145

Babalola, Adeboye, 215
Baldwin, James, 168, 218, 231
Ballagas, Emilio, 91, 92, 205
Baquero, Gaston, 205
Bazile, Castera, 180
Becher, Johannes R., 153
Beecher-Stowe, Harriet, 224
Beier, Horst Ulrich, 63, 66, 69, 115, 152, 158
Benn, Gottfried, 147, 148
Benoit, Rigaud, 181
Bereng, David Cranmer Theko, 199
Beti, Mongo, 212, 228
Bigaud, Wilson, 181
Blanchard, Sisson, 181
Bolamba, Antoine-Roger, 207, 212
Bonaparte, Napoléon, 52
Boto, Eza, 212–13
Boukman, 52
Brancusi, Constantin, 172, 183
Braque, George, 172
Breton, André, 140, 141, 143, 146, 205

Brière, Jean-F., 205
Brooks, Gwendolyn, 218
Brown, Sterling A., 203

Calixte, Charles, 207
Camille, Roussan, 205
Cão, Diego, 58, 117
Carew, Jan, 205, 207
Carpentier, Alejo, 90
Carrol, K., 177
Carter, Martin, 205, 207
Casanova, Giacomo, 89
Cervantes Saavedra, Miguel de, 87
Césaire, Aimé, 113, 118, 119, 121, 135–6, 137, 138, 140, 141, 142, 143, 144, 145, 146, 149, 151, 152, 154, 183, 193, 205, 207, 222, 226–7, 236, 237
Chaka, 197, 198
Cinéas, J. B., 208
Corbin, Henri, 207
Cruz, Viriato da, 212
Cullen, Countee, 200, 201
Cuney, Waring, 202

Dadié, Bernard B., 125, 130, 207, 213
Damas, Léon, 141, 205
Danquah, J. B., 189
Dauer, Alfons M., 40, 164, 221, 224
Davis, Frank Marshall, 203
Dei-Anang, M. F., 207, 215, 226
Depestre, René, 207
Deren, Maya, 61, 98, 110
Dhlomo, Herbert, 210
Dhlomo, R. R. R., 209, 210
Dieterlen, Germaine, 98, 110
Diop, Aliounc, 236

Diop, Birago, 108, 112, 141, 205
Diop, David, 205
Diop, Sheikh Anta, 195
Dorcély, Roland, 181
Dorsainvil, J. C., 32
Douglass, Frederick, 225
Dube, John L., 209
DuBois, W. E. Burghardt, 224
Dufait, Préfète, 180
Dunbar, Paul Laurence, 196, 200
Durand, Oswald, 196
Duvallier, François, 54

Egharevba, Jacob U., 161
Einstein, Carl, 158, 173–4
Ekwensi, Cyprian, 215
Ellison, Ralph, 168, 231
Enwonwu, Ben, 182
Espírito Santo, Aldo do, 212
Exume, René, 181

Fagunwa, D. O., 215
Fanon, Frantz, 21–5, 234
Fodeba, Keita, 83
Friedell, Egon, 17, 26
Frobenius, Leo, 24, 62, 63, 159, 190
Fula, Arthur Nuthall, 198, 210
Fuze, M., 209

Glissant, Édouard, 207, 208
Glück, Julius F., 173
Gourgue, Enguerrand, 180
Grabbe, Christian Dietrich, 145
Griaule, Marcel, 98
Guillén, Nicolás, 62, 91, 140, 149, 205
Guirao, Ramón, 90, 205

Hayden, Robert, 203
Hazoumé, Paul, 213
Hearne, John, 208
Himes, Chester, 168
Himmelheber, Hans, 158, 174
Horne, Frank, 202
Hughes, Langston, 114, 200–4, 217
Hyppolite, Hector, 180

Idah, 182
Idubor, Felix, 182

Imoukhuede, Mabel, 215, 226
Italiaander, Rolf, 179–80

Jabavu, D. D. T., 210
Jacinto, Antonio, 212
Jackson, Rhoda, 181
Jaspers, Carl, 11, 12, 13, 15, 22
Johnson, Fenton, 202
Johnson, James Weldon, 200
Jolobe, James J. R., 209
Jordan, A. C., 209
Jores, Arthur, 128
Joseph, Antonio, 181
Juin, Hubert, 143

Kagame, Alexis, 26, 99, 100 ff., 105, 108, 109, 110, 116, 118, 122, 131, 174, 175, 212
Kenyatta, Jomo, 131
Kibwana, Sahele, 212
Kirchner, Ernst Ludwig, 172, 183
Kjersmeier, Carl, 173
Klee, Paul, 101, 183
Koumouki, Laniba, 177

Labat, Père, 79
Laleau, Léon, 205
Lam, Wifredo, 183
Lamming, George, 168, 208, 236
Laye, Camara, 125, 137, 156, 176, 213 ff., 227
Lazare, Luckner, 181
Leakey, Louis Seymour Bazett, 129
Leclerc, Charles Emmanuel L., 52
Leiris, Michel, 34
Lévi-Strauss, Claude, 185
Lévy-Bruhl, Lucien, 33, 97, 111
Liebmann, Kurt, 147
Lods, Pierre, 179
Lucas, Olumide, 195
Lumani-Tshibamba, Paul, 212
Luschan, Felix von, 161, 173

Mais, Roger, 208
Malinowski, Bronislaw, 14, 15
Malonga, Jean, 213
Malraux, André, 170
Mandisodza, Katie, *see* Hendriks
Mangoela, Zakea D., 199

Index of Names

Maran, René, 204–5
Marcelin, Philippe, 208
Marcelin, Pierre, 208
Mariana, Juan de, 97
Marino, Giambattista, 87
Mason, Mason Jordan, 207
Matip, Benjamin, 190, 212
Matos, Luis Palés, 205
Mbeba, David, 131
Mbiti, John Samuel, 207, 212
McFarlane, Basil, 114, 207
McKay, Claude, 200, 201
Métraux, Alfred, 34, 47–8, 54, 55
Modigliani, Amedeo, 183
Mofolo, Thomas, 196 ff., 204, 209, 229
Molema, Silas Modiri, 209
Moonens, Laurent, 179
Mopeli-Paulus, A. S., 207, 211
Moreau de Saint-Méry, Médéric Louis Elie, 30–3, 80, 89
Morgue, see Sutherland
Moshoeshoe, 199
Mphahlele, Ezekiel, 211–12
Mqhayi, Samuel Edward Krune, 112, 196

Neto, Agostinho, 212
Niger, Paul, 205, 238
Nketia, J. H., 189
Ntara, Samuel Yosia, 209
Nzinga a Nkuwa, 59, 117

Ogotommêli, 26, 98, 110, 124–5, 139, 149
Okara, Gabriel, 207, 215
Ortiz, Adalberto, 140, 149, 205, 208
Ortiz, Fernando, 64–5, 67, 79, 88, 91,
Osadebay, Dennis Chukude, 210
Ousmane, Sembène, 213
Oyono, Ferdinand, 212, 228

Peters, Dewitt, 180
Picasso, Pablo, 172, 183
Pierre, Fernand, 181
Plaatje, Solomon T., 200
Poisson, Louverture, 181
Price-Mars, Jean, 32, 33, 34

Quevedo y Villegas, Francisco Gómez de, 88

Rabéarivelo, Jean-Joseph, 141, 205
Rabemananjara, Jacques, 149, 205
Ranaivo, Flavien, 205
Rigaud, Odette, 38, 49 ff.
Rimbaud, Arthur, 141
Robert, Shaaban, 212
Romain-Defossé, Pierre, 179
Roumain, Jacques, 29, 53, 113, 141, 205, 208
Roy, Claude, 154

Sachs, Curt, 87
Sadji, A., 213
Saint-Amand, Edris, 55, 208
Salas, Virginia Brindis de, 205
Sartre, Jean-Paul, 104, 105, 134, 141, 142, 143, 154
Segoete, Everitt Lechase, 199, 209
Sekese, Azariele M., 199
Selvon, Samuel, 208, 215
Seymour, A. J., 207
Senghor, Léopold Sédar, 93, 96, 112, 113, 117, 118–19, 125, 126, 134, 139, 141, 145, 149, 151, 156, 164, 169, 171, 193, 205, 207, 211, 221, 234, 238
Sherlock, Philip M., 114
Simon, Antoine, 54
Sousa, Noémia de, 212
St. John, Sir Spencer, 46
Sulzer, Peter, 199
Sydow, Eckart von, 161, 170, 173

Tallet, José Zacarías, 90, 205
Tardon, Raphaël, 208
Tayedzerhwa, Lettie Grace Nomakhosi, 112, 209
Tchicaya U. Tam'si, Gérald Félix, 136, 138, 207
Tempels, Placide, 26, 98, 104–6, 107, 109, 110, 116, 121
Tenreiro, José, 212
Thomas, Carey, 190
Thomas, Dylan, 154
Tirolien, Guy, 205
Tolson, Melvin B., 203

Toussaint L'Ouverture, François
  Dominique, 52
Trinidade, Solano, 205
Trouillot, Hénoc, 208
Tutuola, Amos, 103, 104, 113, 138,
  150, 154, 166, 185, 207, 215, 227

Vesey, Paul, 114, 140, 207
Vilakazi, B. W., 209

Washington, Booker T., 224
Wenger, Susanne, 183
Westermann, Diedrich, 24, 190
Williams, Joseph, 31, 33, 34, 46, 60
Wols, 183
Wright, Richard, 185, 192, 230,
  232, 233

Zobel, Joseph, 208

INDEX OF SUBJECTS

Afro-Cuban lyric poetry, 90–5, 166, 205
Agayú, 68
Agitation style, 203–4
Agwé, 43, 44, 45
Ahnen, see Muzimu
Amma, 61, 118, 126
Anacaona, 88
Arada-Ritus, 34 ff., 42
Areíto de Anacaona, 88
Arrollao, 92
Asson, 36, 37, 39
Ayida-Oueddo, 43
Ayizan, 42

Babalao, 62
Babalawo, 62
Babalú-Ayé, 68
Bagi, 34, 35
Baiao, 89
Ballads, blues words, 221 ff.
Bantu people, 100, 107
Bantu language, 100
Baron-la-Croix, 45, 51
Baron-Samedi, 45, 69
Bazima, 107
Bazimu, 107, 116
Beauty, 103, 174 ff.
Bembé, 90
Benin, 192
Benin portrait heads, 161, 163, 173
Bintu, 100, 102, 123–4
Birth, 111
Black Bottom, 89
Blue notes, 220, 221, 223
Blues, 217 ff.
Blues style, 201–3, 225
Bochio, 161

Bolero, 89
Bon Dieu, 41, 54, 61, 63, 104 ff., 118, 218
Botao, 82
Bugingo, 106
Buzima, 106–7, 115–16, 124, 162

Cakewalk, 89
Caille-Mystère, 34
Calenda, 32, 80 ff., 89
Cha Cha Cha, 86, 89
Chacona, 88
Chaconne, 88
Charleston, 89
Chica, 81, 87
Choual, 38, 165
Claves, 88
Conga, 89, 92
Copla, 93
Coumbite, 84, 223
Creole, 194
Crossed rhythms, 165
Cumbé, 88

Damballah, 43, 45
Dance, 78–90, 169 ff.
Danzón, 90
Dead ones, 107 ff.; see Magara
Death, 69 ff., 106 ff., 115 ff.
Determination: of image, 157–63, 169 ff.; of deities, 115–16, 218–19; of men, 124–5, 231
Determinative, 100
Diablito, 69–78
Drum language, 187–90
Dundun, 188

Ecstasy and possession, 37 ff., 44.

45, 47–51, 58, 64 ff., 95, 148, 162, 217 ff.
Egungun, 70, 79
Ekón, 71
Ekué, 70–81
Emancipation, literature of, 211 ff.
Eribó, 75
Erinle, 68
Erzulie, 44 ff.
Eshu, 63 ff.
Expressionism, 146–55

Fable, 221–2
Fambá, 69 ff.
Fandango, 81, 88–9
Fetish, 158 ff., 173, 174
Figure-carving, 173
Foula, 37
Foxtrot, 89

Grand-Bois, 49, 50
Guanabacoa, 91
Guédé, 45–6, 69

Habanera, 89
Hantu, 100, 103, 190
Harlem style, *see* Blues style
Head-foot figures, 161
Hounfort, 34, 49 ff.
Hounguénikon, 37, 39
Hounsi, 36–7

Ibeji, 144
Ifa, 62, 69, 110
Iléocha, 62
Imaguas, 144
Inle, 68

Jazz, 165, 220
Jubilee, 219–20
Juego, 70 ff.

Kanzo, 36–7
Kintu, 100, 102, 107, 151, 158, 239
Kinyaruanda, 27, 99–100
Kizima, 107
Kuntu, 100, 103, 139, 156 ff., 194, 219–20, 238

La-place, 35–6, 37, 53
L'art pour l'art, 135, 143, 150, 175
Laughter, 103, 139–40
Legba, 39, 42, 63, 136
Libation, 35
Literature of tutelage, 198, 204, 209–10
Loa, 34 ff., 37 ff., 47 ff., 218
Loaloachi, 89
Logos, 132–3

Macumba, 219
Magara, 110, 111, 112, 175
Magara-principle, 112 ff., 115 ff., 125
Maître-Cimitié-Boumba, 50–1
Mamaloa, 36
Mambo (dance), 86, 89
Mambo (Voodoo priestess), 35
Maracas, 81, 88
Marassa, 144
Masks, 70, 170–3, 177
Maxixe, 89
Mazon, 39
Mbari houses, 182
Medicine men, 127–30
Merinque, 86, 89
Muntu, 100 ff., 104–7, 121–2, 126, 132
Muntu face, 162–3, 169–70
Music, *see* Dance, Rhythm
Muzima, 107, 169
Muzimu, 107 ff., 169 ff.

Ñañigo, *see* Ñañiguismo
Ñañiguismo, 69–79, 91
Negro churches, 40, 213 ff.
Negro English, 194
Negro renaissance, 200 ff.
Négritude, 141–2, 205 ff., 211
Nommo, 101, 102, 121–57, 168, 189, 194
Nothingness, 131–2
Ntu, 96–120
Nwomo houses, 181
Nyamurunga, 61, 105, 118

Obatalla, 67–8
Ogou, 45, 65

Ogun, 44, 65, 92
Olorun, 61, 63, 118
One-step, 89
Orisha, 62–8, 92, 115, 117
Oshun, 65–6, 67, 68, 83
Oya, 66, 68

Papaloa, 35, 36, 54, 58, 62
Papiamento, 194
Pè, 35, 61
Père-savane, 53, 54
Pétro rite, 34, 42, 49 ff.
Pillar-carving, 173
Placebo, 128 ff.
Pocomania, 219
Polymetry, 164 ff., 218
Polyrhythm, 164 ff., 218
Polytheism, 58 ff., 218
Portrait heads, 161, 163
Possession, *see* Ecstasy
Poteau-mitan, 34, 102
Potencia, 78
Pre-logical attitude, 97–8

Race question, 233–4
Repository, 41, 102, 156
Rhythm, 36 ff., 84 ff.
Rumba, 79 ff., 81 ff.
Rumba brava, 84
Rumba picaresca, 84

Sacrifice, 37–8, 71–2, 111–12
Samba (dance), 86, 89
Samba (introductory singer), 84
Santería, 62–8, 219
Sarabanda, 87–8, 90
Sculpture, 153–63, 172–7, 182
Seguidilla, 89

Sehango, 63, 65–6, 82, 115
She-orisha, 63, 115, 219
Shimmy, 89
Skokian, 14 ff.
Soba, 35
Són, 90
Soul, 104 ff., 109
Spiritual, 200, 201, 220–1, 224
Spirituals, style of, 202–3, 205–6
Surinaams, 194
Surrealism, 104–7, 154
Swing, 166

Tango, 89
Turkey-trot, 89
Tutelage, literature of, 198, 204, 209–10
Twins (marassa), 144

Ubusa, 131
Ubwenge, 122 ff.

Vacunao, 82
Vèvè, 35, 49
Voodoo, 19, 26, 29 ff., 144

Winti cults, 219
Wizards, 130–2, 231
Work songs, 223–4
Writing, 185–8

Yanvalou, 39, 42–3
Ycmayá, 65, 95
Yoruba language, 188
Yuka, 79, 81–2, 83, 84

Zaka, 44
Zombi, 47–130

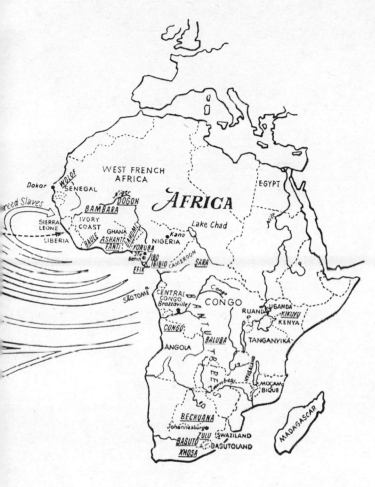

←— = Diffusion of African cultural elements through the slave trade.

◁— = Diffusion of African cultural elements through further migration.

YORUBA = Tribes and cultures in Africa; predominant traces of African culture in America.

CUBA = Countries.

Benin = Cities.